AMBITION MONSTER

AMBITION MONSTER

A MEMOIR

JENNIFER ROMOLINI

ATRIA BOOKS

New York   London   Toronto   Sydney   New Delhi

ATRIA
BOOKS

An Imprint of Simon & Schuster, LLC
1230 Avenue of the Americas
New York, NY 10020

First Atria Books hardcover edition June 2024

ATRIA BOOKS and colophon are trademarks of Simon & Schuster, LLC

Simon & Schuster: Celebrating 100 Years of Publishing in 2024

For information about special discounts for bulk purchases,
please contact Simon & Schuster Special Sales at 1-866-506-1949 or
business@simonandschuster.com.

The Simon & Schuster Speakers Bureau can bring authors to your live event.
For more information or to book an event, contact the Simon & Schuster
Speakers Bureau at 1-866-248-3049 or visit our website at
www.simonspeakers.com.

Some names and identifying details have been changed.

Interior design by Erika R. Genova

Manufactured in the United States of America

1   3   5   7   9   10   8   6   4   2

Library of Congress Cataloging-in-Publication Data has been applied for.

ISBN 978-1-6680-5658-5
ISBN 978-1-6680-5660-8 (ebook)

For my family, and for friends who've
loved me like family.

If you have ever spent any time around seriously ambitious people, you know that they are very often some of the unhappiest crazies alive, forever rooting around for more, having a hard time with basics like breathing and eating and sleeping, forever trying to cover some hysterical imagined nakedness.

—**ELISA ALBERT**

Like so many women, the story of my ambition is a story of power and fear. It is a story of trauma and self-loathing, hope and longing, and the burden of generations of thwarted dreams. The story of my ambition begins with a fish tank, ends on an office floor, and begins again in an Irish hotel. It is not a love story, though as in any good story, there is, of course, love.

Prologue

The first time it happens, I'm standing on a stage. I'm ten minutes into a speech on "authenticity," "power," "finding your path"—the series of platitudes-with-a-twist I've become known for and am now invited to spout—when my voice cracks and the words in my brain no longer come out as sounds from my mouth. It's a momentary glitch in the system; a gurgling gasp, air pushing through tissue where language should be. The episode lasts only seconds, but even then I know it is a signal, a "check engine" light. Something is wrong in my body, and what is wrong feels serious.

It's 2017, early summer. I'm at the height of my career. Earlier that year, I landed a high-powered, high-profile, coveted C-suite job. Two months later, I published my first book—a career guide for misfits—which is well received and positions me to become the thing everyone wants in 2017: a human brand.

Suddenly, people who never cared to talk to me want to talk to me. Suddenly, long-unanswered emails are answered with urgent enthusiasm. For the first time in my life, the people looking over shoulders at parties are looking for me. I field interview requests, get made up for photo shoots, am whisked away to lunches and drinks. I spend chilly predawn West Coast mornings on the phone with East Coast reporters who want to discuss my productivity secrets; what I'm reading, buying, and wearing; how to "get my life." Afterward, I shower, dress, and drive to the fancy Hollywood office where I spend the next nine to ten hours working my fancy Hollywood-adjacent job.

I'd started my professional life late. After years flailing around as a waitress and a college dropout, I land my first office job when I'm nearly thirty. For the next decade, I slog my way up and through the ranks of print and digital publishing during an era of chaos and free fall, the industry's boom times long gone. I endure media recessions, closures, and layoffs; work strategically and relentlessly throughout. I understand the fickle, arbitrary nature of success, how difficult any degree of it is to achieve. I'd watched those around me perform, preen, and paw toward it; claw at and covet it. I'd pined for success too. And here it was. If conventional wisdom taught me anything, I knew that when success comes for you, you show up, no matter what shape you're in. If you don't, it may never come again.

About midway through my book tour, the sides of my neck begin to ache. The pain is dull, but persistent and throbbing. It's as if someone has a light clamp on my throat, or I am being strangled by the world's slowest, most inefficient strangler. I wake up hoarse. By the end of recording a half-hour podcast, I'm panting, each word an act of force. I'd always had one of *those* voices, low and raspy, straddling the line between Lauren Bacall alluring and two-packs-a-day trashy. But this voice is different. I'll read half a paragraph aloud and it'll all sound fine, then inhale and be met with spittle and wheeze, my throat clenched in pain. I know I *should* slow down and stop talking, but I don't. Instead, I pitch, promote, and proselytize. People say I sound "sexy." I banter, quip, and advise.

The throbbing continues. The sounds get weird. I start to worry. Insomnia Google suggests esophageal cancer, ALS, recovery from swallowing a fish bone. Maudlin, I play out my future: *These are my last days of normal human talking.* I'd better make my last words count.

As I have for most of my adult life, I work through the pain.

Careers are a matter of choice as much as a matter of chance. Long before hustle culture entered the social media zeitgeist, long before social media itself, I was a seven-day-a-week worker. I'd made myself indispensable at every company I ever worked for, in every position I'd ever held. At the expense of nearly everything else in my life, I was always—*always*—good at my job.

I started working when I was thirteen. I worked in restaurants and in retail, in temp offices crunched behind a desk and in telemarketing, glued to a phone. In high school, I took delivery orders in on-their-last-legs pizza places, made out with the delivery guy in the storage room in between calls. I sizzled up cheesesteaks in suburban Philly delis, adding the American cheese frantically and too late, hot grease running down my arm. I charged late fees to shame-faced patrons at video stores when there were still video stores, hawked death-and-dismemberment insurance; sold bolero jackets and A-line minidresses to women who wondered if they should buy A-line minidresses and bolero jackets. *Of course you should.*

I found comfort in physical labor, in pushing myself to exhaustion, in earning my keep through a harder-than-necessary day's work. In my twenties, I trod miles in bars and banquet halls, poured pitchers of deeply desired beer, and endured undesired ass grabs by men young and old; scrubbed deep fryers of French fry barnacles until my hands were blistered; wiped deli slicers clean from tacky liverwurst, and sometimes sliced my fingers too. I disinfected toilets full of other people's shit, cleaned vomit and cum from the bathroom floors of trendy French bistros, polished glasses and silver over steaming carafes, married sticky old ketchup bottles and wiped out the insides of the lids, lest the customers suspect their ketchup was not pristine, new, bought just for them. I lifted stacked-plate entrées on wide oval trays and marched them across cavern-ous events rooms until I was sure my elbow would shatter under the weight.

I spent more than a decade *serving,* serving attitude along with extra baskets of tortilla chips, warm-but-not-fresh baguettes, ice on the side, dressing on the side, lemon on the side, extra béarnaise on the side. I served desserts that had fallen on the floor, steaks that had been spit on, caffeine when they ordered decaf. I served and I charged and I poured and I sold and I answered and I obeyed.

As soon as I could manage it, which was not as soon as I'd hoped, I clawed and crawled my way out of working-class life and into the cor-porate world, into executive positions, into the box ticking and paper pushing the late anthropologist and anarchist David Graeber defined as "bullshit jobs." I recognized the bullshit, became quite efficient at navigating said bullshit. I learned to manipulate systems and people within systems and ascended rapidly, ferociously, discovering my ver-sion of the American dream—a Cinderella story with a job (jobs!) as the princely prize.

Soon after that, as the result of a high capacity to navigate bullshit jobs, a skill I learned working (actual) shit jobs, I became—to a cer-tain small sector of powerful and influential people—a *somebody.* These powerful and influential people paid me to write about women and work, to think about women and work, to speak and advise and pontificate about women and work. They flew me to conferences and instructed me to extoll the virtues of productivity, the pleasures of pro-fessional ascent. I dutifully obliged.

For years up until the day my voice went out—and even longer after that, longer than I knew I should—I worked constantly, maniacally. I worked when I was sick, when I was tired, when I didn't want to, when I did. I worked when I was happy, when I was deeply depressed, when I was anxious, when my heart was broken. I worked through full-course-load school schedules and more than one serious health crisis. When I was pregnant, I worked until my due date, worked during maternity leave too, rocking my infant in a carrier on the floor with my foot while staring intently at my laptop, typing away.

When work started giving out phones, I carried two like I was an on-call ER doctor whose all-hours accessibility could save lives. I tended to work after dinner, during late nights before bed, during middle-of-the-nights when I couldn't sleep. I scheduled work over all my weekends (I can catch up!). I worked during vacations; up to, during, and right after family gatherings; planned my honeymoon around when would be best for work. I even worked when I was in work, often working two, or more, overlapping jobs.

Work was an eager lover I never said no to. A constant I could count on. I was good at working and I liked the way it made me feel: important, self-reliant, stable, strong. I worked as a safeguard against failure and financial ruin, to maintain a life station and status I'd hustled so hard to achieve, to keep up professional appearances, to hoard a bit of clout.

Above all else, overwork was a distraction that blotted out the dull but ambient emotional discomfort that was always there, a feeling of unworthiness that I'd been running from my entire life. Work made me feel like I was somebody other than the unlovable monster I was quite sure I was inside. It allowed me to feel that if I cosplayed long enough as a cool and competent professional, I could obliterate that monster for good.

I'd learned about work through systems of power. Capitalism taught me about work, and so did the patriarchy. Second-wave feminism taught me to dream of labor, as did the culture. The eighties movies about the women who could finally—and could not wait to— have it all. The magazine covers featuring businesswomen in sleek stilettos and neutral-toned skirt suits, fresh-faced toddlers peeking out of leather attaché cases, right by their sides. The commercials that told me I could bring home the bacon *and* fry it up for a man while also never letting that man forget he was, in fact, a man. As if any of this was even possible, as if any of us would ever forget.

But, more than from any other system of power, I learned work from my family. I did as I was taught and, above anything else in my childhood, in a myriad of indirect and direct ways, I was taught to work.

Anything You Can Do

M ost of us are quick to judge "bad" parents and "bad" parenting. We feel we inherently know what is right and what is wrong when it comes to raising a child. The truth is, parenting is an emotional cataclysm in the best of circumstances. Add in a few extraordinarily common wrenches—generational trauma, socioeconomic hardship, neurodivergence—and there's almost no way to *not* fuck up your kids. The majority of us are never taught how to live emotionally healthy lives, nor do we consistently treat ourselves— much less parent—with emotional gentleness, presence, and care. None of us get it quite right. The best we can do is show up with good intentions, try to improve a bit on the past.

Like most children of difficult homes, I've lived my adulthood more in reaction to my parents than in relation to them. I love my parents. I've tried for my entire life to protect them from my sadness, from the grief that stems from what happened to me as a kid; have spent nearly half a century blaming myself for their mistakes. I love my parents and I want to be a good daughter and I don't want to drag them into this, yet it is impossible to tell the story of my ambition without telling at least some of theirs—believe me, I've tried.

My parents were teenagers when they met at a party in Southwest Philadelphia around the winter solstice of 1971. On the night they meet, my dad's a seventeen-year-old high school dropout with a barely there chin-strap beard and a sixties-Beatles Caesar haircut, bangs a little too short. He'd left high school after ninth grade and spent his days working at a local corner deli, where he sliced lunch meat, assembled hoagies, and packed up groceries for the neighborhood's old Italian ladies. He also sold cigarettes, which my mother sometimes came in and bought. He took notice of her; you couldn't not. At sixteen, she was already tall and striking—wide smiled, clear skinned, dark brown hair almost to her waist. Despite a rebellious streak, she was mostly a sweet kid, a loyal friend, even if life had already knocked her around a bit.

When my parents meet, my mom's committed to another boyfriend, her first. But my dad is smitten, not giving up. Early the next year, when she comes down with mono and is kept out of school for weeks, the boyfriend she liked so much barely shows her the time. But my dad shows up. He brings her flowers, plays her Stevie Wonder and Roberta Flack records, sits by her side. He seems attentive and kind, a young man you can count on, a person to love and be loved by. My grandmother likes him. So do my mom's friends. By that spring, my mother breaks up with her boyfriend, chooses my dad instead.

Within the year, she's pregnant. With me. She drops out of high school, too. Weeks later, my parents are shotgun-married in their neighborhood Catholic church. My mom wears a gauzy white prairie dress with a ribbon tied at the waist; her hair loose, her head covered with a short white veil. My dad wears the baby-blue polyester suit he wore to take her to junior prom, a white carnation pinned to the lapel. They look like kids playing dress up, which, in a way, they are.

The reception is held in my maternal grandmother's tiny Southwest Philly row house. Most of the guests are teens. In the few pictures that exist from this day, my parents and their friends radiate ecstatic joy, romantic hope. On their faces is the thrill of attending your first-ever friend wedding, that nervous giddiness you feel when the adult world is new. My parents are taking a big bet on each other, on love. In this initial bet, at least, my mom has more to lose.

I'm born in 1973, the same year as the Supreme Court's *Roe v. Wade* decision, though my mother insists abortion was never a consideration. The great unsolicited assurance of my life is how I was unplanned but desperately wanted, my mother's pregnancy a year before her high school graduation nothing but the happiest of surprises. This line was repeated by my mother, by my maternal grandmother, and by most of my mother's friends, usually without prompting, always when I didn't ask.

My mother was a smart kid, a fast learner, a decent student, not necessarily academic, but savvy with people and systems in the way that a person actually needs to succeed. If she had ambitions for her young life that were not motherhood, we've never discussed them. When I've asked if she ever wished she wasn't a teen mom, she's reacted with outrage and offense, though, as with many of her responses, I'm never able to tell if this is a performance. I'm often unable to discern the truth in my mother's answers to my questions. Like many smart, complicated, wounded mothers dealing with smart, complicated, wounded daughters, she is a woman uniquely skilled at conversational litigation, twisting words and meanings and narratives to suit her agenda; at outmaneuvering unwilling opponents in a game only she seems to be playing and, therefore, only she can win.

In my mind, my mother could have and should have been more than a person saddled with a baby before she was an adult. At times, when I've attempted to hold her to account for the events of my childhood, she's responded sharply, defensively: "What? Should I have had an abortion? Is that what you want?"

The answer, though I've never articulated it, is yes and no. No, I am more than grateful for this life, which I have worked hard to make the most of, in part because I am acutely aware of the sacrifice it took to bring me into this world. And also, yes: Abortion would have made things easier for both of us.

Then again: Who said life was supposed to be easy?

———————————

Our first family home is with my grandmother, my mom's mom, and my uncle, my mom's younger brother, in my grandmother's tiny house. My mom, my dad, and I all share one room, my mom's childhood bedroom. I sleep in a frilly bassinet. My dad gets a new job stocking produce at a local grocery store. My mom takes care of me, though she's not completely alone. In the early seventies, Southwest Philly is a tight-knit working-class community; most of our relatives live within blocks. My mom's four closest female friends live in the neighborhood too, and we hang out often, a kind of "teens and a baby" gang.

In the afternoons, we head to their houses. We navigate cranky middle-aged mothers, manage to avoid even crankier old cats on our way up to teenage bedrooms to meet my mom's friends, still in their school uniforms. They are cool girls of the seventies, decked out in heavy eye makeup and glossy lips; uniformly stylish and tough. When they're not sitting on bedroom floors talking about boys and sharing mascara tips that involve separating one's eyelashes with a pin, we all head out to the playground together. Some days there's a spontaneous trip to the zoo. I'm dressed like a hip seventies doll—David Bowie T-shirts, red corduroy bell-bottoms, sunglasses too big for my face—and carried to concerts and Mummers parades, passed around at parties. In these early years, I am lavished with teenage attention, adored.

My dad works. My mom watches me, sees her friends. For a while, our young family's experiment works.

Like most people in their teens and early twenties, my parents are sorting out who they are. Their personalities change constantly, and fast. By the time I'm three, my dad starts slicking his hair back, wears a gold chain and a wide-collared leather jacket, and often doesn't come home until long after I'm in bed. When he's home, his attention goes to things that are not me. When he pays attention to me, it's mostly to discipline, and his discipline is harsh. Once, after I dip my fingers into a stick of butter, he tells me that this is a disgusting way to handle butter and, if I do it again, he'll smack my hands until they fall off. My father is a simple man, a man of his word. Days later, I do it again and he sits me down, tells me to hold out my hands, proceeds to smack them until they are red.

My dad is smart, hyperobservant of his surroundings, doesn't miss a trick. He's a quick study with a burgeoning entrepreneurial streak. His days as a stock boy are short-lived. He's noticed how the grocery store owners price fruit and vegetables higher than they need to make a profit, even if the quality is not always there. He thinks he can do better. He's just into his twenties when he starts his own business, selling cases of produce he buys wholesale at the Philadelphia Produce Market directly to customers on the street.

Around this time, my mom starts working too, as a Clinique beauty counter girl at the fancy John Wanamaker's department store in downtown Philly, enrolling me in a local daycare during her shifts. Between both jobs, my parents manage to save a bit of money. They put it all into a faux-brick and aluminum-siding HUD house that's next to a dive bar, a bare-bones Southwest Philly row home we furnish with mismatched hand-me-down furniture. The first nine hundred square feet of our own.

My parents, now fresh out of their teens, are smokers, drinkers, partiers. They're experimenting with all sorts of things, but mainly how to have a kid without sacrificing too many of their freedoms, while remaining young and fun. Once we move into our house, they're the only people in their friend circle with their own place, so the parties are mostly held there. My dad's built a party-ready cinder-block shelving system, which holds rows of albums, a turntable, a set of bongos, a flute, and a ceramic bong that's shaped like Richard Nixon's face. I attend these parties until bedtime and, more often, until long after I'm supposed to be in bed. I sit on the bell-bottomed laps of heavily perfumed women in tube tops. I dance alone to disco, to Donna Summer's "Love to Love You Baby" or my favorite, "Funkytown" by Lipps Inc. Mostly I like to eavesdrop on the adults, listen in as they grow wild and loose, make up stories in my mind about what they say, use these stories to escape the realities of the grownup world I'm immersed in, a world that's too overwhelming for me to understand.

It's the seventies and everyone is talking about sex and crank and ludes. I hear about Gary, who lost all that weight because he's doing way too much coke. I hear men ask women if they'd like to fuck. Once a man passes out at our house and a woman, his girlfriend, kneels next to him and motions me over. "He seems like he's sleeping but watch how much he kisses me because he's drunk." She bends down and begins to kiss him and, it's true, the asleep man is no longer asleep, but up and gyrating his body and kissing.

Once when I am in the bath before bed and there's a party downstairs, a man with a beard and tinted aviator glasses opens the door to use the bathroom. He doesn't come in but stands silent in the doorway, stares at my naked body for too long. I wasn't more than five.

Once a couple who've just broken up are both invited to our house by mistake. The man is angry at the woman, he wishes they hadn't broken up. He's mad enough when he sees her that he punches her in the face. My mother screams at me to go upstairs; when I come back down, she's on the floor cleaning up blood.

Once, I sit outside a circle of my mom's barefoot, cross-legged friends and one man, who is asking them to lift their tops so he can see their breasts. He wants to have a competition to see who has the best ones. I am sitting next to a pile of the women's platform shoes, my back up against the couch. A few weeks before this, at a small party at our house that was maybe not a party but still the ashtrays were full and the wine was flowing and there were more people there than just us, my mom decided it was time to read me the sex ed book *Where Did I Come From?* and now I am drawing pictures of naked men with hairy dicks. My mother turns around out of the party circle, sees the hairy dick drawings, and says, "What are you doing? Stop." But I don't stop. I am obsessed with my mother and her approval but am also obsessed with men and sex and hairy dicks, and I know this makes me a bad, dirty kid, but I cannot stop.

One of my earliest memories is of dancing around the narrow kitchen of our new house with my mother, singing a duet of the Ethel Merman song "Anything You Can Do (I Can Do Better)." I do not know "Anything You Can Do (I Can Do Better)" is a show tune composed by Irving Berlin for the Broadway musical *Annie Get Your Gun*. We're not a Broadway musical family. My mother plays David Bowie and Teddy Pendergrass records while she cleans; my dad listens to Rick James and Jethro Tull when he's home. On the day we start singing "Anything You Can Do (I Can Do Better)," my mom and I are just back after running errands. When we're out, I am an extension of my mother, never not by her side, immaculately groomed like she is, closely attached. I follow her around dutifully. She calls me her "little duckling," which I like. I'm aware from a young age that my mother's and my situation is unusual. I know this from the old ladies on the street who tsk "babies having babies" as we pass; from the store clerks, waiters, and bus drivers who ask if we're sisters, who express disbelief when I call out "Mommy" to my mom.

The galley kitchen in our new house has rust-colored carpet that's rough to the touch but fun to dance around on. I know that my mother likes this song and likes when we sing it together, and I like to please my mother. She is long and lean and lanky, now wears her dark wavy hair in a wide, puffed-out bob. When we dance to and sing this song, she lifts her arms wide like a scarecrow's, makes herself bigger, really goes for it—stomps toward me using a loud, nasally voice, scrunches up her face and fixes her eyes so she appears clownish, wild. We don't know all the words, so we just sing the same verse again and again.

———————

"Anything you can do, I can do better, I can do anything better than you," my mother sings.

The song is a call-and-response argument. I yell out my disagreement next, sing about how I *can* do things. As I sing, I jump around and dance.

It goes on like this, a few rounds at least, until I pause and look up at my mother towering over me, features distorted, eyes dark, pitch too shrieky and high. The overhead light in the small kitchen is suddenly too bright, my mother's voice is too loud. I place my hands over my ears and start to cry.

"STOP! STOP! STOP!"

I don't like this song anymore. I don't want to be better than my mother and I don't want her to be better than me, I don't want us to compete. My mother laughs off my reaction; she wants to keep playing, she's having fun. She wants me to keep doing my part.

But I can't. My dad's working and we are alone in our house. It's early evening, the doors are locked, the lights are on, the room is comfortably warm. I am at home and with my mother and I should feel safe, but I do not feel safe. I live in a house where it feels like anything can happen at any time, a playhouse for adults that rarely feels safe for me, a kid.

"Come on!" she says and starts up her part again. But the moment has passed, the game is over. She tries to nudge, but I'm too upset to sing. I don't even know my next line.

————————

"Anything you can be, I can be greater . . . sooner or later I'm greater than you."

Bullies

W hen he's young, my father is always asserting dominance—over other men, over my mother and me, over his
employees, over the wild alligators we encounter on dirt
roads on our frequent road trips to Florida. The drive from the center
of Philadelphia to southern Florida is just over a thousand miles long
and takes—depending on a number of factors (weather and traffic;
the health of your vehicle; gas stops, pit stops, how many passengers
you're carrying, and how many breaks from the road they require)—
twenty-two hours, give or take.

"Winter is not a season, it's an occupation," Sinclair Lewis
famously said, a sentiment with which my parents agree. They hate
East Coast winters, hate the snow, the windchill, the bundling, the
sleet, the cleaning off your car in the morning, the shoveling, the coats.
We make it through Christmas just fine, the lights and the revelry
and the tradition and the Italian-Catholic familial obligation all there
to carry us through, but by mid-January, at least one of them is itch-
ing to pack it up and quit town. Because my dad is self-employed,
we can.

My parents aren't planners, at least not in those days. They're
impulsive; they don't give a damn about my public school's schedule;

and they resent authority—cops, my teachers, the man. We're (briefly) vegans before there's a word for vegan, pro-choice, pro-cannabis ERA supporters, Nixon and Reagan haters. There's a sense that the rules do not apply to us, unless I myself break them. Still, these trips to Florida always come as somewhat of a surprise.

We drive down Interstate 95 with my parents' friends, in an old metallic green station wagon we name the "War Wagon" for its ability to stand up to our wear and tear. For a time, the War Wagon is missing a window, and we cover its open space with an old plastic bag. We pack the car with fruit from my dad's produce stand and camping supplies and a few other twentysomething travelers eager for a warm-weather retreat. Our destination is always the same: the Florida Keys, a place that in the 1970s feels lawless, the country's southernmost point, the end of the line, a last-resort island paradise for retirees, vagabonds, and drifters looking to get lost.

The Florida Keys are an archipelago of more than a thousand islands off the coast of Florida, though only thirty are inhabited. They're connected by a series of bridges and contain one of the country's largest national parks—the Everglades, a protected wetlands that's home to hundreds of species of wildlife, including panthers, manatees, exotic birds, and both crocodiles *and* alligators, the only place in the world where you can find the two animals coexisting in the wild.

In these early trips to the Keys, we arrive and set up camp at a state park called Bahia Honda, a hippie campers' idyll where you can pitch a tent directly on the sand, just a few steps from the sea. I'm bursting with anticipation the entire trip, thrilled to run to the water's edge once we land.

The sand at the Bahia Honda campsite is pale white, fine, soft as a cloud. The ocean is bright turquoise, calm and clear; giant pelicans fly above, diving to snatch a fish, a fresh catch squirming inside an oversize bill. While my parents set up camp, I wander around alone, traipsing through the rainbow village of tents, collecting rocks, bugs, sculptural white coral, and peach-colored conch shells the size of my forearm. Later in the evening, before it gets dark, my dad's shirtless, short-shorts-clad friends scale palm trees, shake them for loose coconuts. Afterward, they knock the furry brown fruit open with a knife, offer some to me.

There are benefits to having young parents. The spontaneity of youth is its own magic. On their best days, my parents are enthusiasts, deeply invested in life's pleasures and delight. Their impetuousness builds a sense of possibility inside me that never leaves, disrupting traditional ideas about structure, rules, and even time. These spontaneous trips to Florida become a cornerstone of my ability to adapt easily. Our fly-by-the-seat-of-your-pants travel style teaches me to take risks. I develop a belief system that things will work out even if you don't know how; that sometimes you just have to pick up and go. An early childhood with few conventional boundaries allows me to understand the rewards of living outside of the fold, even though I know, even then, that I am not built the same way my parents are, that their fun comes at the expense of my feeling protected, and that, even when surrounded by adults, I often feel unseen, other, and alone.

In Florida, like at home, my father seeks out danger. He's handsome, gregarious, makes friends wherever he goes. Some of those friends are looking for trouble, too. In a motel late one night after many drinks, he jumps over our balcony to a new friend's balcony, a six-foot distance between them, a three-story drop to the ground. He and his new friend are playing a game; they try this stunt again. Back in our room, my mother screams for him to stop. He does not stop. He also does not plummet to the ground.

Driving down through the Everglades, we see alligators along the side of the road. My father and his friend want to get up close.

They jump out of the car, tease the beast with a stick, poke at it, and then they run. The gator chases them along the dirt road, its squat legs surprisingly fast. My mother's barefoot in a string bikini and cutoffs, she and a female friend shrieking from the car for this assholery to end. The alligator is ten feet of brownish green scales, with beady eyes and a mouth that is snapping and angry and huge. The windows of the car are open, but inside it feels airless, muggy, and hot. I sit in the backseat and stare out the window, perfectly still. I'm too young to know the stakes of my father's recklessness, but I'm old enough to internalize panic. The gator closes in, getting nearer to us and nearer to the car and nearer to my dad until it's right at his heels.

"OPEN THE DOOR! OPEN THE DOOR! OPEN THE DOOR!"

My mom's friend opens the door. My dad and his friend slide in, quickly slam it shut.

My mom is in the driver's seat, peels the car away fast.

"That was fucking stupid," she says.

"Yeah, but we didn't get caught," he says, reaching an arm over the front seat and shaking her shoulder.

He looks over at me and winks. "We didn't get caught."

The agenda for these Florida tours is always roughly the same: A day trip stop at Disney World on the way home, off-season and midweek, empty enough that the whole park feels like it's ours. We buy and all wear cheap plastic Mouse ears. We chase down Mickey and Pluto and Goofy and Minnie and linger over hugs. We rent a golf cart outside the park, and I get to drive. We eat ourselves full of ice cream and caramel corn, go to It's a Small World, ride the tea-cups over and over until we're sick. *Let's do it again!* They always say yes.

There are other highlights too, not all sparking joy. There's the poor judgment of not fully formed brains, the poor decisions made from poor judgment, like the night my parents meet a strange hippie couple at the campground with whom they party too hard and too late. I don't know exactly what happens or what is consumed, but we wake up the next morning to find the strange hippies have stolen most of our stuff.

And there's the ambient rage, always simmering just underneath the surface, always threatening to blow. My parents argue often, over anything, everything, anytime. They drink too much and fight over drinking. They flirt or are flirted with and fight over flirting. There are quick bursts of fury, gritted teeth, a reflexive smack, a quick punch, too fast driving, jerky turns, a too hard acceleration, slamming of the brakes and the gas.

The narrow Seven Mile Bridge that connects Knight's Key and Little Duck Key always feels precarious, like one false move and we'll careen over the edge, a sensation exacerbated by my parents' nonstop bickering. When my father is angry, or even annoyed, he drives recklessly. When it's her turn to drive, my mother, who is terrified of water and drowning, holds her long tan fingers tight on the steering wheel until her knuckles turn white. No matter the circumstances, I stay quiet when we pass over the bridge. The ten minutes feels like an hour, the way time seems to stand still when you're scared. We look to our parents to let us know what's safe or not, rely on their emotional regulation to regulate ours. When my parents are angry, I'm anxious. When they're worried it won't work out—whatever "it" is, driving over a bridge, their young marriage—I worry the same, but more intensely, the fear growing into my bones.

My parents want me to be tough, but I'm not. When we're not in Florida, I walk the eight city blocks each morning to my Philadelphia public elementary school starting when I'm in first grade. My father tells me to speak and stand up for myself, but it's not my way. At five, I am clumsy, emotional, and soft. At my mother's insistence, I wear my blond hair in blunt bangs attached to two prissy pin-neat braids. We are a young family of little means, but my mother knows instinctually how to milk what we have: good looks, good manners, always appearing neat and clean.

In first grade, I attract a bully, a girl who follows me all the way home each day, calls me names, threatens to hit me with her metal lunch box. One day she does start hitting me with her lunch box, hits me harder when I cry. When I confide this to my mom, she tells me to fight back. When I explain the situation to my dad, he teaches me how to throw a punch. My parents are working-class survivors. They don't suffer fools. And they won't tolerate weakness, not in themselves, and certainly not in a kid they're teaching to be in the world.

One of my mom's friends has a new baby I desperately want to hold, a fact which is used as a lure. I'm told I can hold the new baby if—and only if—I stand up for myself and punch the bully in the face. The next day after school, I come home, feigning pride. I lie and say I've defeated the bully, describe an elaborate, victorious scene. I have no power, but I'm learning to manipulate power to protect myself and still get what I want. I'm learning how to tell stories about my life and perform being a person I'm not.

Secretly, I spend every day after school trying to outrun the bully, mapping out elaborate, circuitous routes home. One afternoon, when I finally arrive at our house, my mother wants to know what's taking so long. I confess, and she becomes enraged. Tells me to get in the car, says we're going to find this bully, stand up to her once and for all. We drive around slowly, block by block in the neighborhood, scanning kids' faces to identify the perp. Somewhat miraculously, we spot her on the street outside her house. My mother over-brakes the car to a halt, tells me to get out, slams the door, marches up to the bully, points for me to stand next to her. I look down at the ground while she sizes both of us up.

"Oh my god, she's not even taller than you," she says to me.

Then, to the bully: "Don't mess with my friggin' kid again."

Window of Tolerance

The wall-size fish tank arrives one day. I don't know how or when or why; I'm a kid, distracted by other things. I like dolls, but mostly I like destroying dolls, matting their hair until it is ragged and rough, removing their dainty doll clothes, scrubbing off their cherubic face paint with my mother's sweet-smelling nail polish remover. My mother comments on the dolls, mostly when we're in public, mostly when people can hear. "Can you believe what she does to a perfectly good doll?" she says. Everyone looks at the dolls like they're tiny plastic monsters. I'm beginning to think I'm a tiny monster, too. At five, I've started to assert a personality. I'm not as "easy" as I used to be. No longer everyone's baby, not my mother's duckling or doll.

The tank stands empty for weeks, collects dust in our living room until one afternoon we pile into my father's new-to-us Chevy Nova on a mission for new pets. It's winter in Philadelphia, but inside the fluorescent-lit fish store, it's the humid balmy tropics, albeit with a turtle poop scent. We tour aisles of mossy tanks and choose our fish—two broad, flat oscar fish for my mom and me, an albino catfish for my dad, and a bag of assorted goldfish to fill things out. No one researches the fish, what they might need, how they'll get along. We pick what looks cool, and purchase on a whim. At home, we have three other pets, including, temporarily, a squirrel. Whims are our way of life.

We manage to keep the fish alive longer than you'd think. Especially if you know fish. Oscar fish are fast growing, temperamental. Albino catfish can grow to the size of a human leg. By summer, the goldfish are long gone, replaced several times over, gobbled up one by one. By July, the fifty-gallon tank has just three inhabitants, all cartoonishly large, bloated, and insatiably hungry. By the end of the summer, the fish will be at war.

My parents' young marriage is now constant combat, a struggle for power and dominance, a fight for survival. My father's away from the house more and more, gone late nights or overnights, or longer. Kids, like pets, don't understand time. When he's away, my mom talks about the life she and I will have together, alone, how we'll leave this place, how we will become models. She will be a grownup model and I will be a kid model, she has it all planned. She's still young and strikingly beautiful, emotionally reckless in a way those who are young and beautiful are allowed to be. When I see my dad, I tell him about the modeling. I don't know it's a secret, that I'm tripping the wire. But later, when I'm in bed, they argue violently late into the night.

Between them there is jealousy and infidelity and infidelity born of jealousy, but I am too young for complex realities. I can see the sharp-edged map of their marriage, but I'll never truly understand the finer textures of its terrain. All I know is what I overhear in my mother's long talks with her girlfriends, the "fuck *hims*" she spits over red wine and ceramic ashtrays filled with powdery gray ash. Later, in her conversations with my dad, the chorus of accusations, the "fuck *off*s" and "fuck *yous*" she scream-shouts and shrieks.

While he's gone, my father's albino catfish grows bigger and stronger, prowling, its red eyes darting for food, no matter how many thin bright orange goldfish it swallows, no matter how many begrudging trips to the store my mother makes for more plastic baggies of prey.

One morning, my mother and I wake to find the larger of the oscar fish dead, floating, half-eaten. The other is alive but barely, bitten badly and swimming sluggishly, a slow-motion skeleton, an almost-corpse. It's a gruesome centerpiece, imminent death floating above my toys, next to the round wooden table where I often eat alone, across from an old white piano no one plays. We often have people at our house, but the night when the second oscar fish dies, we are alone; it is just us, my mother and me.

After she makes and serves me dinner, washes the dishes and wipes down the table, counter, and stove, my mother turns around, pauses, and stares over at the catfish. Then she stomps down the stone cellar stairs. I hear her flick on the lightbulb string, flick it back off again. When she returns, she's carrying an industrial-size bucket and a gallon of Clorox bleach. She pours the bleach into the bucket and removes the lid of the tank.

She takes two flimsy fish nets on long shaky sticks, which are not quite strong enough for the job, dips them into the water, and lifts the catfish—unexpectedly muscular, fleshy—out of the water. The catfish flips up and out of the tank, thrashes forcefully within the netted sticks until he arrives by some divine energetic vengeance, and with an assist by gravity, into the bucket. Away from the tank's neon pebbles, he looks more creamy than white. His almost translucent beige body splats and splashes and thrusts in the bleach. In a few minutes that feel like hours, the catfish is dead. My mother marches the bucket upstairs to the toilet, flushes its contents down the drain. She tells me to put on my pajamas and brush my teeth. I get into bed and my mother reads me a story. Then I go to sleep.

In a house where violence is normalized, there's little room for grief. After the tank is removed (a man with a python takes it off our hands), my mother and I move on quickly. The catfish becomes a symbol of admired retribution, might in the face of betrayal. It's a family punch line, a joke we all laugh at, the despair and desperation behind it never mentioned or explained.

In the next year, our dog will run away, our iguana will hide behind the couch and die, I'll perform in my first tap-dance show, I'll have a birthday party and one of my classmate-friends will vomit on our stairs, my mother will birth a second child, there will be a fire in our house. My dad is absent for most all of it.

Before we leave this house, my mother will kick in the metal bottom of the screen door until it is permanently dented, bang the plastic phone on the receiver until it breaks, smoke so many cigarettes the walls will turn yellow. She will tell me to fight back, be tough, stand up for yourself, stand your ground while running all our family's errands, performing every household chore. She will sit behind me folding clothes while I watch *The Flintstones* and say, "The way Fred talks to Wilma is not the way men should talk to women." She will tell me to have a career of my own, to make money, to never be dependent on a man, and I will listen. She will kill a catfish, a mighty beast, one night in a bucket of bleach and never look back. There will be tiny bleach spots in the blue carpet that never come out, next to the tiny leftover blood spots nearby under the dining room table that no one but me knows are there. There will be a legacy of strength I'm expected to maintain. And secrets I'm expected to keep.

The term "window of tolerance" is used by psychologists to help patients learn to mitigate, minimize, and react appropriately to the stressors in their lives. Our windows of tolerance represent the emotional margins within which we are able to process stress in a healthy way without flooding the brain with stress hormones or entering into hyperaroused states of panic, rage, or even emotional collapse. Depending on the person and the depth of unprocessed trauma, once the brain is flooded with stress hormones almost anything can happen, including, and often likely, emotional and physical abuse, a state experts often refer to as being "offline." Like a cornered animal, an individual outside a window of tolerance will usually engage in one of four trauma responses: fight, flight, or freeze, which most of us have heard of; plus the fourth, a behavior you've probably seen but not known the name for—fawn—when we use over-the-top people-pleasing to avoid intolerable conflict at any cost.

My sister is born in the summer of 1978, in the sixth year of my parents' marriage and into my sixth year of being alive. Our precarious family system soon strains under the weight of this new addition. We move quickly and collectively out of an already narrow window of tolerance. We begin barely tolerating anything at all.

My mother is no longer working. Before she became pregnant with my sister, she'd briefly gone back to school to be a hairdresser, dyed her sleek bob dark disco purple; made new friends, went away with them overnight to a fancy hair show. But she drops out of the program before receiving her certification, abandons this independent life before it begins—the combined factors of her own insecurity and a lack of support at home dooming the enterprise from the start. In this and any new venture for my mother, my father is clear: He does not like her hanging out with new people, especially men—*Who's this fucking guy? I don't care if he's gay!*—and he is too busy with his business to pick up our household's domestic slack, even for one kid, let alone two.

As small business owners, our financial picture is ever-changing, hard to predict. Money is sometimes scarce. My dad gets our fresh fruit and vegetables for free, which means we are never food insecure, though there are times when our fridge holds just two items: one shelf full of oranges and another of beer. My mom buys the rest of our groceries at a downtown hippie food co-op that smells of stale carob and is filled with oversize buckets of bulk grains. The co-op bears a number of handwritten signs, including one next to the toilet in the bathroom: "If it's yellow let it mellow, if it's brown flush it down!"

I eat broccoli and a baked potato for dinner, bring thermos beans to school for lunch. I have two pairs of pants and they're both hand-me-downs. Getting a new pair of sneakers is a big, exciting deal. When we buy a new refrigerator, it's a celebration. I turn the box into an elaborately decorated fort, place it in front of our house, just off the street, and play in it for months.

At this time, we are part of the plastic-on-the-furniture but never-without-a-fancy-Easter-outfit class, the can't-quite-pay-our-taxes-but-our-TV-is-new class. The richest people we know live in a row house nearby with a glittery white popcorn ceiling, a finished faux-wood-paneled basement with a bar, and an aboveground pool in their backyard. We spend what money we have; there's little context for what "having" money means.

There are times after my sister is born when I look at my mom and I know that she is scared. Of what, I'm too young to know. She's worryingly thin, smokes now more than ever, often in the kitchen while staring out the window with a faraway look. She is twenty-two with two kids. She has no money of her own, no marketable skills, no high school diploma. The women she's closest to—her cool friends I love—graduated high school but skipped college, partnered up instead. They now have their own new families to contend with, their own man problems, each one of the dudes they've married objectively worse than the next.

How do we fight our way out of a corner? What will we sacrifice in order to survive? As my father's recreational indulgences take him further and further from home, my mother fights back. She scrambles and schemes, tracks him wherever he is, plays against his jealous streak, manipulates, taunts. The combat required to maintain her marriage takes up most of her attention. My sister is still a baby. There's little left of my mom for anything or anyone else.

She's harder and sharper with me now, expects more, tolerates less. I miss my mother *and* I resent her lack of attention. I resent my new sister more. My sister's room is right next to mine, just big enough to fit a crib given to us by friends, painted yellow by my mom. Next to her room are the carpeted stairs, which go two down, then a turn on a small landing, then twenty down to the first floor. I know this because I often creep out of my room at night to sit on the landing and listen—to parties, to Johnny Carson's monologues, but mainly, when my father is home, to my parents' increasingly violent fights.

I'm a hypersensitive and reactive child. I throw screaming tantrums until my face is hot and my tears sting. The intensity of my young anger makes me feel afraid. I start hiding, both myself and what I consider to be my myriad screwups, my mistakes. At night, before I fall asleep, I cover myself in blankets and carefully arrange my stuffed animals over the bulge of my body to make myself invisible, so no one knows I'm there. In my room is a wooden doll cradle, where I keep my dolls and my bad report cards, the ones that give me an F in conduct. For months, I meticulously hide these and other bad school papers under my dolls and their thin gingham mattress, tucked in tight with a chevron-stripe blanket knitted by my great-grandmother specifically for the dolls. The blanket matches the poncho I'll wear to church on Easter later that year, which matches the poncho my sister will wear too. We'll both have on white Mary Janes, and ruffled socks cuffed over, and matching white Easter hats. On the outside, we look pretty, pristine. Under this immaculate surface, however, I feel increasingly foul, soiled from within.

I'm lying to my mom about my report cards and about how poorly I behave in school. I'm lying to my dad, when I see him, about who my mom sees when he's not home and what she does. She's started going out with friends and getting the babysitter more, but I don't care because the babysitter is a teenager who lets me wear makeup and watch as much TV as I want. I do care about the lies, though; there are so many, I can't keep track.

In the winter, my father takes a trip to Florida, without us this time, for longer than we usually go. When he calls and wants to talk to me, I don't know what to say. One afternoon when I'm with my mom, I slip about the report cards. I'm not a sophisticated wordsmith; the slip is obvious and dumb. My mother marches me up the stairs, rips apart the doll bed, and holds my report cards out with a shake. She grabs me by the arm, pulls me over, and makes me look at them the way you would a dog who'd defecated in the house.

A few days after this, she trips down our stairs and sprains her ankle, which, on top of my father's absence and the constant care-taking of two kids—all of it—is the final straw. A few days after that, she heads to the airport with her sprained ankle and wheels alone in a borrowed airport wheelchair to fly to Florida and retrieve my father for good. She leaves my sister and me with one set of my great-grandparents, the paternal ones with the once-glamorous Italian-born great-grandmother, who now has early Alzheimer's and thinks I am a young version of my uncle, my father's half brother.

While my parents are away, Valentine's Day arrives. My teacher asks me to make a card for my dad and I tell her he's away and she says then make one for your mom, and I say she's away too. The inner-city Philadelphia public school teacher, who does not seem to like or enjoy children, will not know what to do with this.

At my great-grandparents' house, I grow an intricate, lacy red rash that starts on my arm but a few days later spreads all over my body, accompanied by a fever high enough that it cannot be ignored. Another grandparent arrives to take my hot, splotchy red body to someone who identifies what I have as a thing called fifth disease. I recover swaddled in a thin crocheted blanket atop a couch still wrapped in the plastic it came in. My great-grandmother dotes on my sister, who she calls "the baby"; but she calls me "the bad one," even though she thinks my real name is my uncle's. Later, everyone will laugh about this, and I will pretend to think it's funny too.

When my parents finally return, they bring us presents from the road. They seem happy, relaxed, in love. My mom arrives with a golden tan and a big smile; my dad with clear eyes, a beard, and a renewed commitment to our family. He never leaves again.

There's more to this part of the narrative, secrets and side plots, stories in the rearview mirror of my parents' marriage that are not mine to tell. Years later, when I mention these stories to my mom, she swats at me like you would a fly, tells me to get over it.

"None of it was actually *that* bad."

How much do we need to endure early in order to justify feeling messed up later?

If the situation wasn't *that* bad, was it something wrong with me?

Am I too much to manage, inherently awful?

It's the wrong question to ask. It's the question I never stop asking.

Everyone Loves an Italian Girl

In the early aughts, when I first moved to New York and into the elite, ultrawhite world of New York publishing, Urban Outfitters made a faux vintage T-shirt with the words EVERYONE LOVES AN ITALIAN GIRL scrawled in seventies-style cursive letters across the front. I had very little money for clothes (or even food), and so, when the shirts went on sale, I bought two in a size smaller than I was, cut off the necks and sleeves, and wore them an inappropriate amount—to bars and parties, mainly, but also to work in offices where women did not wear such things. I was a rough-around-the-edges working-class Italian-American girl in an Ivy League world, still grappling with what that meant and how I could possibly fit in.

Up until the point when I embarked on a white-collar career, my understanding of work was merely as a means to survival, holding your nose while performing whatever good-enough employment you could get, muscling your way through. I was the first person in my family to graduate high school and, eventually, college; my siblings followed suit. My early models for adult womanhood did not include take-charge career fulfillment or even contented homemaking, but were shaped by the unrealized lower-middle-class lives of the Italian-American women I grew up around—women I both loved and feared.

On all sides of my family, I am Italian American, fourth generation, but, because our generations are short, growing up, I was close with all of my immigrant great-grandparents, most of whom were in my life until I was well into my teens. I grew up with a hard-stamped Italian-American identity, including the cliché movie and TV depictions you know: tomato vines growing in buckets in cement backyards, an always-simmering pot of homemade red sauce called "gravy," homemade pasta my grandparents called "macaroni," homemade basement barrels of red wine that'll fuck you up worse than moonshine, Feasts of the Seven Fishes on Christmas Eve, ricotta (pronounced "ree-gut") pie on Easter, ravioli, cannoli, spumoni, boundaryless aggression, rough and regular affection, constant confrontation, theatrical levels of emotion, guilt diffused like air. And a few identifying features you may not be as aware of, the more unpleasant reveals: under-the-surface darkness, suspicion, rage; a sense, imagined or not, that we are different, that there's prejudice against us, that we can't rely on others who are not our kind.

My grandparents were deeply distrustful of non-Italians—there was talk among them that non-Italian white people thought of us as dirty dagos, greaseballs, wops. My father is arrested once, pulled off the street with slicked-back wet hair fresh out of the shower, physically nabbed and thrown up against a car by a cop, frisked, brought in when they find the tiniest end of a joint in his front jeans pocket, booked. Everyone in the family believes this happens because he's Italian. No one talks about how much worse it would've been if he weren't white. All we know is that my great-grandfather couldn't find a job because he was an Italian immigrant, that, in response, my great-grandmother did backbreaking work until she became wheelchair bound, that Italians are still getting hassled on the street for looking too dark and slick. All we know is our own pain.

Around my extended family's table, the greatest insult is to be called an American. Except in our houses, it's pronounced "medigan" and is used to describe everything from putting cheese on pasta with seafood ("What are you, a medigan?") to the non-Italians anyone dares to date or bring home ("What are you doing with a medigan?") to public figures we hate ("Friggin' medigans"). My great-grandparents speak in broken English, they say "fungool" for "fuck," they call coarse, piggish men "gavonnes." When I shop with my grandmother at the Italian corner market, she speaks a language of vowels that I never understand, sounds that look different than the words: "loo-CAH-tel" "gal-a-mad," "scun-gee-lee," "brAH-jol."

Daughters don't matter much in most Italian-American families, at least they matter less than sons, who are worshipped, revered. Daughters are expected to be in service—of their mothers, fathers, husbands, brothers, sons, all men. They're meant to do all the elaborate cooking, and all the immaculate cleaning, and all the meticulous laundering, all the Catholic church–going, all the extended-family caretaking, and all the child rearing, such as it is. My grandmothers were both born in the 1930s, both younger sisters to older brothers, both deprioritized, both treated harshly, as less.

At Sunday dinners, held at my great-grandparents' homes, we crowd around dining tables with leaf extensions that render them too big for their rooms. At these dinners, the men are spoiled with whatever means available, doted on, well fed. My great-uncles are given freedoms at a young age, and encouraged to pursue lives of possibility. My grandmothers—both smart, beautiful, capable women who will never see themselves this way—are taught to be good Catholic girls, to marry Italian men. Along the way they are regularly ridiculed and demeaned, especially by their moms.

As a teen, my mom's mom, Jean, was spirited and rebellious. She made friends easily, liked singing and dancing the jitterbug, loved Frank Sinatra so much that she accidentally yanked off her friend Ida's poodle skirt when they went to see him live. Jean first fell in love with an Irish boy, who loved her back but who her father said she couldn't marry. Instead, she was set up with a slick Italian-American man her dad liked, a man who seemed to enjoy her parents and other women more than he ever liked her, a man who took off abruptly one day and left her alone with two kids, including my mother. Behind Jean's tiny Philly row house are train tracks, and across the street are nosy neighbors who sit on their front porch and stare at and judge her life as a single mom.

Throughout my childhood, Jean lives with my uncle, my mom's younger brother, who is what might have been referred to then as "troubled"—though no one has the emotional clarity or the financial resources to sort out what the trouble is. Instead, we live in denial, minimizing the quite serious situation. For people so compulsively direct, so much is never said.

———————

Into his young adulthood, my uncle doesn't go to school, and he rarely works. Instead, he spends his days scribbling line drawings of Jesus in black Magic Marker all over my grandmother's cellar walls and buying lottery tickets at the corner store at the same time every day. He never misses the live lottery drawing at 7:00 P.M., even if you're watching something else on my grandma's TV. He eats family-size portions of pasta faster than anyone you've ever seen, talks in a monologuing loop, argues with you if you say he cannot dance as well as Michael Jackson, which he can't.

When I'm at my grandmother's house, my uncle gives me unsolicited advice about grownup life that is not the kind of advice a kid should hear. He talks to himself constantly, yells at my grandmother often, loudly, abruptly, out of the blue. Sometimes he loses control with her, physically strikes.

Jean is single, but she doesn't like it. She has an on-again, off-again boyfriend named Ed, who takes her dancing sometimes. When I see him, he plays the game of "I found this quarter behind your ear," which I don't like because when he leans in, I can smell his breath, which reeks of old whiskey. Ed is always in and out of the picture, and when he's out, my grandmother waits by the phone for him to call and cries. I spend a lot of time with my grandmother, who is soft and tender like me, but I know, even then, sadder and more broken than I'll ever be. Whenever I see her, she tells me to pray to God. Sometimes, she takes me to church on Sundays. She has little art on her walls except pictures of her children and grandchildren and a painting of the Last Supper, a braided and dried palm leaf left over from Palm Sunday, a signed picture of the Pope and, in the dining room, a single gold-painted cross.

Jean works in Center City, Philadelphia, as a clerk at a corporate insurance company, a dead-end, no-advancement job that has a good pension. She takes the trolley to work every day. On the weekends she sometimes takes me to the movies and we ride the trolley together and when we go to the bathroom she tells me to put paper on the toilet seat before I pee. I love my grandmother, she is gentle and kind, but she is not a person with whom I can feel safe. When I am small, she has one of many severe depressive breakdowns, is carted from the house in a straitjacket, leaving my mom to decide whether or not to try electric shock. She does, but my grandmother is still sad afterward, still prays to God to make the pain go away. She'll live to be eighty-four but won't like herself through most of it, will call herself stupid through most of it. A lot of it won't seem like living at all.

During his childhood, my dad's mom, Dolores, is also single. She lives just a few blocks away from my mom's mom in an apartment above her dad's barbershop. She works for decades as a factory worker at the Mars factory, where they make M&M's, though what she's really good at is art. When I visit her, she draws me pictures of exquisite women in expensive clothes, ornate designs that look like fashion sketches, hair and makeup perfectly styled and soft.

The pictures always seemed to me models of herself, the self I think she'd wished to be. From puberty on, Dolores is voluptuous and tantalizingly beautiful, brazen, independent, foulmouthed, and ballsy. Nearly everything about her as a woman in the 1950s is not socially acceptable. When she's in her early twenties, she meets a thick, macho, cigar-smoking, married Italian-American guy, who may or may not be mob adjacent, not that we are ever allowed to talk about the mob or mob adjacencies.

They'll fall in fiery, problematic love. In the only surviving picture of them together, my dad's parents sit in one oversize armchair. My grandmother wears a sleeveless, body-hugging blue shift dress, her black hair teased high, her black eyebrows thick, her lips full and painted coral red. My grandfather is in a high-sheen silk button-down shirt and crisp trousers, his thick, also-black hair brushed back, legs draped over the body of my grandmother, his date. They're both scowling; an expression that says, "Don't fuck with me." They look like two gorgeous, dangerous, bull-headed jerks. A few months after this picture is taken, my grandmother is pregnant with my dad. My grandfather eventually tells her he'll leave his wife for her, says he'll marry her. She tells him not to bother. She'll have suitors after this, some kind, some not, some my dad likes, some he doesn't. For most of her adult life, Dolores avoids settling down, avoids the trappings of mid-twentieth-century domesticity for a woman. Misses out on the safety of it, too.

She'll live with her parents and my dad until her mid-thirties, when she meets another man, this one with not even a paper cup to piss in. She'll get pregnant again and, to be near the man, moves into a one-room apartment with black cement floors in a run-down part of Jersey.

The night Dolores goes into labor with her second son, her new man is not around, so my dad gets her to the hospital when her water breaks. He is eleven. After this, he'll run away, back to Philly, and sleep on rooftops until my great-grandparents finally agree to take him in.

Dolores stays with her second baby's father, even though when she moves back to Philly, to the apartment above my great-grandfather's barbershop, this man doesn't always come home. When he does, they yell in the efficiency kitchen about where he's been and who he's been with. She pushes him against the wall, against the refrigerator, howl-

screams in his face. They argue so loudly when she's babysitting me at her apartment that I scooch the red pleather beanbag chair closer to the TV so I can better hear *Love Boat*.

For the eighty-six years before dementia hits her, Dolores is the baddest bitch I know. She hates housekeeping, loves the casino, and calling people "assholes." She raised my dad as a single mom in a time when this was rarely done. She made him learn to dress up and go out to fancy places, even though they didn't have much money. She wore red lipstick every day of her adult life until the day they put her in a home. She also regularly criticized, ridiculed, and shamed her sons into submission; made herself difficult, near impossible to know. I watched my grandmother work her entire life for so little, never ask for—or receive—what she wanted or needed, and yet she never gave up the ship. When she finally dies at ninety-one in a nursing home, some of her last words are "I fight, I fight!"

It's a family anthem. In time, I'll start singing it too.

A Different Story

When I'm young, my father does many things that keep him from fathering, but most of those things are related to work. He works constantly, day and night, weekends too. When he's not working, he's talking about work, and when he's not talking about work, he's quietly stressing about it.

While he may lack a high school diploma, he more than makes up for it in good sense and grit. Within a few years, he builds his produce business from a stand on the street to a refrigerated truck he parks in a rented parking spot to a big warehouse store a few blocks from our house in Southwest Philly. Eventually he'll expand to four stores throughout Pennsylvania and South Jersey and, in the process, elevate our financial profile to an upper-middle-class level no one in our family had experienced before.

My father is special—he knows it, we know it, everyone who encounters him knows it. He's the kind of man who changes the energy of a room when he enters it, that combination of innate charisma and old-school magnetism, and the rare good sense to know what to do with it. He's got a solid build, a confident, swaggering gait. Dark hair, dark eyes, the Italian-American good looks of the day—*Taxi*'s Tony Danza with more edge; *The Deer Hunter*'s DeNiro with less bite. He's generous, a good tipper, a person who'll come by with his pickup and help you move something heavy, someone who tells service staff what a good job they're doing, a guy who knows the basics of car maintenance, how to fix a leak in your sink.

He visits his grandmother on weekends, goes to church on Christmas morning. He's great at a party, is a fun drunk (for everyone but my mom), one of those gifted storytellers who effortlessly commands attention but not selfishly or for too long. Always hits the right tone, goes for the right laugh.

Throughout my life, gay men cruise my father, women we know and women we don't swoon over him and, when I'm old enough, so do my friends. He knows how to dress—and when he's dressed up, he looks, in a literal sense, sharp. Sharp creases along the legs of his pants, crisp shirts, shined shoes, a gleaming gold chain. My father is warm, discreet, one of those rare men both women and men want to be around, a man everyone believes they can trust.

He's also, at this time, moody and impatient, quick-tempered, stubborn, emotionally unavailable, and hard to know. At his worst, with those closest to him, he can be judgmental and cold, bordering on cruel. You want to know my father, but you don't want to cross him. I idolize and want to be him I suspect from the moment I was born.

———————————

For decades, my father wakes up at 3:00 A.M. every day to go to work. He does this whether or not he's hungover, in sticky-hot August and negative-ten-degree windchill winter mornings, when it takes a half hour to warm up the car. He buys product from the Philadelphia Produce Market each morning before dawn, before the good stuff's snatched up, when he can still get the best price. He's skilled in many areas of his business, but particularly at haggling, swiftly sizing up a negotiating opponent, alternating between careful pressure and charm to get what he wants.

For most of his career, my father's labor is grueling. He's often loading and unloading trucks full of heavy boxes and doing it fast, is regularly injured on the job. He bags produce when he's short a bagger, drives the truck when the driver doesn't show up, works an extra register when the line gets too long. The work is ever-changing, full of (literal) moving parts. I remember few times in my childhood when he's not overwhelmed by work, when he's not on the phone managing one crisis after another in the business of perishable goods.

My dad's sense of honor, his role in our family, all rely on his keeping up with backbreaking work. After my sister is born, his work differentiates us from the close relatives around us whose lives begin to collapse. The family members my parents describe (when they think I'm not listening) as "on the shit," the ones who become lost to heroin or meth or crack, whose new babies sit in piss and filth just a few blocks away. The ones my mom whispers and worries about, the ones we can now afford to bring diapers to and food and clothes, solutions we know will help for only so long.

The slide in this country from middle class to lower class to abject poverty is swifter than most people imagine. Unless you see it up close, it's difficult to comprehend the speed with which a person can lose grasp of a life within a system that undervalues dignity, a system that makes it close to impossible to gain that life back. As a child, I watch relatives sink deeper and deeper into poverty, see them sponge off their mothers' Social Security, never pay their own rent. Family members get locked up for stealing cars, lose fingers scaling fences while running from cops. Cousins die by suicide, by heroin overdose, by falling off a roof. Addicted gamblers lose entire pensions in the flashing ding-ding-ding of Atlantic City slot machines. Family grifters attempt to pull a fast one on life, try to get by on scams—scam lawsuits, scam jobs. In the end, they wind up with next to nothing at all.

My extended family was a cautionary tale. My father's work allowed us to tell a different story about ourselves. His business gave my family the resources we needed for ascent; it kept us from succumbing to and being subsumed by the darkness that was part of all of us, the addictions and mental illness in our blood. It eventually helped us get OUT, out of the inner-city HUD house with the old men urinating on the street outside the dive bar next door, away from the neighborhood park where my father was jumped one night and came home so beat and bruised he required an emergency room visit. The next morning, I woke up to Grandma Jean, blank-faced on the couch, the only sign of my parents is my father's bloodied undershirt left on the floor in the hall.

My father's work made my parents heroes. It created employment in our extended family, helped keep people fed. On Fridays, my father delivered boxes of fresh produce to all of my grandparents, always for free. He hired friends and out-of-work relatives and paid them well, even though they often thanked him by leaving his cash registers light. He employed a family of down-on-their-luck Irish brothers, one of whom was upstanding, the rest of whom were garden-variety lushes, one just straight-up shooting meth. Despite my father's generosity, when we visit their family on Christmas Eve, the brothers' Irish mom sits in a corner and mutters "Ugly dago family" under her breath.

Watching my father, I see work as an act of force. I learn work has the power to transform. I am told, again and again, that a good work ethic is the highest form of exaltation, that working hard is what makes you worthy; it keeps you safe. My nuclear family occasionally went to church but we had no religion. We prayed to the God of work.

When I am young, I spend little time with my father, but when I do he imparts powerfully held beliefs about how I'm allowed to be, who I should grow up to be:

The most important thing you do in this life is put food on your table and a roof over your head.

Stop worrying about other people, worry about yourself.

Play the hand you're dealt.

I hate liars and I hate sneaks. Don't be a liar or a sneak.

The worst thing you can be in my dad's mind is a person without common sense, a "dope." He frequently talks to me about what makes a good (and bad) person, but it's most often through the lens of what makes a good employee, about how he discerns who to promote, who to trust. I hang on his every word.

I'm seven when he buys his first store. It's a cavernous space— two double-wide buildings merged together—on a nondescript corner of Southwest Philly down the street from our church, equidistant from my grandmothers' homes. In the middle of the store's warehouse is a yellow-painted metal staircase that goes up straight for two stories without stopping for a landing, a staircase that seems to float in the sky and leads to my dad's office, the office of the boss. From the top of the stairs, you can see all of the store and the warehouse: the forklifts and the wood skids piled high with sacks of potatoes, the mountains of onions in orange mesh bags, the front counters and the deli cases, the back drains that smell of rotting vegetables and bleach.

I want to see my father more, I want to know him. When I reach my earliest teens, I go to work for him so I can feel close to him, so I can see him in his world. My mother is too available, too suffocating, too much. I want what my father has. I want the power to leave. I want to be the boss of everyone and everything.

The business is rough—the men who work in it, the work they do, the streets that surround it, a community in decline. Philly's a tough place, a city where people are in-your-face confrontational, kind but not nice. Especially in our neighborhood, in the early eighties, there are streets you don't want to walk down at night. At least once a month, the outside walls of my dad's store are tagged with graffiti and the store needs to be repainted, and each time we talk about how the neighborhood is getting worse. My father closes up at night and collects the heavy zippered bags of cash to make the bank drops. He carries a gun. In his car is a machete, a metal bat, and an atomizer of pepper spray, which I spray at my neck once, thinking it's perfume only to have it accidentally land in my eyes. In our basement at home is a wide metal safe, with an old-school dial, filled with cash.

When we finally move, it takes four men to lift it up and carry it away.

Surrender Signal to Space

When I am nine, my family moves to the suburbs. We find an old farmhouse twenty minutes away from Southwest Philly, in a small, leafy town called Lansdowne, which has a health food store, a diner, a one-screen movie theater, and an old-timey commuter train station made of stone. It's bordered by a creek and scant woods and surrounded on all sides by generic, sometimes scummy and rough, lower-middle-class suburbs. Comparatively, Lansdowne feels like its own quaint island, a breezy-bucolic pretend-land.

The house is weird and wonderful, with three bedrooms, two and a half baths, worn hardwood floors, a fireplace, and a laundry chute my sister and I will eventually misuse as a portal through which to toss stuffed animals and, sometimes, the family cat. The outside is painted red and white and resembles a children's storybook barn. It's a major upgrade for us, and it feels to me—and to members of our extended family—like my parents have somehow become rich. What I don't know is that we can't quite afford this house, that my mother arranged a complicated balloon mortgage with the elderly owner, who took a shine to this young, persistent woman and her young, trying-to-make-it family. But the owner's son isn't so smitten. In the mortgage close meeting, he stares at my parents like they're trash, looks straight at my dad and says, "You better sell a lot of bananas," with a preppy-boy scoff. In the next few years, my dad, never one to back down from a challenge, opens three more stores, sells a literal ton of bananas. *Fuck that guy.*

Our new house is nestled on a narrow street in a pocket neighborhood that's filled with stately stone houses and fancy cars. Some of the neighbors are working-class Italian Americans like us who made it, bigger than we did—contractors, mostly, who build white pillars on their front porches and elaborate pools in their backyards. The rest are architects, pharmacists, college professors, and, occasionally, public school teachers who got in early on this special secret neighborhood with its charming lanes and hills. The white-collar neighbors form a twee neighborhood association with a twee name and gather each month to sip box wine and eat rubbery cheese, a gathering my mother attends precisely once before deciding it's not her scene.

The move marks the halfway point of my childhood, the first class jump of my life, a shift in how we live. The move marks a shift in my mother too. It's the eighties. She gets red acrylic nails and an extra-curly perm, wears gold jewelry and elaborately designed sweaters from Macy's. She finds new interests in new age philosophies, in crystals and incense and pendulums, in self-help books by Louise Hay and Shirley MacLaine.

My mother relishes the life she can now provide for us, driving to the store multiple times a week like it's a fun hobby, stocking our new pantry with doubles, triples of everything we could possibly need. She begins her suburban stay-at-home mom life in earnest by methodically upgrading any imperfection around her she sees: the backyard's unruly shrubs, the kitchen's uneven floor, ill-thought-out storage systems, chipped-paint baseboards, the unfinished basement; eventually, my sister's and my clothes, our hair, and, especially, her own late-twenties body, even though she's gained maybe five pounds and looks beautiful and the same.

My dad buys her a long silver Cadillac, a classy new ride to match our classy new life. The car is plush and luxe, automated in a way that feels futuristic for the time. It has soft, pale gray leather seats, which my sister immediately takes to biting, leaving behind tiny, slobbery tooth marks even after she's repeatedly told not to, even after she's been threatened and scolded and shamed. At four, my sister is bullheaded, obstinate, makes a fuss when she doesn't get her way. Her reaction to my parents' might is immovable resistance, a strategy that wins their respect, or at least exhausts them—a strategy it never occurs to me to try.

Once my sister, mother, and I are in Burlington Coat Factory, a cavernous warehouse-like store with racks upon racks of marked-down designer coats, ladies' sportswear no one wants, and dress-up outfits for holidays that, as a kid, you'd rather die than wear. It's a warm, late-summer, pre-back-to-school day, or maybe a warm, spring pre-Easter day; either way there is sun and enough heat to feel uncomfortable standing under it for an extended time. It's not a pleasure trip; we're on a mom errand, shopping for something we need to find.

Inside the store, my sister spots a coat she wants, a coat that is too small for her and too expensive and that we are absolutely not going to buy. When she's told no she immediately starts screaming for it, says she *must* have it, drops to the floor like the coat is Romeo and she's Act IV Juliet. My mother threatens to leave her there if she doesn't stop this foolishness. When she doesn't, we, my mother and me, start to walk away. But my sister—wily, wise beyond her years—calls my mom's bluff. Behind a forest of rainbow puffers and dressy Rothschild wool, she sits motionless, determined, arms crossed. She's not going anywhere.

They've reached an impasse. My mother, a woman not to be trifled with on her best day and especially not by her *own ingrate child* making these types of *bullshit* demands, grabs my arm and we storm out of the store, through the parking lot, back to the car. She's wild with fury, but it's clear she hasn't planned this far, doesn't know what to do next. I'm in the backseat crying. My mother pounds the steering wheel three times, screams "FUCK!" shifts into drive, floors the gas, and propels the car forward so fast and with such force we fly over the unseen median laid out in front of our spot.

A few seconds later our long, classy car is hovering over the long cement block in a way that can't be reversed, no matter which pedal my mother hits or how hard she tries. We're suspended in air, like a Cadillac seesaw, the car and the median making a plus sign, a surrender signal to space. My sister remains inside the store.

My mom and I carefully open our doors and make our way off the seesaw, which is easier than I think it will be, the drop just a few inches to the ground. We march through the parking lot and back into the store, where we immediately find my sister at the entrance in the arms of a kindly-looking middle-aged Burlington Coat Factory worker decked out in the store's latest dress slacks and a polyester business-casual blouse. She's holding my sister at her hip and cooing at her like she is the world's cutest snot-faced koala. My sister is cooing back, lapping up the tender-concerned attention like it's emotional soft serve.

"THERE you are!" my mom announces with relief, as if we've been looking for her the whole time. "You must have been so worried," says the Burlington Coat lady. My mother reaches for my sister, kisses her cheek, gently rubs her head, thanks the lady profusely. We can't thank her enough. We're all smiling now, all playing our roles in the charade that we're nice. The lady lets us borrow the store's phone—car trouble!—and, a half hour later, a group of burly men from my dad's store, the same ones who moved the basement safe, come and lift the car off the median. On the drive home, we're quiet. My mom's been trumped by a four-year-old who sits calmly next to me on the bit-up leather backseat while passively sucking her thumb. "Look how smug she looks," my mom hisses to no one in particular, but I can see in the rearview mirror that she's grinning a bit too.

––––––––––––––––

Into my tweens and teens, my mother often treats me with contempt. She says things like "You're lucky you're pretty because if not, no one would like you because you're such a bitch." She kicks me for accidentally breaking her new Spiegel-catalog lamp, and I fall backward, down a (short) flight of stairs. As our relationship worsens, I start snooping through my mother's stuff. I read her journals and her Jackie Collins novels, try on her makeup, perfume, and clothes. I am trying to connect with her when I cannot connect with her, take on her identity when I have none of my own. When she's not awake before I get on the bus to school, I go through her pockets and steal her cash. I am a terrible sneak and she's a wonderful detective and I almost always get caught. My mother begins telling a story about me: "You know how Jenn is," she says to her friends, to my friends, to my siblings, "with Jenn, you have to walk on eggshells." I begin telling a not-great story about myself too.

The times are often good. There are roller-skating-rink birthday parties, new bikes for Christmas, art supplies when I express an interest in learning to sketch. With little complaint, my mother engages in the constant, consistent, invisible, and mostly thankless labor of creating a home for us, a life. There are framed school pictures, clean sheets and made beds, a linen closet full of neatly folded blankets, washcloths, and fresh towels. She never forgets a holiday or special occasion, keeps a drawer full of blank greeting cards, always sends a note when someone's celebrating or in pain.

We eat dinner together at the kitchen table, which is a picnic table that's pushed into a nook. Most nights, it's vegetarian recipes from *The Moosewood Cookbook,* but we order in pizza on Fridays. We buy a grill and deck furniture and put up an aboveground pool, host countless family barbecues; we celebrate birthdays, communions, confirmations, graduations surrounded by family and friends. The seasons pass, the leaves fall, the ground smells like mulch. My mom plants bulbs, and, by April, there are flowers all around our house. In the fall, we trick-or-treat in the neighborhood; the lady down the street hands out the type of homemade candy apples that could break your teeth. Our neighborhood resembles John Hughes's Chicago, an eighties suburban dream. It's a life like any other, bound to the people in it. There are funny, tender moments. There is care and there is love. Even if that love often feels conditional, a reward for behaving as the children my parents wish us to be.

Still, my sister and my brother, who's born when I'm eleven, grow up differently. In this new life, there are no big house parties and psychedelic drugs, no creepy lurking dudes, no arms pulled out of their sockets when they run too far ahead in the street, no dislocated collarbones because someone threw them in the air and didn't catch, no flashlights in their crying infant eyes as a joke, no smacked-until-they're-swollen hands for touching the butter with your thumb.

My parents are growing up, becoming better parents, better people, healing from old wounds. What's unspoken is that we've moved on and I'm supposed to get over it, my memories inconvenient to this new narrative, a reminder of misdeeds everyone else would rather forget. I'm a hyperemotional relic of their past; difficult to raise; a mouthy student with undiagnosed ADHD; a stress case with a forever aching jaw, teeth I'm slowly grinding down to nubs. I demand to be heard and witnessed, seen at almost any cost. My parents nurture in a way they think is enough. It's never enough of what I need.

Nine years is a long time in kid years. Even the shallowest understanding of attachment theory will tell you the foundation of who we are is set between ages one and five. My family moves to the suburbs, but I never really leave our original house. I'm trapped with my memories, no matter how many healing drum circles my mom brings me into, or how much sage is burned. I still feel different and wrong. There are people in all of our lives who seem to almost chemically trigger our worst impulses, remind us too much of our deficiencies and pain. It sucks when this is someone in your own house, your own kid, a person you can't, at least for a few years, avoid. I'm spiky and volatile, full of feelings no one knows how to place. Unlike the rest of my family, I never know what's good for me. I'm constantly, as my parents tell me often, pushing my luck.

My sister has her own way of dealing with our parents. She's built to both stand her ground and, at the same time, keep the peace. My brother is a boy, and that's special—it matters less what he does or how he behaves. My father often refers to my brother as "my son," as in "What do you think you're doing to my son?" My sister and I get this when we paint my brother's nails, when we make him dress up in our old clothes, when we tease him too much.

My brother's childhood is exclusively suburban, upper-middle-class. He attends private preschool, sleeps in Marimekko sheets, is outfitted with the latest high-tech toys, his every interest indulged. He's our family's prince.

In our new life in the suburbs, my father moves freely in and out of the house. He plays full-court basketball twice a week. He goes on far-flung Caribbean fishing trips with his friends, where they smoke cigars and take pictures we'll later frame, of them holding up giant fish. They catch sharks on one of the trips, and my dad has one of the sharks stuffed, but my mother says he can't hang that in her house and so instead the shark hangs over the deli case at his store. My dad works hard and he works long hours. When he's home, he watches TV to unwind, including all four seasons of sports. When he's watching TV he's not to be disturbed.

One night he's watching a hockey game on my parents' square, blocky bedroom TV. It's early evening and my brother is full of energy, running back and forth in front of the screen.

"Will you do something about him?" my father yells.

"Why don't YOU do something, he's YOUR son," I say.

And with that, my father's feet are on the ground. He is on the attack. He is nimble and strong, and I am aware I am outmatched and so I run. I run out of the bedroom, but I cannot possibly make it to my room down the hall and so I just stand, and wait. Within seconds his fist is on my face, just against my cheekbone. Before I can blink, my face is smashed into the picture frame that's right above my head. Seconds after that, I have the beginnings of what will become a small black eye.

For the next week, I don't go to school. I refuse to go to school. I record a message on a cassette tape on my pink boom box demanding my father apologize and telling him all the reasons he was wrong. I push the tape under the bathroom door while he's showering. I don't hear about it for days. When I do, it's begrudging. We're in a power struggle, one he'll never let me win even if I'm right. His is an old-school parenting style, less concerned with emotional safety than with asserting dominance, a demand for his children's blind respect. In this system, he'll never give an inch—what if I take a mile?

Who knows if ruthlessness is born or made but the truth is I'm just like my father. My own competitive, distrustful spirit is built on situations like this one. I learn most every foundational thing I know about the world from him, but mainly: how to size up an opponent. Into my adulthood, I rarely play at anything unless I think I, too, can dominate and win.

———

By high school, I start going out more, in part to avoid the tension at home. I've acquired a group of female friends, all a little offbeat, unidentifiable by any clique. My best friend lives in a trailer just a few miles away from our school. In the afternoons when we hang out at her place, her mom serves off-brand Pepsi, fills most of her own avocado-green plastic cup with rum. One of our other friend's dads is cheating. Another's doing too much coke. Someone's sibling is sick. In our homes, my friends and I have crises too big to talk about. But away from home, we have each other.

We hang out constantly, are close in the way you're close only in your teens, when life is emotional chaos masked as profundity and, if you're lucky, you get loyalty, companionship, and a few really good inside jokes. We share the same music taste and the same high school enemies. We support each other through unrequited crushes and clumsy first hook-ups. After school, we take the trolley six stops to Planned Parenthood to procure free condoms. When we're old enough, we teach each other to drive.

The fun we share is mostly innocent. That is, until we start stealing alcohol from our parents' liquor cabinets, skimming just enough so they won't notice, refilling the amber-hued bottles with water when we accidentally skim too much. We combine dusty schnapps and gifted-holiday whiskeys, special once-a-year ports and too-sweet sherry no one likes—whatever there is, whatever we can find. We transport boozy medleys in rinsed-out shampoo bottles hidden in the oversize pockets of the J. Crew barn jackets we got for Christmas. We're on our way to parties in the woods we've told our parents are school functions that don't actually exist.

When the skimming gets too risky, when we've skimmed all we can, we find ways to acquire our own six-packs of Zima and Yuengling lager, scoring cheap vodka by the handle, liters of Southern Comfort as a treat. By our sweet sixteens, we're drinking a few days a month until we vomit, often in the designated driver's backseat. Or until we black out and pass out on neighborhood lawns, waking up only when the sprinklers go off.

Some weekends, we drive the nine miles north to Villanova to pick up college boys hitchhiking to parties. Or we crash dances at all-boys high schools. Most of the time we stick together, but on wilder nights, just two of us branch off. Two of us are risk takers with darker impulses, two of us rely on the others to pump the brakes. Of the group, I'm the riskiest risk taker, reckless, attention needy, often thrill-seeking at my friends'—and my own—expense.

At school, I know I *should* care about keeping up with assignments, but I don't and my parents don't seem to either—they were fine without high school, my mom tells me, I will be too if that's what I choose. I fail math, I get Ds in science, I cheat to pass history. The only class where I excel is English Lit.

After school, I hold down a series of part-time jobs, make enough money to feel independent, to pay for clothes, gas, and going out. Even from the start, there are aspects of working I particularly enjoy: the pageantry in being the first person to turn on the lights in a store or a restaurant, the intrigue in any kind of behind-the-scenes job secret, the power of knowing how a particular business *really* operates. Work feels like a grownup game I want to master. From the jump, I find work fun.

On Saturdays when I'm not working, I take art classes at a college in downtown Philly on the recommendation of my high school art teacher, a woman I like and respect. I test into Advanced Placement art classes and briefly join the staff of the school literary magazine. But I don't really commit to anything except boys. When they like me, I feel worthwhile, a feeling I chase as often as I can. I lose my virginity in sophomore year to a nineteen-year-old car detailer in his (extremely clean) Dodge Dart. After that, I date older boys and younger ones too, rough foster kids, boys who are gay but don't know it yet, creepy stalker boys, boys from other schools. I'm never not caught up in some kind of boy drama, to the extent that it annoys my friends, and to the distraction from most anything else.

One night, I head out alone to a classmate's party, chasing down a current crush. I get there late; most of the girls have gone home, if they were ever there. I'm by myself and I'm nervous, so I drink too much; the people and the party blur fast. Later, I open my eyes and discover my body behind a strange door in a strange bedroom under the strange form of a boy from school I do not like and do not want. I don't remember saying yes. I don't remember saying anything at all. But I do remember his hot breath on my cheek and in my ear, the weight of his lacrosse-trained arms, his bare, fleshy belly, round and heavy with beer.

I don't know how it ended, or what I did when it was over, or how I got home. But at school on Monday, everyone knows what happened because the boy—who is loud and ugly and vile—tells them. When I try to explain, I don't have the right words, and even my friends don't believe me. I don't tell my parents because I'm ashamed. I'm also aware of the chaos I'll unleash if my father and cousins take matters into their own hands, a melodrama I wish to avoid. The year before, after I confessed to my dad that another boy was harassing me, he tore off to the kid's after-school job, held him by the neck against a wall, and threatened his life.

Eventually, I stop trying to explain what happened the night the boy raped me, stop saying anything about it at all. For the rest of the year, the cute boy, the one I'd gone to the party to see, no longer looks at me. For the remainder of high school (college, beyond), there will be many more nights with many more drinks and many more boys. Unable to disentangle pleasure or even desire from sexual trauma and Italian-Catholic shame, I experience sex mainly as a performance, an acquisition of male approval. I am a girl without a compass putting on a sexy-power show. I'm a girl I never wanted to be.

How do we know what to dream? Where does ambition first spark? What defines want?

In my real life, at home, I have little reference for the life I want, but I'm beginning to see what I don't. The suffocation of suburban, heteronormative domesticity, the constant sweeping of the kitchen floor, the obsessive wiping of fingerprints, the banal monitoring of dishwasher cycles, the built-up resentment in a house where the person working hoards the freedom and you do all the work. All of it feels too small, caged in. I want a bigger field on which to play.

I am interested in art but, even more, in books, especially the old editions of classics I begin collecting in Philly's used bookstores. I like them as design objects, admire how they smell and look, revel in the way owning stacks of them makes me feel. We were never a *literature* house; my mom read self-help and romance; my dad, occasionally, thick volumes on U.S. presidents and, sometimes, war. Our main source of information is local TV news or *People* magazine, which we subscribe to and fight over who gets to read first every week.

Now, venturing out further on my own, I tear though prose and poetry collections. I am buoyed by Ernest Hemingway's short stories, Emily Brontë's dark take on romance, Stephen King's plot twists and turns. I love tracking the patterns of sentences, the way a single comma or a simple line break transforms a plot. I grew up surrounded by skilled Italian-American raconteurs, my father especially; spent a childhood fighting to be heard at tables of tough men and women who made you earn the floor. By the time I'm a teen, I can spot the spine of a well-told story with an ease I don't yet know is a skill, a clarity I don't know is unique.

During the summer I am seventeen, I take the New Jersey Transit commuter train from Philly to New York's Penn Station with a popular, charming friend who is a catalog and stock-photo model/aspiring actor, a kid whose picture we see in frames at Marshalls all the time. He's headed to the city for an audition and wants company. I'm more than game. After his audition (at an office in midtown where I am thrilled to spot redheaded actor Seth Green), we walk to Times Square and procure fake IDs at a deli, a thing you could still do in Times Square in 1990 with ease. The lamination's still warm on our cards when we use them to buy a fifth of Smirnoff at the liquor store next door, smuggle it into a booth at a nearby peep show, and take turns swigging it down.

We're loopy and giddy as we exit the peep show into the August sun. We stroll the city for hours, all the way downtown and then all the way back up. It's my first time in Manhattan and I relish every second of it. I feel uncharacteristically calm inside the city's storm, in the wildness of it, the street art and style, the people expressing their full freak selves. New York soon becomes—and will always be—the place I feel most at home.

When the fall comes, I show up to take my SATs hungover, eke out a grim 980 out of 1600. Take them again, it's worse. On my report cards, I barely skate by. But outside school, I'm listening, reading, and learning; rapidly absorbing new ideas in whatever media I can find. Chief among these discoveries is *Sassy* magazine, the first issue arriving by surprise, a thoughtful gift from my mom, who found it through *Ms.*

For a certain kind of teen girl in the late eighties and early nineties, *Sassy* was a life raft, an edgy-indie counterpoint to the era's rah-rah mainstream publications like *YM* and *Seventeen*. Instead of pushing girls to be pretty and (God forbid) palatable to boys, *Sassy* encouraged us to have brains, to pursue offbeat interests, to be ourselves. It was staffed by a group of wildly smart, funny, and irreverent writers in their twenties, the cool big sisters we wished we had. Writing in a casual, first-person voice that set the standard for and would later become de rigueur in women's blogs, the *Sassy* staff revealed a world we all wanted to be a part of, a culture we identified with, a place where we felt we could belong.

From *Sassy*'s first issue on, my friend Heather and I devour each word it publishes. The magazine influences everything we read and listen to, the way we dress, the makeup we use, and the slang we speak. We wait all month for our new issues to arrive. When they do, we lie side by side on Heather's bedroom floor, poring over page after page, noting each style tip and band recommendation, each film the *Sassy* editors think we should see. When the editors announce a "Sassiest Girl in America" contest, Heather and I apply posthaste, my first submission involving a hand-rendered six-foot-long scroll. We want to be the fearless *Sassy* writers, to inhabit their beyond-cool New York lives. The magazine is my first true taste of my own ambition, my first clue toward a professional dream.

When I'm not memorizing e. e. cummings or obsessing over *Sassy*,

I listen to 10,000 Maniacs, Tori Amos, R.E.M., the Violent Femmes, New Order, the Cure alone in my room on my Walkman, to the same favorite songs again and again. On Tuesday nights, I watch *Moonlighting* on TV while simultaneously breaking down the plot on the phone with my charming model friend. On weekends, Heather and I see films like *Dangerous Liaisons* in an art house theater downtown. I'm discovering new worlds and new ways to say what I think. I start to pick up a bit of confidence, my own point of view. But none of it feels like it matters. I'm still stuck here.

One afternoon I call my father "condescending" and he doesn't know what it means and thinks I'm being a wiseass so he slaps me across the face. One night I call my mother a bitch and, in the smack-yelling aftermath, she wakes my father, who races out of bed to kick me, scream-spitting that I am never again to show such disrespect. They are a unified team and never let me forget it, a parental one-two punch. I'm told repeatedly that I exaggerate, that I'm too "dramatic." I'm taught that my feelings are inconvenient, that my sense of the truth doesn't matter, that I am the problem. I internalize all of it, a slow rot building inside me, my heart a cauldron of rage.

Into my senior year, my mother tries too late to set me in the right direction, cheerleads my few academic accomplishments, encourages me to apply to artsy schools we can't afford, says we'll figure it out. I don't. Instead, I'm accepted into precisely one state college, allegedly to study art therapy because I'm too scared to say I want to work with words. At this point, I believe writing is the career of *real* intellectuals, that I'll never be smart enough to articulate my thoughts on a page. No one's told me that it's a skill you develop over time, that, with the right guidance and focused effort, I'll inevitably get better. That it's possible to learn.

I slog my way through the last months of high school and graduate in a daze. I spend the week after graduation at a Jersey Shore house rental for senior week, drunk every night and up to no good.

By the time college rolls around, I'm thrilled to get out on my own but almost comically emotionally ill prepared. I leave my parents' home directionless, with a handful of creative interests eclipsed by a belief I am unlovable and inherently bad, that my chief value is how I look.

Lowlights

I start my twenty-first year in a college bar with my closest college friends downing shots with names like woo-woo and mind eraser. They're the same girls who bailed me out of jail with a bag of change when I was arrested for public drunkenness a few months before. It's the group that, earlier that semester, I drove to Manhattan one night at midnight while high on cough syrup because someone knew someone at Hunter College who said we could stay in her dorm (true!) and also that we could just "walk up" to Allen Ginsberg's house in Greenwich Village and he would let us in (not true!).

I'm into my third year of college at the state school. I live in a basement apartment with a roommate who was raised born-again Christian but is now involved in an elaborate sexual role-play relationship that includes redecorating the apartment with various art supplies so it appears as a jungle or, sometimes, a ship. Her musician boyfriend lives with us too, though he doesn't pay rent and, according to our landlord, is not supposed to be here, but we justify his staying rent-free because he still has a dining hall pass and comes home a few times a week with a backpack full of stale bread and blocks of thick orange government-issue cheese he's lifted from the caf.

The two have a white mouse they rescued from a punk show where the band was electrocuting mice onstage. Now we have a twitchy mouse who runs sideways in a clear plastic ball they've bought for him because they're worried he'll be retraumatized by spending too much time in his cage. One night while my roommate attends a Green Day show, I accidentally kick the ball and it bangs into a leg of a table. When it cracks open, the mouse runs out sideways and twitches under the stove and, despite searching every nook of the apartment with a flashlight for days, we never see him again.

Like most twenty-one-year-olds, and probably a bit worse, we are messy in most every way a person can be a mess. We drink most nights, particularly forties of Mad Dog 20/20 because it's the cheapest option. I take most drugs I am given; fortunately, I am offered few. My roommate swipes empty whipped-cream cans from her job at a diner so we can do whippets when she gets home. We love Bob Dylan's "Last Thoughts on Woody Guthrie" enough to write out the entire poem on giant poster boards and hang it all over our walls. We smoke so much weed and have so little money we offer to clean out other people's bongs so we can collect the resin and smoke that too.

Beyond the partying, I'm accomplishing little. My GPA drops to a 1.4, a steady decline, semester over semester, year after year. I'm not dumb, but I think I am. Away from school, I like reading and discovering new writers, debating ideas. But I have fuck all for academic confidence. I'm too anxious, scattered, and easily overwhelmed to keep up with assignments. Undiagnosed ADHD works against me, nascent addictions finish the job. I haven't sorted out yet that school (and life) is mostly a perception game, that if you show up and look like you care, you're halfway to a win. Instead, I've stopped attending all classes except Spanish, because somehow, despite my garbage GPA and no money, I've secured a spot in a summer student exchange program to Costa Rica and this Spanish 5 or 500 or whatever arbitrary number it is, is a requirement for my trip. I started college as an art student, but now my major's Public Relations with a minor in Spanish. But really my major is acting out, with a minor in getting fucked up.

I may fail to show up appropriately at school, but as always, I show up for work. I work four days a week at a local Pennsylvania Dutch restaurant that serves chicken and waffles and various root-vegetable-based mushes. I head there early in the morning, usually hungover, and scrub the bathrooms, the soda-sticky servers' station, and around and under all the booths while the owner follows me with a flashlight to see how I've done. The restaurant requires employees to wear a uniform shirt with their name embroidered on it, but the owner says the shirts are expensive and he doesn't know how he feels about me, and until he does, he wants me to wear Becky's shirts. Becky is the boss's favorite waitress, the one who gets the good shifts, the shifts when you might make seventy-five dollars in tips. I am working weekdays, when you serve soft foods to senior citizens and make twelve dollars. When the customers ask for watery decaf coffee refills, they call out "Becky" and I respond, lackadaisically. *Who cares.*

We are in that stage of life when living just seems to happen. When you might be stoned on Tuesday afternoon and wind up at the movies with a group of people, half of whom you don't know, and later find yourself at a party dancing to the Lemonheads' "Mrs. Robinson" and then a bar where you meet and go home with a broad-chested boy who writes safe and sensitive poetry even though he is not sensitive or safe. I'm listening to the Velvet Underground for the first time; "White Light/White Heat" blows my mind. I'm reading Adrienne Rich's and Sylvia Plath's poetry and still writing bad poems of my own. I rendez-vous with a painter who keeps a cat skeleton in a vintage suitcase so he can study the anatomy closely; sometimes he just has it out on display. I start sleeping with a local novelist-janitor who communicates with me mainly through letters he drops at my apartment at dawn after his overnight shifts, who uses words in combinations that sound dreamy but, under any scrutiny, fail to make sense.

My friends and I are small-town, small-time creatives living in a predigital age, wandering through life like we're the stars of our own low-budget indie movies, which sometimes, because one of us owns a VHS camcorder, we are. We think what we're experiencing is special. Like our understanding of time as endless and energy as boundless, life has yet to disabuse us otherwise.

I meet my soon-to-be-new roommate Beth at a party where it's rumored they're passing around joints filled with angel-dust-laced hash. She lives next door in a multistory flophouse, home to six art students in total, each room smokier and more cluttered than the last. Beth is beguiling, a combination Louise Brooks and Sinéad O'Connor if she lived in the thirties and was photographed by Man Ray. She has a jet-black cropped pixie cut, a closet full of showy vintage outfits, and delicate stick-and-poke tattoos on her upper arms. She listens to Enya and Sarah McLachlan and lives in the front of the house, with two windows and a giant dark-wood armoire that's always overflowing with fabric, art supplies, and clothes. We're drawn to each other immediately. She's one of those solid savior people who collects human strays, who will take you in no matter what shape you're in, someone who's stable and generous but independent enough to not be spineless and cool enough to never scold or judge. Truly the best kind of friend.

I live with Beth a week before she asks if I'd be interested in working with her at a restaurant in the high-end chain hotel the next town over. The servers there are pros who wear pink and gray bow ties with their tuxedo shirts and make a hundred dollars a night and don't have to clean pissy bathroom floors. She thinks she can get me in. I say *yes, please!*, nail the interview, and buy a sixty-dollar herbal concoction, mix it with two gallons of water, and swallow it down over two days in order to pass the drug test—a test I find out about after quite literally puffing on a joint—and somehow, miraculously, I do.

It's May of my twenty-first year and school's out. Beth and I sync up our restaurant schedules the best we can and plan out a month of road trips for our days off. We drive to the hotel along wide country roads with the windows down, blasting *Last Splash* by the Breeders again and again. Our hair is fresh-from-the-shower wet and our skin is young and, even though we are heading to work, work has a beginning and an end.

In the car, the late-spring air moves and floats between us. Sometimes Beth naps in the seat next to me and I feel perfectly at ease. When we're together, I'm my best, most authentic self, our friendship so flawlessly calibrated it lends a kind of safety and peace I will not know again for (many) years. We're acquainted with a group of boys a few years older than we are, and on some nights we grab our roommate Vicki and drive the three hours to the boys' downtown Philly apartment and sleep on the floor. One boy is a writer and one is a musician and one is a cartoonist and they are cool Gen X boys listening to cool Gen X music and we like them enough but Beth and I never leave each other's sides. Other days we drive two hours to the beach to briefly sit on the sand and splash in the water before we head home again to make it in time for our shift. We rinse out our work shirts in rest stop sinks and hold them out the windows of the car to dry while the other person drives. When we arrive, we rush to the bathroom, comb our hair and snap on our bow ties, dab our lips with lip gloss, our eyes with mascara.

"How do I look?"

You look great.

One night the boys from Philly are in town and we're all watching *Thirtysomething* reruns and Beth decides we should dye everyone's hair platinum blonde. We've got an old cassette of Nina Simone playing in the bathroom's soap-scum-clogged cassette player but the "a" is smudged and I think it's Nino Simone. We all emerge hours later untoned and color-stripped bright yellow blondes. That weekend, the first in June, I'm walking in Philly in a vintage men's plaid cowboy shirt and short-shorts, a bandanna in my hair. A man calls out: "Hey, Blondie, you're fresh like summer," and I am.

By July, I've started dating Troy, who is a man Beth knows from high school. He's also our boss's boss at the hotel-restaurant and a well-liked food and beverage manager at the hotel. Troy has thick brown, wavy hair and nice teeth, wears double-breasted Men's Wear-house suits in various shades of olivey brown-gray. Troy is charming in that popular-kid-in-high-school-who-peaked-too-early kind of way. He's twenty-five, drives a red Miata mostly with the top down, seems grownup in a way we are not—a straight man to our artsy types, a nice guy who doesn't take himself too seriously, fun to tease. One night, we have no customers in the fancy pink-bow-tie restaurant and Beth's shift is cut, and Troy offers to drive me home so she can take our car.

At the end of my shift, he picks up two six-packs of beer from the big, locked walk-in in the back of the industrial kitchen and a pack of Marlboro Lights from behind the front desk and winks at the front desk clerk as he does it. He puts the beer, save two bottles, in the trunk of his Miata next to his golf clubs, tosses the pack of cigarettes in the console between us, opens the door to my side of the car, closes it behind me, and drives me home, drinking beers along the way.

We stay up all night talking on the fire escape/porch and he tells me about his life. He dropped out of college after attending on a golf scholarship, worked various shitty jobs until they took a chance on him as a busboy at the hotel. He has hustle, instinctively knew how to charm the guests and, like most charming hustlers, he quickly moved up. He's now the youngest manager at his level in the company. The hours are brutal but he makes good money. He still lives with his parents and thinks he probably shouldn't, but his mom cooks and does his laundry and he's always at work and never home. The arrangement just makes sense.

I don't know how I feel about Troy, but I can tell Troy likes me. After this first night, he sends two dozen long-stemmed red roses cradled in baby's breath along with a tiny teddy bear, a move clearly meant to impress. I'm not impressed so much as curious—he's not my type, but maybe he should be? I agree to go out with him again. Great, he says, pack a bag, I have the perfect idea.

On our first official date Troy drives me two hours away to attend a softball game at the college he went to on the golf scholarship and—

I'll find out later—quickly drank himself out of ever attending again. He arrives wearing a polo shirt and khakis, looks extremely adult, a Ben Stiller from *Reality Bites* over the Ethan Hawkes I usually dated. Shiny, spiff. We meet his friends at a bar before the game—all big guys, rowdy guys, guys who smack asses and like sports and frats. Our arrival is met with enthusiasm, cheers. Troy is a jovial man with a killer smile who never forgets a name, well liked and well received.

We attend this softball game, a college tradition apparently, one where you drink a beer every time you land on one of the bases. Troy is not a large man, not as large as the stocky central Pennsylvania dudes who are his buds, and by his fourth time around third base he seems more than mildly buzzed. I ask, "Hey, are you drunk?"

He says he is not, insists it as if I've suggested the ocean is dry. An hour plus later, when the game is finally over, he insists he's fine even when I tell him he shouldn't drive, even when his friends want to take his keys. "They're just joshing," he says, and I think I know what joshing means, but also in this case maybe not? His friends drive away before we do. I have no idea where we are, alone in this field, outside of rural-college-town nowhere. I can't drive stick but ask if I can try. He says no. I want to push the subject but I want to seem cool more. I'm afraid to make a scene. I've been groomed since birth for just this kind of moment, to cow to a misbehaving bad boy and put his needs before my own.

We drive along the back roads outside this central Pennsylvania college town with the top down, pickup trucks everywhere and not much else. Everything seems fine until there's a red light in front of us and a gold pickup stopped at it and instead of looking at the gold pickup, Troy is looking at me or past me and I say his name slowly and quietly, and then louder and faster and louder and faster until BOOM, we crash. Airbags are not required yet and the seat belt's got enough give that my forehead crashes hard against the windshield before the belt thrusts my whole body back and I thwump into the leather seat.

Without missing a beat, Troy backs the heavily smashed-in Miata into reverse, guns the car around the gold pickup, blows through the now-red-again light, and speeds down a side street and then another side street and then into the driveway of a house, the car sputtering and smoking the whole time. He stops the car and knocks on the door of the house and opens the garage door and hides the almost undrivable, fully-dented-in convertible in the garage in a way that is so calm and so cool and so smooth that it's not until months later that it occurs to me: this isn't his first time. Troy might have qualities that look good on paper; he's also an alcoholic liar who collects DUIs.

A week later I'm on my way to Costa Rica with a group of exchange students on an international flight where you can still smoke. In the six weeks I'm there, Troy will try to call both the school I'm attending and the house where I live. He'll attempt to send me flowers, twice. The gestures feel relentless, invasive, not sweet. Each missed call and failed delivery requires extensive translation with my host family in a language I can't really speak. I'm already feeling awkward, alone in another country for the first time, further from home than I've ever been. Traveling abroad is more uncomfortable than I'd imagined. The other students in the program are intimidatingly worldly, both more academic and more comfortable in their own skin than any people I know. My confrontational beer-bong brand of confidence is out of place in this environment. Too American, rough. I haven't yet learned to shape-shift. On the first get-to-know-you night out, I drink more than everyone else and embarrass myself, my attempts at connection unintentionally alienating and coarse.

Still, there are a few good moments, glimmers of how this could go if I could get out of my own way. On weekends, I find a guide to take me on a hike to swim under a waterfall, the biggest I've ever seen. I make a friend and we take a trip by bus to an active volcano, stay overnight in a cheap straw palapa, hitchhike to a hot spring.

But by week three, I'm so homesick and struggling so much at the school I start hiding in the narrow twin room of my host house and reading the books I've brought instead of going out with the rest of our group. I sleep late, missing class. When there's an opportunity to extend the trip and move on to Nicaragua with my friend, I pass and head home early instead, defeated and ashamed. I'm not the person I thought I was, the up-for-anything girl, game for adventure. I don't know who I am, where I fit, what I'm supposed to do next. By the time I make it home to Pennsylvania, Troy feels like the only clear path forward. Like a destiny I can't escape.

While I'm in Costa Rica, Beth gets wrapped up in a new life dating a moody iron sculptor who she'll soon run off and marry (and have two kids with and remain married to, to this day). Old roommates in our shared house move out and new ones move in, including one who hates me because she thinks I once stole her chambray shirt (I did). Everyone is busy, back to school with full course loads, that good September feeling, a fresh start.

But not me. I've returned to a letter from the college dean explaining that, due to poor academic performance, I'm officially kicked out—a D in the Costa Rica class the final nail in this slacker coffin, a confirmation that I'm intellectually inferior, like I'd thought. When I head back to work, the servers who covered for me at the fine-dining pink-bow tie restaurant hold on to my primo shifts. Instead, I'm offered work at the all-you-can-eat crab leg and pasta buffet next door, a demotion to glorified busboy, which I take because I'm broke. On my first day back, the boss hands me an oversize Hawaiian-print polyester shirt, my new uniform. "Put it on and then go clean up that puddle of Russian dressing under the salad bar."

I manage to dodge Troy at work the first few days, but he leaves enough messages on our house phone that my roommates get annoyed and I finally, dutifully call. I know we're not right for each other, the relationship is not right for me, but I don't say this. Instead, I'm awkward and avoidant, say maybe one of the sentences I really mean to say, pad it out with other words I don't mean. I never mention the accident, or the fact that we both have drinking problems, that his are worse. I'm not adult enough for any of that. Instead, I string him along. I'm a hungry baby and his attention is something like food, even if it's not the flavor I want.

Troy asks if I want to go away with him for the weekend to Ocean City, Maryland. He has the hookup through work. We'll stay in a standard king room with nonstandard champagne and chocolate-covered fruit, I won't have to pay for a thing. It's the kind of romantic getaway women of a certain American class are trained to want, the kind of trip every woman I grew up around likes. I feel weird to not want it, like there's something wrong with me for not wanting it, like I'm a fucking snob, like I think I'm so great. *What, you're too good for this nice guy and this nice trip? You think your shit doesn't stink?*

Class is about so much more than money—it's about taste. Inexplicably, from the time I'm young, my taste is precise and exacting. I have a clear and unambiguous personal aesthetic, an almost obsessive eye for detail in both storytelling and design. This extends to my own sense of style, but also to places I aspire to travel and see. My taste is a powerful tool once I allow it, a pull toward what I'm naturally drawn to, where I feel most comfortable, where I might belong. But for a long time, it's something I bury, too afraid of where it might take me and, more, what it might take me from.

––––––––––––

Taste is always subjective, a matter of access, education, and personal preference. But preference itself is a privilege, one few people get—no one's thinking about lamp design when they're trying to keep the house lit. When I'm young, and, honestly, maybe to this day, the force of my own tastes feels classist and wrong, something for which I should be ashamed. As a teen, I'm smacked in the mouth when I use words I like that my father doesn't understand, ridiculed if my interests become too rarified, if I express myself too creatively and act like a "ham." I'm raised salt of the earth but what I like is artistic and cultured—it's not about acquiring more money, per se, but about living a creative life of taste, something that's often intangible to the working class. Effete.

Troy's a nice-enough, handsome-enough, hardworking guy from a working-class family with a good job. He drinks too much, sure, but so did most every man I grew up around—including my dad, especially at Troy's age. That's not what I don't like about him. I'm repelled by the fact that he's unimaginative and uninspiring, that his favorite movie is *Dumb and Dumber*, that he watches only golf on TV. That I aspire to more than his red-roses-chocolate-covered-strawberries Dockers-dude affection feels like a preference I'm wrong to assert. Not a problem with him, but with me.

I say yes to the trip and it's an okay time, even if I'm performing a bit, trying to be a person who can have this kind of fun. When we arrive, we eat dinner in the hotel restaurant, I order the fried seafood platter, we gossip about work. Troy drinks craft beers, orders me a buttery California Chardonnay. The next day we go to the beach and it's cloudy. Even so, I manage a sunburn so deep I develop blisters on my nose that last for days.

That night, the temperature dips. Troy takes a picture of me with my red face and my still-platinum hair wearing a sweatshirt from the college I no longer attend. I am an adult woman, but my face is still that of a child. It's early September of my twenty-first year and my features are soft and pliable because they are not fully formed, and neither is my brain. When you don't have a lock on who you are, you'll let all the wrong things in. At the hotel, I oblige a few rounds of fast, disconnected sex, not because I want to but because I think I should. I become pregnant that night.

When I tell Troy, he's psyched. He wants to get married, says this is how it's meant to be. You're directionless, he says. Come on, here is a path. It's what God wants. He's Irish Catholic to the extreme, comes from a family so church-devoted he served as altar boy into his late teens; became an altar man. He's so sure and I'm so lost that I agree without really thinking, get caught up in his fantasy of the wife and mother I can be. It's hard to argue I'm throwing my life away—really, what's there to throw?

The next weekend we tell my parents. They're happy for us. They're meeting Troy for the first time, but they like him already. I introduce him to my friends from home and they like him too. For the first time, I see him through other people's eyes, how they view him as a catch. He's a normal guy everyone wants to drink a beer with, easygoing, patient, polite. I'm perceived by friends and family as difficult and volatile, a "handful." I think of myself as a lost loser, a rotten freak. What no one understands, honestly, is why a guy like this likes *me*.

Troy and I get an apartment closer to the hotel where he works, on the only retail strip for miles, across from the only bookstore, which is New Age–themed and serves coffee and is also where I get my next job. I walk across the street in the early mornings, fire up the industrial-size cappuccino machine for the three people a day who request coffee with foam. I restock shelves with *Chop Wood, Carry Water*, the *I Ching*, and *The Celestine Prophecy*, but mostly I sit around. I gain sixty pounds in four months, am sick nearly all of the time, start wearing Troy's old jeans and oversize flannel shirts, a pissed-off pregnant lumberjack guiding those seeking easy enlightenment to the SARK posters, incense holders, and chakra books.

One morning Troy struts into the bookstore café with a bottle of sparkling apple cider and a De Beers princess-cut ring. He gets down on one knee in front of the counter. All four of the store's New Age customers gush. I say yes. What else is there to say?

In mid-December, three and a half months into my pregnancy, I go to two appointments:

The first to fix my platinum hair, which is now half blond and half brown, the poor person's ombré. The second, two hours away, is to my mother's gynecologist to check on the baby.

I look like hell. I'm bloated and pale with dark circles under my eyes. I don't work much, and instead I stay home and watch the O. J. Simpson trial while balancing food on my expanding chest. I'm not smoking cigarettes, so I fill the gap with pizza and ice cream and chips and ice cream with chips. I'm eating for two and I take this seriously, as if the fetus growing inside me will be better served if I eat for five.

I head to a local hairdresser's, Sally's, and tell Sally I want my hair something close to my natural color because I'm pregnant and I don't think you can dye your hair when you're pregnant and she says: "You know what you need? *LOWLIGHTS*." She's excited, she hasn't done these before! She grabs a flesh-colored rubber cap from the back and tugs it roughly onto my head until I look like a human condom with a bloated sad-lady face.

Sally methodically pulls strands of my hair through holes in the rubber cap with a long, hooked pin, section by section, my head resembling the dolls I used to destroy as a kid. She dyes the hair on top of the hair condom toffee brown and leaves the hair underneath yellow blond and when she finally washes and removes the cap and blows the hair dry, the result is a dark dishwater beige, in some places a configuration of cheetah spots, in others, stripes. "Aw, I think I was supposed to get that cap on tighter," Sally explains.

At my second appointment that week, I see the gynecologist who delivered two of my mother's children and is now approximately 717 years old. He gives me a pregnancy test (positive) and takes out a hand-held device that looks like a phone receiver and runs it over my bloated abdomen. It makes a squish-squish wavy ocean sound but not a thump-thump one. He doesn't detect a heartbeat on the phone receiver device but says that's probably okay because the phone receiver device doesn't always pick up the heartbeat through a thick stomach this early on. He tells me to make an appointment for the next week, but I'm twenty-one and not used to making appointments and then it's Christmas and New Year's, which I spend with my family. Troy works both.

In between we see a Catholic priest who lives two hours from our house because Troy wants to get married in a Catholic church and we're trying to get the priest to marry us without the six-months-long Catholic-marriage course you're supposed to take first. We are Catholic marriage delinquents, hiding that I'm pregnant and also that we've ever had sex.

I blow off the doctor's appointment until the second week of January. When we finally set it, my mother asks if she can tag along. It's at a big hospital near her house with one of the new fancy ultrasound machines. She wants to see her grandchild and also, afterward, we can do more wedding stuff!

I hate the wedding stuff. I hate my David's Bridal clearance-rack dress. I don't want to talk about wedding favors and cake toppers. The wedding feels like my mother's party, not mine, which makes sense since she's doing all the work. But it also feels, intentionally or not, like she's showing me up, better at this kind of practical living than I will ever be. I'm petulant and sullen throughout, a dour bummer, make every detail annoying and unfun. Everyone blames my mood on pregnancy, but really it's that I'd failed to calculate wedding planning into my new domestic duties, which now include taking over where Troy's mom left off as his personal chef, housekeeper, laundress. I already feel like I'm on my own with the baby growing inside me, the zygote I've started talking to each night. I'm already apologizing for how unhappy I am, rubbing my stomach in the hours we're alone, saying it will be okay, even though I'm not sure it will.

When the day of the fancy ultrasound appointment finally arrives, Troy manages a few hours off work. My mom comes, too. It's a crisp, sunny January morning. My mother, who is about to be a grandmother at thirty-eight, is practically bouncing with joy. She skips into the hospital while singing the lyrics to "Kooks," a David Bowie song about young parents making a go of it, one she sang to me when I was a kid.

We're shown to a room, and the ratio of people to space is awkward and tight. We make jokes, the technician laughs. But a few seconds into the procedure, her smile drops. There's suddenly palpable tension around the fancy machine. The technician has already explained she's not allowed to tell us anything, so we sit in silence, watch the fuzzy screen, and listen to the beeps until my mother grabs my knee hard and whisper-yells, "*ASK HER.*" I don't but she does, and even before my mother says, "What are you seeing?" I know it's all gone sour and wrong. The technician takes a pause before looking down and says, "I'm not seeing a heartbeat." Troy says, "That will develop, right?" I sit on the table with my legs up and slowly, softly cry.

I'm seventeen weeks pregnant and getting married in a little over a week and the baby in my body is dead, has been dead. We schedule surgery to remove the dead baby from my body for Thursday, but it's only Tuesday now.

Outside in the parking lot Troy says, "You know, babe, I have to head back to work—why don't you stay with your mom?" My mom agrees this is the best idea and with that, he rides away in the maroon SUV he's just traded his Miata in for, the one with the high safety rating and the four-wheel drive. The next day my parents go to work and my brother and sister go to school and I lie on the floor of my parents' kitchen and stare at the ceiling and wait, for what I don't know. I can't believe I am back here and wonder if I was ever really gone and if I'll ever get to leave.

On Thursday, my mom drives me to the hospital and Troy shows up as the nurses are prepping me and the anesthesiologist is explaining everything. When they're about to wheel me out for surgery, I hear my mother tell Troy she wants to go to lunch.

"Just be here when I wake up, okay?" I say.

After surgery, I wake up in a pleather armchair directly next to a man with a tube in his nose. I have a tube in my nose too and my mom is not there and Troy is not there and when they return forty minutes later my mom says, "That was FAST! I didn't know you'd be done so fast! WE had an *excellent* lunch."

A week later, I wear a rhinestone and lace veil over my mottled-brown hair and a hospital-grade menstrual pad under my baggy-in-the-waist gown. I walk down the aisle on my father's arm, kneel at the altar in front of God, kneel in front of a statue of the Virgin Mary, stand up, sit down, eat the wafer cracker that is the body of Christ, sip the fake wine meant to be blood, stand up again, and say my vows.

Later, I'll smile by a crudité plate, have my picture taken in front of an ice sculpture that's shaped like a hollowed-out heart. In these pictures, I appear pale and lifeless, a bridal ghost. I've just lost a baby, my brain's on ice, my heart's hollowed out too. Before the night is over, I'll smush frosting into my stranger-spouse's face, throw a bouquet. I'll slow-dance under a spotlight to our wedding song, "I Love You" by the Climax Blues Band (his choice), while 150 of our parents' closest friends whisper and stare.

"I Love You" is all about a man who was down and out—quite literally, *HITTING THE BEER*—until a woman walked into his life and made him right, stole his heart, straightened him out. It's a song that lays bare the most pernicious woman-as-martyr archetype, woman as patient and saintly savior, woman as fixer, magical woman who can transform the brokenness in man just by walking around the planet with a smidge of logic, a shake of sense. No thought to what the woman walking into his life and attempting to do all that mending might need, only that the man now has someone to take care of him, he now has it all.

When I hear this song today, I can still feel how it felt hearing it that day, how it felt to be thought of in this way. Even in the moment, I wanted it to feel better than it did. I wanted this life with Troy to be enough. When we danced to this song, Troy rocked me back and forth in exaggerated motion, dramatically lip-synced the song's lyrics in my face, a big show of love. I was twenty-one and living a certain kind of girl's fantasy, the kind of girl I thought I was supposed to be, the girl I think my parents wished me to be, making the kinds of decisions and sacrifices they themselves had made, following their same romantic leaps of faith. But this was not my fantasy, dancing awkwardly with a man who was surely drunk—a man I barely knew—swaying to a song about relationship imbalance, a song where only one person in the partnership matters or wins. Is it a good time to tell you that this song is too fast to slow-dance to? Is it important to know that this song is more than four minutes long?

Once we return from our honeymoon—a timeshare in Disney World, a wedding gift from my parents—Troy takes control of our life. He makes most of and manages all of the money, pays all the bills, which are all in his name. One night when he's working late, I look at his checkbook and see he's been balancing it into the negative for pages, writing and calculating minus signs for weeks. There they are, in a row. Minus $27, minus $89, minus $223. One afternoon I find a case of empty beer cans in the backseat of his SUV. When I ask him where it came from, he says he doesn't know. One night I find multiple empty beer bottles carefully hidden under other garbage in the trash; the same week I find an empty condom wrapper near the couch. Another night I am at the bar down the street from our apartment and the bartender says, "Oh you're the missus? We love Troy around here, he's always buying rounds!" She laughs as she explains she's never had a customer give her his PIN number before.

None of it is enough, and none of it is okay. There's no target yet for my ambition, but I know one thing for sure: There has to be more than this.

Connecticut

Troy and I stay married for nearly four years, mainly because neither of us can handle the failure of less. We move around a lot, mostly for his job. When we move, we initially live in hotels, in standard-size rooms, sometimes for months at a time. Troy's a corporate food and beverage director, but mainly a fixer, sent to fix failing hotels, which put us up for free. We rarely see each other because he works seventy-hour weeks. Or tells me he does.

I am in one of the squishy stages of life—not just because I'm young, but more because I'm lost, which is a condition I'll later learn can happen at any age. I have no college degree so there are limits to where I can work, what I can do, be. I wait tables at night and babysit in the afternoon. I try for a telemarketing job misadvertised in the paper as work in a publishing office, a job that is actually part of a pyramid scheme. The requirement for this job is not a degree but an intense level of enthusiasm, reading both *The Seven Habits for Highly Successful People* and Dale Carnegie's *How to Win Friends and Influence People,* and then taking a quiz. The job is run by a rah-rah blond evangelist who promises a six-figure salary once you're in. I don't read the books and I walk out in the middle of the quiz—I'm desperate for my own money, but not desperate enough to enter the business of scams.

When we are living in a hotel in Stamford, Connecticut, I briefly meet a woman at the end of her adult life who transforms the beginning of mine. I'd been looking for apartments in this state I'd never been to before, a place where I know no one, a city an hour outside of Manhattan that I cannot, for the life of me, understand. The rents in Connecticut are too expensive for us. I am waiting tables in the hotel, but it is often slow—not many solo business diners want a revolving rooftop fine-dining experience that looks out over a highway, the reality of it just as depressing as it sounds. Troy makes money, but I don't know where it goes and whatever's left is not enough to stretch here. I can't find an apartment in our budget that's not either an hour away or a total shithole, so now we're looking into alternative housing situations, open to shares.

The woman I meet—a former artist and art history professor—placed an ad in the local newspaper for a caretaker to come live in her guesthouse. She's looking for someone to do basic grocery shopping and tidying, to make sure she takes her medications on time, someone to generally be present and useful and around. The idea of living with an artist is appealing, at least for me, and I've recently started thinking more about me.

I call and inquire, the woman agrees it might be a good fit, gives me directions to her house in the woods. When I pull up the driveway, I see a canopy of bright yellow ginkgo trees dotting the property. It's early November; just enough leaves have fallen to create a golden path to the house. I ring the bell; the woman shows me inside. Her midcentury home is small but feels spacious, filled with ornate wood furniture, fine art, books, and plants. The kitchen has a large skylight, which is covered with an orange film. There's a stone pool in the back, completely mossed over, and beyond that, a one-room cottage with its own tiny kitchen and an even tinier bath. It was once her art studio, the woman explains as she walks slightly ahead of me, while I keep her careful pace. Now it's a place people could live. Nothing about the property signals wealth, rather a life of aesthetic precision, independence, pleasure, and care. It's the first house like this I've ever been to, its careful curation signaling a broad, well-traveled existence; a life-size diorama of the kind of independent adulthood I'm realizing for the first time is something I crave.

We land back in the main house kitchen and the woman tells me about her life—she was a painter, a sculptor, and once a professor, though she's too old to teach now, too old for many things she used to love. She needs help at home but isn't interested in an outside nurse or medical care, which she says is unnecessary, and she doesn't want to burden her family or friends.

The woman wears billowy burgundy silk pants, a matching silk top, and an ornate silk scarf wrapped around her neck. She is the kind of thin that happens only to the very old or very sick, and on her head is a grayish brown wig that's not very good. She makes us tea in a delicately crafted teapot and we talk for an hour. She was married once, but that didn't work out. She found she was happier on her own, never had kids. She's lively and smart. I manage to make her laugh, which feels like a gift. She gives me a tour of the main house before I leave; we pass paintings and sculptures, various ephemera from her travels, a framed photo of her, much younger, smiling while wearing a white sundress, in what looks like Greece. "This could work," she says at the door, "come back with your husband, we'll see."

A few days later, I return with Troy, who stomps in with his khakis and his golf shirt and his thousand-dollar smile. His slick, shallow charm is enough to move him successfully into and through most rooms, but not this one. It's immediately clear he doesn't belong in a space like this, even if, for the first time, I know that I do.

The next day the woman calls to tell me she's afraid it won't work out; she liked meeting me but I'm not in the appropriate stage of life for what she needs. I don't know better not to argue: Is she sure? I could change, I could be more than she's expecting, do more? I make promises, but she's older, wiser, smarter—she knows. "No, I'm afraid this won't work, but here's my advice, Jennifer: Go back to school, sort yourself out for *you,* find out what is it you want and like to do."

I break the news to Troy. He tells me the place was creepy anyway— we can do better, I'll see. Three weeks later we pull up to the place he's found: a charmless split-level in Rye, New York, and move into a room that's really a den. Our roommates are three male snowboarding buffs and their large pets. The floors are covered with brown wall-to-wall carpeting, which consistently smells of wet dog, old pasta water, and men's shoes; its entryway is cluttered with snowboarding gear. In the two months we live in that house, I'm not sure what will keep me from not dying there. By January we're back in Pennsylvania. Troy has a new job, and we move into a two-bedroom apartment, our own.

Once we're in Pennsylvania, I take the Connecticut woman's advice and go back to school, enroll in community college classes as soon as I can. Among my first courses is Intro to Writing. My professor—an older hippie woman with long, witchy salt-and-pepper hair—tells me I have potential as a writer, if that's something I'm interested in. I am. She hooks me up with the town's local paper, a pamphlet really, one of those papers you find rolled up in your driveway for free. I start writing book and local theater reviews. They're barely edited, they go to print with typos, the tone is derivative—I haven't yet discovered my voice— but I like doing them. I can't believe I'm finally writing. It feels like a direction, some kind of sign. I'm thrilled.

Troy is not as thrilled. When I told him I thought I wanted to be a high school English teacher he'd seemed okay with it, but he can't wrap his head around this. He loves me, but really he's in love with an idea of me, this offbeat girl he chased because the others came too easy. Since we lost our baby (a topic we never discuss), he's held on to a domestic dream of our life, even as this dream recedes further and further from view.

When I float the idea of moving to New York after I graduate to pursue writing, we both check out of the conversation before it begins. If we were more honest with each other, we'd laugh. It's absurd to imagine taking this marital show on that road. But it's the road I increasingly know I want to be on, even if Troy's already told me he won't pay a dime for school, even if he yeahs-yeahs me from the couch, where he's watching sports, when I tell him about the programs I'm applying to, the degrees that'll broaden my skill set, set me up better for an entry-level job. Six months later—with my straight As from the community college, a recommendation from the editor at the local paper, and enough transferred credits that I'm halfway to a bachelor's degree—I'm accepted into Emerson College's Writing, Literature, and Publishing program. When I make clear that I'm going with or without him, Troy's condescending comments end. It's real.

He says he's actually interested in Boston. He asks his company for a transfer and there's a broken-enough hotel right outside the city that justifies it. We move in late summer, to an apartment right on the Freedom Trail, just as all the students are back. The city's bustling and full. I enroll in a rigorous eighteen-credit course load, six classes spread over five days a week. Into our second week in town, I play up my scant Spanish skills and land a job as a waitress at a tapas restaurant on trendy Newbury Street. I'm hired on the spot, handed a sequined vest, and told to purchase black hot pants before I return.

The end of our union is as swift as the beginning. Troy's reverse-commuting outside the city, my new life is centered within. Days go by without us seeing each other, then weeks. It's fall, then winter. I start studying at the college library in my free hours, lingering at the tapas restaurant at night over shift drinks. Troy starts drinking at work, too. After the first DUI he receives a warning; after the second, he's screwed. He loses his license and is offered a choice by his company—leave the job or transfer. He decides to transfer to another hotel in Pennsylvania, the corporate boys looking after their own. Before he can even ask, we both know my answer. I've already managed my way off the map of this relationship. For better or for worse, I'm free.

The Brokenness

There's a story about the writers Mary Karr and David Foster Wallace and a coffee table that I heard years ago and think about a lot. There are lots of stories besides this, how Wallace pushed Karr out of a moving vehicle, how he wouldn't take no when she wanted to break up, how, after they broke up, he followed her five-year-old son home from school. Wallace was a problematic Gen X man and, according to reports from female students he allegedly harassed, an often hideous one. He was also, sadly, let's face it, no worse than many in an entire generation of white, cis, able-bodied boy-genius men in America, who were, even more sadly, better than the generation before them. From all accounts, including his own, Wallace was depressed and often angry; impulsive, intense, and also really fucking clever, manipulative, and smart; a combination that, for a certain kind of woman at a certain time in her life, has historically proved irresistible, for the adrenaline rushes alone, the stress spikes we mistake for passion and connection, the ones many of us learned in childhood are a requirement for love.

In Karr's telling, toward the end of their dating, Wallace visited her apartment. They had a fight and, within that fight, he broke her coffee table. She sent him a bill for a hundred dollars. He paid, and then asked for the remains, since he'd bought them, after all—a small act of astonishing pettiness, an example of how rejection can reduce even the most distinguished male brain to desperate, abusive trash. Karr refused, telling him she'd burned the coffee table in a fire—the remains had been used as firewood—explaining, "The only thing you bought was the brokenness."

For the last years of my twenties, after I leave Troy, I trade almost exclusively in brokenness. Guilty, unsure, and too afraid to make it on my own, I alight my ambition upon a series of clever maniacs, artistic sociopaths, B and C thinkers who, because I have no context for such men, I am quite sure are As. I am magnetized by creative men who know more than I do, or pretend that they do, men who are going places or say that they are, men who've been to places I've never gone before.

I have dreams of becoming a published writer but still have little context for what the path looks like. But even more than becoming a writer, I dream of becoming a *somebody*, of achieving success that is unambiguous, the kind that lets the world know you're okay, that you made it, that you're better than they all thought you were. The kind that might make you feel that way about yourself, too.

At night after school and work, I spend hours studying in the cramped North End apartment I now share with an incontinent Siamese cat and two roommates, one of whom is a part-time dominatrix who makes her own leather whips and hangs them all over our walls. I start keeping journals with lists of words I hear others say but I don't understand. Later, in my room, I look them up in an old Webster's dictionary I lifted from the school library, use them in sentences, say them aloud. When I'm not studying or looking up words, I'm trying to shake my thick Philly accent, changing the shape of my mouth as I pronounce "WAH-ter" and "BAHd" instead of "wudder" and "bade" again and again until I'm too tired to speak.

I'm twenty-five and it feels like it's now or never—there's a race to make something of my life, and it still feels like I have a long way to go. I've begun commingling the personal and the professional, begun the faster-than-you'd-imagine process of defining myself by who I know and what I do. I seek love and attention and acceptance from men not because I like or want or even necessarily feel attracted to them, but because I like and want and feel attracted to their class status and their lives, their (often unearned) swagger, the ease with which they're rewarded and allowed to move through the world. I'm looking for a decoder ring to the life I want, a partner to accelerate my ascent.

What's more romantic to a hungry young woman than adjacency to greatness, even if it comes at a cost? I wasn't in love with these men. I wanted to be them. Educated white men got all the attention, hoarded all the connections and success. Proximity to them felt intoxicating. Like a grunge-era Eliza Doolittle, I'm looking for my own Henry Higgins, for a magic carpet ride into my own unrealized dreams.

The first man I date post-Troy is an aspiring photographer, a blond wisp of a person, skinny, German, just my height. He's a Niles from *Frasier*–type dandy, a man who likes midcentury architecture and design and, before we meet in Boston, lived in both Sweden and an exotic place I've never heard of before, Taos. He's stylish, refined, the first man I've met of his kind. The night we meet, he's decked out in head-to-toe baby blue: blue polyester bell-bottomed pants, a blue polo shirt buttoned to the top, baby-blue tennis shoes. He's the roommate of a waitress friend. When he comes to visit the restaurant where we work, he keeps his orange-lensed sunglasses and oversize shearling coat on, even though it's dark and warm and we're inside.

He stares at me while sipping sherry at the bar, follows me with his eyes as I pour bottomless glasses of sangria to pretentious Harvard jerks, the restaurant's main clientele. When we're introduced at the end of my shift, he asks what else I do and I say I want to be a writer. He tells me he sometimes photographs parties for a local nightlife magazine, says he thinks he can get me a writing gig there. What he lacks in physical heft he makes up for in bitchiness and a wicked tongue. He's funny, he's mean, he's a snob and a freak. It's love at first sight.

On our first date, he takes me to see Stereolab at a grimy music hall located in the shadow of Fenway Park, owned by hometown sons Aerosmith. Before heading in, he rolls a joint as thick as a thumb and we spend the concert pressed up against the back wall, staring and laughing at each other, intermittently making out. I'm facing the stage and he's facing me and the club's blue-purple-green strobe lights flicker across both of our faces. When he tucks my hair behind my ear, leans in, and whispers, "I like you," I am sure nothing before this moment mattered. This is the beginning of the rest of my life.

I follow his lead on how to cultivate this new life. I buy clothes that look like his clothes, clothes that he wants me to wear. I dye my hair blond like his hair. We see movies he wants to watch—art house films from directors I've never heard of that I don't yet but want to understand. We go to outdoor sculpture museums, drink expensive wine we can't afford in candlelit bars. He wants to see me all of the time. I'm a full-time waitress and a full-time student; time is on neither of our sides.

———————————

By our fifth date, we're fighting. Big fights, make-a-scene fights; loud, teary, cruel. One night after a fight when I tell him I don't want to see him anymore, he scales the side of my building on the fire escape to the apartment I'm sharing, bangs on the window of my bedroom with a scratched-up hand. I let him in and we fight and then have sex and afterward he gets angry because I tried something new. *Where did you learn that* he says.

By our tenth date, he comments on what I eat and how I eat and talks about how historically he hasn't enjoyed sex with women if they gain, he's not sure where the line is, five pounds? He doesn't like women who let themselves go, he explains. I move in with him a month later, pay our security deposit with my waitressing tips, eat less, smoke more, resolve not to let myself go anywhere.

Our new apartment is in the South End of Boston, on a street paved with rust-colored bricks. The front window faces a dance school. In the winter, at dusk, when the lights come on, you can see the ballerinas practicing and performing, in sync—arms up, legs bent, pliés. Across the street, I practice and perform a careful dance too.

As tempestuous as he is, I am often in awe of him. I like how his hands get tan and rough in the summer, I like the way he chops vegetables while making dinner, and I like that he can cook. I like that he is small, physically unintimidating, not traditionally masculine with a capital "M," like the men I'd grown up around. Once when he is out, I try on his pants and they don't fit. I realize I like this, too.

We buy two old bikes and lock them in front of our apartment and, when I don't have to work, we ride across one of the Charles River bridges at night. We head out to Walden Pond and camp in a tent in a friend's backyard. We take a road trip and hike the Appalachian Trail; it's too smoky to see anything at the top of the Smoky Mountains, did you know? We take a road trip to Miami and drop Molly when it's still called ecstasy and dance in a club lit up with glow sticks and shiny bodies. Before we go, the photographer buys me a silky black bandanna shirt from a vendor on the street that is basically a napkin with attached strings and tells me to wear it. I do. After, we have sex in the bathroom at a party and break the sink.

On my days off, he wants to photograph me. He puts me in sheer sixties caftans, tells me to take off my underwear, to stand next to a borrowed Eames chair, tells me to relax my arms, relax my face, tells me to tilt my head left, no right, asks me, *Why do you look so weird? Why is this so hard for you?* tells me *You're doing it wrong.*

In the mornings, at home, he instructs me to wear shorter skirts, show off my legs, yells when I come in too late from work, yells when I make too much of a mess, snaps when I don't immediately shower after a restaurant shift. Our apartment is directly above the office of the building's management company. The floor and the walls are thin. When I pay the rent, the receptionist looks at me, smiles with her lips closed, says, "Are you okay?"

Yes, of course, why wouldn't I be?

We go to lots of parties—I'm interning for *Boston* magazine, he's still working unpaid for the nightlife magazine—and we meet lots of people. We're an enterprising young couple with aspirations for creative power in a WASPy, uncreative, second-tier city. I'm still in school, still working nights, now freelancing too. When I'm gone, the photographer is bored. He takes half our furniture to a new studio space, where his focus is Scandinavian fashion and Scandinavian design and Scandinavian models, and where he photographs all of the above for free and sleeps with the models, presumably for free too.

One afternoon, when he's telling a story and gets caught in a lie, I confront him. I am wild with jealousy, a rage machine. He tells me I'm crazy and berates me for being crazy, puffs his chest, slams his hands on the counter, slams and reslams the bathroom door. I keep interrogating. He comes out of the bathroom, pushes me against the wall, and wraps his whole tan, rough hand around my throat.

I kick at him, squirm, manage to get away, run into the bedroom closet. The berating and shaming continue through the closet door while I crouch under a rack of his shirts, rocking back and forth with my hands over my ears, chant-crying "stop stop stop." He softens his voice and asks me to come out and I do and we have sex and, afterward, he gets up and wipes himself off with a towel and walks to the kitchen naked for a glass of water and it's just another Tuesday.

That Christmas he gives me a framed copy of his favorite of his own photographs and a copy of *Infinite Jest*. It's inscribed: "To the best writer I know. Let's move to New York and get rich. Love, S."

After two years, I'll get up the nerve to leave the photographer, but only after I no longer believe in his usefulness to my future, only when there's another man in place. The new man is an aspiring writer and musician who wears many silver rings across his Irish-white fingers. We meet one night when he sits at the bar in the restaurant where I work, a rare night when I'm not waiting tables in a uniform but am instead dressed up in street clothes, playing host. He has a curly-haired bob and an almost-handsome face and sports a black leather jacket that looks new. He reads Bukowski and quotes Rilke and Rumi and, once we start sleeping together, expects me to talk about how much I like his penis. "You never talk about how much you like it," he starts one morning, after asking if I'd like to know what he's been writing in his dream journal.

We date for eleven months, most of them drunk, many of them stoned. He's a rich boy from a rich suburb; a prep school kid trying on a struggling artist cap; a banker's son who's playing poor. His friends are writers who do not write, artists who don't make art, musicians who don't play. He has many opinions about writing and writers, art and artists. These opinions are forceful, unequivocal, confident, strong. He's well read, which makes me think he's smart; he can quote so many things. The writer-musician thinks I have potential, thinks I need to be shaped. He's mad that other men haven't "taken better care" of me. He's tall and broad and strong, and when he puts his arm around me, I feel safe. Until, of course, I don't.

We talk about moving to New York, how we'll get an apartment in Brooklyn and a rescue cat too. He'll support us while I'm just starting out as a writer, he says. He has money, he can pay a big chunk of the rent. But no plan's ever put into place. Mostly he wants to lie on the floor of his apartment, smoke cigarettes, ash into dirty cups. Sometimes he wants to read passages from poetry books aloud. Sometimes he wants to listen to Mazzy Star. He met her once. She was too drunk to do her set, he says. She slurred the lyrics to "Fade into You." Afterward he saw her backstage and she was crying over something, a mess.

"I don't want to see you drunk," he tells me, somehow oblivious to the fact that, since my divorce from Troy, I drink most nights of the week. I respond to his request by changing nothing: I work, I study, I drink.

The writer-musician doesn't want to see me drunk, but he does want to take me to Europe. He's been, but only with his parents, only a couple of times. You'll love it, he says, and I'm flattered that he thinks of me as a person you take to Europe. I take time off from my restaurant job, we fly across the Atlantic, travel around for three weeks, staying in hostels and living off cigarettes and bread. In London, he takes us to Damien Hirst's bar in Notting Hill because he's read that you can drink absinthe there. Afterward, we head to the West End and dance in a club. He's territorial, overprotective, accuses other men of flirting with me, makes a scene, won't let me go to the bathroom alone.

In Amsterdam, I get so high on a space cake I run into a cyclist and puke in the canal. In Paris, I stay back at the hostel, drink a bottle of red wine, and read *One Hundred Years of Solitude* while the writer-musician visits Jim Morrison's grave, each of us practicing our own brand of performative ennui. He photographs the grave with black-and-white film. Later, he photographs Oscar Wilde's grave too. He photographs the entire trip in black and white. When we return home, he develops the film, makes me copies, charges me $125 for the privilege of my set. The pictures are comically pretentious, art-school-cliché composed. In them, we look forced, pouty, a parody. We look like the poseurs we are.

Once we're back in Boston, I go to a party after work with my restaurant crew and eat enough magic mushrooms to believe I'm not sitting in a beer-can-strewn Allston apartment but floating in a painted desert in Santa Fe. I don't have a cell phone and the writer-musician can't reach me, so he drives around looking. When he doesn't find me, he assumes I'm cheating, so he pisses on the door of the restaurant where I work and calls me the next day to accuse me of cheating and tell me about the pissing. Somehow the pissing is a bridge too far and I break up with him. A few days later, he sends me a photocopy of his middle finger scrawled with the note, "I now look at you as only a receptacle to put sperm." He'll leave me answering machine messages on our house landline, the entirety of which are him scream-crying "YOU CUNT YOU CUNT YOU CUNT. I HATE YOU, YOU CUNT."

Later than this he'll record a stupid album under an even more stupid pseudonym and he'll email me to say he's visiting New York and ask if we can have a drink for "closure." I'm still emotionally dumb, think I owe him something, I agree. In a dark bar in SoHo, he'll hand me the album he's just finished and tell me there's a song on there about me.

He'll tell me this with a grin on his face that suggests he's been just a little bit naughty. I'll look at the CD and find the song he's written for me. There it is, spelled out in Copperplate Gothic, 1999's most popular menu font, a track entitled "Hiroshima."

Around the time I am twenty-eight, still living in Boston, post-graduation, just post-dating the musician, my life hits another stall. I'll attempt to jump-start it by applying to a summer publishing course in Cambridge that's mostly a finishing school for mostly well-off young white women to network, gain a professional community, and, the holy grail, land a just-above-poverty-wage, entry-level publishing J-O-B. The brochure touts *a 90 percent job placement rate! Alumni spread out across top positions in magazine and book publishing! Editors in chief! Managing editors! BOOK AGENTS!* Oh my!

I hear about the course through an editor at my internship at *Boston* magazine. The cost is three thousand dollars—an astronomical sum for six weeks, nearly double if you live on campus, more if, say, you require meals. "It's *soo* worth it," the editor, who grew up in a rich Boston suburb and uses "summer" as a verb, tells me. "It's a foot in the door."

I barely have feet in this business or any other and for sure no door, and so I fill out the application, request the recommendations, collect the transcripts, send in the nonrefundable application fee, and hope for the best. Admissions are competitive, the course assistant warns when I call, thousands apply for just one hundred spots. But, apparently, a divorced, late-twenties Italian-American woman with nary an espresso cup to piss in is an exotic enough type of white person in turn-of-the-twenty-first-century American publishing to make me stand out. I get in.

In order to save for the publishing course's tuition, I land a second restaurant job, this one at a place that serves lunch and, on weekends, brunch. I request a full schedule at both jobs, fill in for other servers, so that I work most every shift in the week for three months. At night, I count up the stacks of cash on the floor of my Jamaica Plain apartment until there is finally enough.

When the course starts, it's a half hour by bike, but then my bike is stolen and it's an hour on two subways and a bus. At my Cambridge restaurant job, I meet an eccentric MIT boy with a flowing Euro-style mullet. He's twenty-two and just back from a school research trip in Antarctica. His major is something like "Art Meets Ice." We start sleeping together, he tells me dramatically, poetically that I remind him of a praying mantis; he recommends books I should read if I want to be a "real" writer. Sometimes, because it makes life easier, I shack up with him.

I have not recovered from Troy, I have not recovered from the German photographer, I am still reeling from the pissing dream-journaler. I've for sure not reckoned with my childhood, my miscarriage, or the fact that I settle for emotional crumbs given by terrible men to validate the idea that I am terrible myself. I keep stuffing it all down, packing the powder keg, drinking it all away.

But now, I have a single, driving mission: to get myself to New York, enter a career, and leave the mess of my life behind.

The publishing course is broken into two parts: Magazines and Books, three weeks for each. Most of the instruction time is spent listening to panels of publishing luminaries trade jokey-jokey insider barbs about their work. Some of it is spent listening to publishing luminaries explain how they do their jobs, how a book is published, how a magazine article is made.

Even more time is spent in a cavernous lecture hall listening to editors tell tall tales of career journeys, the idea being *if you just do what I did you'll make it too*. It's the year 2000, a decade before the professional world turns millennial girlboss pink. No one has a sense of what's about to happen, that the internet will render most of this collective career wisdom pointless and obsolete. That, soon, most of these jobs they're waxing on about will be eaten by greedy tech titans and their even greedier algorithms. No one knows that in just a few years these fat-cat editors will begin to die off, figuratively but also sometimes literally, expiring midway through three-martini expense-account lunches at the kinds of plush, see-and-be-seen media-power restaurants that will also soon cease to exist.

I find the book people mostly stuffy, and the pace of their part of publishing too stodgy, set in its ways, slow. But I cannot get enough of the magazine editors. I'm mesmerized by every nerdy inside detail they share; electrified by talk of columns, rubrics, slugs. I've wanted to work at a magazine since my days reading *Sassy*, but I'm open to any opportunity. I'm here to find the connections to transport me inside anywhere, I just need someone, *anyone* to crack open a door.

The night the next bad decision I date comes to town, there's a buzz surrounding his arrival. He's a "cool" publishing guy, a maverick. A bigwig who's been known to find jobs for many of the students. His networking largesse extends beyond the course's staid "sherry hour" into hosting the entire class for drinks at a local dive bar, an annual tradition everyone looks forward to, what fun. What's more, it's rumored that each year the maverick hooks up with one of the publishing course girls and that girl always gets a publishing job. Many of the girls want to be that girl.

I want it to be me, but I don't tell anyone this, don't even know if I fully admit it to myself. After the maverick publisher teaches his class—books he's published, deals he's landed, a name drop of Raymond Carver except he calls him "Ray"—we head to the bar. The maverick publisher dives right in, orders and passes out drinks, makes a big show of putting down his credit card, says, "All the drinks are on me." He slaps earnest male students on the back, spills mild literary secrets, drops more major literary names. He's in his forties, big and bellowing, enthusiastic, confident, cool. The female students who've lined up waiting their turn for his attention are all twenty-two, overdressed, glossy-lipped, pastel-cardigan clad. They stand prim against the wall adjacent to the bar like young debutantes, their fresh faces marred by the red glow of off-season Christmas lights that serve as the space's main décor. I'm at the other end of the bar in tight jeans, a tank top, and no bra making riotous conversation with anyone but the publishing maverick, pretending to be unimpressed by and oblivious to his scene. By this point in my life, I've waited on enough big-shot white guys to know there's nothing that attracts them more than being ignored.

The strategy works. By the end of the night, I've caught his eye, grabbed misogyny's brass ring. He approaches, a little slurry. I attempt banter, make a joke, play. I'm far from the smartest person in the room—I can barely talk books or business or the business of books—but I have a thing the others don't: on-the-job training for how to manage a mark in a bar.

Within the hour, I've got all his attention; everyone else has gone home. We close down the bar. He orders what I remember as two Heinekens for the road, asks for them unopened, leaves a bigger tip so the bartender will oblige. In one swift motion he slides the beer into the inside pockets of his expensive summer blazer, twirls to look at me, breezes open the bar door, holds it for me to pass through.

It's 1:00 A.M. in Cambridge on a balmy night in June; the air is sticky and smells sweet. We stroll through a mostly empty Harvard Square. He offers me a line of coke, which I decline; he proceeds to snort a pile off the top of his hand. (Later that summer, *The New York Times* runs a story about the drug's "comeback," asserts, "Cocaine is back for the thirty- and forty-year-olds!" though for this man I don't believe it ever left.)

He wants me to come back to his hotel, to drink the beers in his room. I tell him I can't. I'm in a wedding in Pennsylvania that weekend—an old waitressing friend—and I have to get home. He is fully drunk now, stumbling a bit. He's the same age as my dad, a fact that should make him gross, but in this state he's surprisingly vulnerable, disarming, sweet. He offers to take me to the wedding by helicopter, is emphatic, excited, says he makes a great date. "I'm very rich, you know," he explains, as if all the hints hadn't added up. I walk him to his hotel, take his business card, make out with him at the door. "Look me up when you get to New York," he says. "I might be able to help you find a job."

That fall, I move to New York. I sell most everything I have, including my engagement ring from Troy, to afford the deposit on an eight-hundred-dollar-a-month room in a stranger's apartment that I find on Craigslist, a room where I can touch the walls from my bed. The apartment is across from a nursing home in a sleepy part of Brooklyn. The neighborhood's not so much unsafe as it is desolate, which, in a city like New York, can make things unsafe. I'll get mugged while walking home within the month.

I'd been offered better housing shares with some of my publishing-course classmates, people I like and might like to live with, but decline after hearing the cost. Their rents seem unfathomable on an entry-level salary; I can't make sense of how they can afford it until it occurs to me their wealthy parents are the ones paying. The obvious explanation, though no one says as much.

I drive down from Boston to Brooklyn on a rainy afternoon in late September. Summer's mugginess is hanging on, but there's a chill behind it, just hitting the air. I'd booked a U-Haul van for the move—I've got just a futon mattress, clothes, a lamp or two, a few boxes of books—but when I arrive to pick it up, I'm escorted to a considerably larger vehicle, the only one left, apparently, one that's passed off as an upgrade when I protest. "They all drive the same," the over-it guy behind the desk explains in a way that suggests he's stoned. For all my truckin' experience (zero), the fifteen-foot ride may as well be a big rig, but it's my only option and I don't want to delay.

The normally four-hour drive down Interstate 95 takes seven hours. The rain's fogging up the side mirrors enough that I can't see anything in the rear-view, so I turn on the flashers and take it slow. Somewhere in Connecticut I have to pee and can't hold it. I'm too overwhelmed to find a rest stop and park, so I pull over onto the shoulder, scooch to the passenger-side door, and head into the woods.

When I return, the rain's really coming down. I crack the truck's window, light a cigarette, and wait. New York's classic rock station has the best reception on the AM/FM radio and I tune it in. The DJ's just teed up Lynyrd Skynyrd's "Free Bird"—a song about commitment-phobic men and their freedoms, a song I'd always hated. But hearing it in this context, alone in the smoky cab of a truck, rain pelleting the windshield, my clothes and hair drenched, it sounds more mournful than chest beating. For the first time, I understand "Free Bird" not just as a corny-macho guitar anthem but a song about sorrow, the loneliness of perpetual change.

Since leaving my parents' house, I'd lived in seven different cities and towns, in more than a dozen apartments, with more roommates than I can remember, including several homes with different men. I don't feel free so much as on the run—from home, from an ill-thought-out marriage, from grief, from memories, from bill collectors, from friends who no longer feel like friends. I'm running to stand still, to finally find my place. If I can make it work, New York is where I get to stop.

The downpour subsides. The song's tempo ticks up. I flick my cigarette out the window, flip on my turn signal, pull out into traffic, and drive the too-big-for-me truck into my new life.

The New York Groove

The publishing maverick and I date on and off for a year. He sets me up for an interview for a job with his friend at *Men's Health,* for an interview with his friend at *Rolling Stone,* for an interview with his friend in the marketing department at Random House, none of which is a job I'd be any good at, none of which is a job I get. After dozens of interviews and maxing out credit cards to pay for basics like shampoo and toothpaste, I land a position without his help as the editorial assistant at an internet 1.0 start-up. It's a website and adjacent print magazine about the business of media and culture run by one of the guys who brought you *Spy* magazine, a venture that's both before and too late for its time. It's also a company staffed with earnest, avuncular media veterans who need and want help. The perfect first job.

The maverick takes me out to celebrate—to a new-cool restaurant, Pastis, where we sit close in a leather booth dipping French fries in mayonnaise and day-drinking champagne cocktails with his friends, who are also middle-aged publishing people. I tell them about my job and they share gossip about my new bosses and the industry at large. The waiters see the tab ticking up and respond by meeting our every need—we're one of *those* tables, and for the first time, I'm on the other side. Around the booth, the booze is flowing; no one holds back.

The publisher's friends have been in the business so long, they have so much dirt to impart. I'm a rapt audience, giving fresh attention to stale anecdotes they've been dining out on for years; a pretty blonde wearing a twelve-dollar vintage green-collared minidress, lace tights, and patent leather Payless boots. It doesn't matter what I say: my age and enthusiasm are enough to earn my seat at the table. I make these old men feel cool.

Later that month, the maverick calls again. He asks me to meet him at a nondescript restaurant on West Ninth Street called Marylou's, a place that, late at night, becomes an old-man coke bar for the rich and famous and criminal, a place that Jay McInerney will fictionalize in one of his books. We sit at the bar with his friends again, but this time he doesn't talk to me, behaves as if I'm a nuisance, even though he'd invited me out. The bar has a mauve-painted ladies' room with a large-mirrored makeup area in which a well-turned-out woman in her fifties hands me her Chanel compact, tells me to keep it, tells me it'll look better on me, tells me I'm too young for this place and the man with whom I've come. It's not the ghost of future me, but it might as well be. Instead of going home with the publishing maverick that night, I head back to my six-by-eight-foot room, where I sleep on a futon on the floor.

When I'm with him, I start doing coke, not because I like it, but so I can keep up, so I can stay up late and not be too drunk. I'm not even sure I like him—he's patronizing and self-centered, doesn't shoot straight. But I'm too in awe of his power to trust my own judgment. I'm on my own and out of my depth with New York publishing people, can't yet sort the wheat from the pretentious-asshole chaff.

And whether I like him or not, I like the way the relationship looks for me, how people think I'm something just because he's decided I am. I bring the insider gossip I hear when I'm with him back to my colleagues at work cautiously, strategically. I'm just an assistant, but high-level secrets give me value, make me seem plugged in. I'm smart enough to know this, to play the cards I'm dealt. At this first job, my entire focus is making myself stand out. I work all day and long into the nights, one of the first into the office and the last to leave, my days an unbroken cycle of phone messages and faxes, memo passing and package sending.

But I also push my bosses to let me take on tasks that will help me learn more than clerical work. No one wants to edit the reader letters page—a necessary but tedious brainteaser that requires balancing out feedback in a limited, one-page space with an exacting, Tetris-like fit—so I claim the job and, in the process, work with the art department and learn about layout and design. I start pitching subjects for *Tech Talk*, the monthly Q + A column about which gadgets media people use, a vapid assignment I've calculated that none of the more established writers cares about, a column for which I can easily tap the publisher's fancy media friends. After a few months of delivering compelling enough subjects and transcribing interviews conducted by senior staff, I ask to take on *Tech Talk* myself, with my own byline. My boss agrees. It's my first New York clip and I'm privately giddy over it. I ship out copies to my parents and friends affixed with Post-its scrawled with fifty exclamation points each.

I spend most of each week at work. On the weekends, the maverick publisher takes me to clubs—mostly a place called Moomba, where they know him at the door, where we slip through the line that's wrapped around the block, breeze past the bulky bouncers with ease. Once inside, we're served VIP drinks at VIP tables with other VIP New Yorkers. I don't know any of them; I haven't been in New York long enough to care about New York celebrities. One night I'm crushed at the end of a booth with a meek man wearing a pastel yellow sweater tied around his neck who is drinking seltzer, a square. He tells me about a project he's struggling with, gets granular on the details, city permits, how hard it is to shoot anything in New York. The story is boring, I want to drink more, I want to meet more people, access more of the scene. I climb over the back of the booth, crawl away, accidentally hit him with my purse on my way out.

It's Wes Anderson. He's filming *The Royal Tenenbaums*. I'm so dumb.

The maverick publisher's West Village apartment is small, dark, and plush; an eighties time capsule, with floor-to-ceiling pale blue drapes and wall-to-wall pale blue carpet and overstuffed couches and a smoky-gray glass dining table at which it looks like no one has ever sat. We stay up late smoking cigarettes, talking about his authors, talking about his new books, talking about celebrities he's kissed who are bad kissers, talking about him. Once he asks me to slow-dance with him in his living room when there's no music playing. Another time, he tears up and tells me he doesn't think he'll ever be a dad. Late one night, he'll summon me over when he's wasted, ask me to take off my clothes and sit around his apartment in a robe, the nicest robe I've ever worn. Later we'll get in his bed, and I'll notice his skin smells sour. In the dark he'll tell me this could be special. I'll lie awake feeling the comfort of his expensive sheets, the weight of his expensive blankets, and the awkward proximity to a stranger's skin.

One morning he'll sit up in bed, ask if I can get dressed. He'll open his wallet, hand me money, tell me to go to the store. He needs a pack of cigarettes and a special kind of fresh-squeezed orange juice from the deli down the street—*No not that one, the other one.* When I bring the juice back he's still in bed. I pour him a glass and walk it to his room. He tells me to set it down, he tells me I can keep the change. He asks me if I could leave. *Could you please leave?* When I call him again he doesn't answer. When I leave him messages, they're not returned. I'm stung by the rejection, but I move on quickly. Easy come, easy go.

Once I move to New York, I date only men I work with or meet at work parties because I've become obsessed with my career and mostly all I do is work or go to work parties, so I date only writers and editors because those are the only people who are there. I date men who are emotionally unavailable, who don't actually like me or want to get to know me, which at this point at least, suits me fine. I don't actually like or want to know myself either. I'm still in my twenties. I'm hooking up feverishly, haphazardly; using industry gossip as foreplay, submitting to sex not for pleasure but as an extension of my résumé, a gathering of useful information, a performance of independence, if not solely a means to numb out.

It's the early 2000s. I fuck shitty media men before we call them "shitty media men," their brand of shittiness exotic to me, different from the boys I grew up around. The men I meet are intimidatingly accomplished and outwardly polished; their predatory behavior initially difficult to parse. I date a series of foppish boy-men playing rapscallion, literary Gen X nerds flexing scant industry power to see how much they can get away with and, as it turns out, they can get away with a lot, at least with me. I go home with book critics and beat reporters, novelists and business journalists, *New Yorker* feature writers, fellow publishing assistants. I let a clumsy *New York Observer* columnist feel me up in a corner of Bret Easton Ellis's overcrowded holiday party while keeping one eye on Parker Posey across the room and never putting down my drink. At the after-party for one of the first-ever Webby Awards, I smoke a joint and later leave with a *Mother Jones* editor who's fifty-three but tells me he's forty. As a matter of principle, I don't date married men, but I date men who are too unavailable for any degree of emotional intimacy—too involved in other relationships, too narcissistic, or just too obsessed with their own dicks.

When I meet Gideon, I'm the assistant to the editor in chief of a new magazine. It's a demotion from my first job, at the internet start-up, where I was editorial assistant, but that place went under after just four months and I was lucky to find another gig as fast as I did. At this new magazine—which is, I shit you not, a magazine about magazines, the early 2000s were so dumb—I'm more like a secretary. I keep all the editor in chief's appointments, and his secrets too.

Gideon is a tenacious staff reporter who wants those secrets in order to land better assignments and get ahead. He's cute enough, but his real appeal is in how he's pushy and incorrigible, dangerous in a way most boys in offices are not. He visits my desk a few times a day, sits on the edge sometimes, asks me what my boss is up to, asks me what I think of this story or that. The magazine where we work is only my second job in New York. I'm mostly a "schedule maker" and an "expenses filer," but I want what Gideon has. I want to get paid for my persistence. I want to report long stories. I want to exclusively write.

I've lived in the city for less than a year and I'm already on my second roommate-filled apartment deep in Brooklyn. My assistant jobs pay half of what I made working as a waitress full-time. Making ends meet is near impossible. After I pay essential bills, I'm usually down to eighty dollars a week for food and cigarettes and anything else. I'm savvy, make the three-dollar rice-and-beans side from the Burritoville on Twenty-Third Street last for two meals, sometimes three. Meanwhile, Gideon gets sushi for lunch, wears designer shirts, and lives solo in a three-bedroom on the Upper West Side, though mostly he lives at the office, and so do I.

One weekend when we're both there on a Saturday afternoon, he calls my extension and asks if I'll come look at something he's working on. I meet him in the conference room, sift through the papers he's handed me, which I immediately sense are a prop; he doesn't want or need my help. A few seconds later, he leans in to kiss me, then pushes me onto the boat-shaped conference room table and we have sex next to an ancient phone. I don't understand how inappropriate this is; I'm not thinking about an imbalance of power. The attention feels nice.

After a weekend or two like this, Gideon says it's too risky, and I start meeting him at his place. This works better, he tells me, as he likes to shower right after. He's got a lot of neurotic ticks, which I find endearing. And he seems broken somehow, which I find familiar. I have few friends in the city, and the ones I have are mostly fellow assistants, younger than me by years. We mostly only ever talk about work. I'm surrounded by people, but I'm lonely, too.

Whenever Gideon calls, I make myself available. I bring him small, carefully considered, and quickly discarded gifts. I listen to his problems, try to offer him advice. Sometimes I run his errands and, when he's out of town, I watch his cat. When I'm in his apartment alone, I walk through all the rooms, peer out each window, look down at his view of the street. I spend hours examining his books and CDs, opening and closing his cabinets and closets, running my fingers along his fine glassware and heavy stone mugs, stroking the rough silk of a dress left by another woman, from the looks of it, someone more refined than me. When he's home, we spend enough time together in his space that I think I know and maybe even love him, but I'm never there overnight and, at his insistence, we never meet in public. Once, when he has dinner plans with friends and is rushing me out the door, I ask if I can come along.

"What, I'm supposed to just bring you with me? Don't you realize how weird that would be?"

I don't. When we're together, he corrects my pronunciation of words, interrupts my stories to explain that an adjective I've used does not mean what I think it means, fact-checks me constantly, in real time. I ask if he wants to see a new artist's work at the Gagosian gallery and pronounce it "Ga-gah-SAN," which is wrong and he tells me so, looks embarrassed for me, never answers whether or not he'd like to go. When there's a junior writing job I want and he's friends with the editor who's hiring, I ask if he could put in a good word. He says he doesn't know me well enough to recommend me for a job.

This is not to say Gideon was all predatory-man bad and I was all innocent-lady-victim good. Truth was, we were built similarly. We were both ambitious, frenetic, and combative; trusted few people and were untrustworthy ourselves; craved the rush of pointless drama and conflict even when it served us no good. There were differences between us, of course, the biggest being that he was an Ivy League boy from a nice educated family, with nice educated connections, which had buoyed him from the start, his roughest go-getter qualities just more charming assets in an already stacked professional arsenal, the swaggering cherry on top.

We were the same age, but his career was already miles ahead of mine—book deals, high-paying magazine contracts, access, opportunity, everything I wanted. I studied him and what he had fanatically, eavesdropping on his work calls, sitting on the floor of his office while he typed. I accepted the scrawny nub of a relationship he gave me, the unfeeling ways he spoke to and about me, in exchange for the privilege of this intimate view of his life. My attraction to him felt ferocious, blinding, bigger than me. I wanted to crawl inside his skin, inhale the pulse of his success. I told people about him, even though he'd asked me not to, though of course I didn't tell them this.

The arrangement with Gideon lasts past our time working together, longer than it should. I hate being a personal assistant and I hustle to get out from under it as fast as I can, taking on additional tasks for editors who are not my boss, making myself useful, indispensable, start building the foundation of a good reputation for myself, and a good name. Within a few months, through a connection at my first job, I manage to land a position as a fact-checker, move myself away from assisting for good.

The job is at *Talk*, a splashy mess of a magazine edited by Tina Brown and financed by none other than Harvey Weinstein, who rarely comes into the office except to yell, usually while he's mid-eating and therefore spraying crumbs everywhere, his ill-fitting sweatshirts never without evidence of food. *Talk* is a big-budget spectacle from the jump, the launch party—held at the Statue of Liberty, a guest list that included Madonna, Joan Didion, Paul Newman, Sarah Jessica Parker, *and* Henry Kissinger—is almost a parody of itself, a circus of excess.

But despite (or because of?) the New York media hoopla, the magazine begins to fail pretty much right out of the gate, and will close less than a year after I arrive. It's a $50 million debacle, the kind of buzzy-schadenfreude business train wreck people can't seem to hear enough about. At this point in my career, it's exciting to work in a place like this, a place at the center of intrigue. The day-to-day operations at *Talk* are bedlam; editorial direction changes with the wind. The staff is regularly kept in the office until midnight to accommodate the caprice of higher-ups. I'm often verifying ages and spellings even later than this. I'll spend weeks fact-checking a feature by a famous writer, only to find the story scrapped, last minute, on a whim. One hour it's Dan Rather on the cover, *No, nix that; it's Hillary Clinton; No, it's Mariah Carey; No, that interview's bad, now it's Gwyneth Paltrow—Harvey wants to promote her new film*. The work is intense, but it's the kind of disorder I'm built for; the kind of all-hands-on-deck chaos where if you're paying attention, you learn the most, and you learn it fast. Though they're led in all the wrong directions, the staff I work under is top tier—editors and writers at the height of their careers. I quickly identify those I respect and want to learn from. My job is to talk to them about their editorial decisions all day, a boon.

One morning a few months after I start working at *Talk,* Gideon publishes a gossipy item about the magazine. Later that day, one of my famous bosses discovers it is I who leaked a small but key detail; an innocuous but funny secret involving a celebrity. It's a secret Gideon had badgered me into giving—we're still fucking—the source of which he barely bothers to conceal. ("You didn't say off the record!" he jokes.)

The place is just dysfunctional enough that, after reprimanding me for a full day, the publisher lets me off with a warning. There are clearly more important fires to put out, but also—and this is a crucial, intangible aspect to most all success, especially mine—my bosses like me and wish to keep me there. After decades with my father in my ear, I know instinctually how to be a good employee here and most anywhere. At least outwardly, I'm socially supple, compulsively adaptable and reliable. I anticipate my superiors' needs, go out of my way to make myself seem cool and unobtrusive, pleasant to be around. I've actively, obsessively cultivated my bosses' goodwill, and the effort pays off just as I need it to.

Outside of work, I'm still seeing Gideon, but not just him. I'm tangled up with multiple suitors, my red Nokia phone buzzing with "u up" texts late into the night. In my work life, I am diligent, strategic, calculating, eyes on the prize; but after work, I'm sloppy and not at all self-preserving; a pretend life-of-the-party girl, a girl who pretends she doesn't care, the last person standing wherever I land. I can't handle solo time with my brain so I triple book myself most every night I'm not in the office; start at a work event to network and, after, meet editor-writer friends to gossip, to network more.

We gather at Manhattan bars—Cedar Tavern, The Magician, Punch & Judy's, Milk & Honey, Von, Library Bar, Art Bar, Holiday Cocktail Lounge, XOXO, Max Fish—and spill our secrets, talk shop. Later, if I'm not going home with a man, which is not often, I take a cab or the subway across the river, land in Brooklyn, head to Boat, to Great Lakes, to Superfine, to 12th Street, if it's a truly fucked night, to a place called Loki, whose back room is a low-lit, rapey, multi-sofa'd hell. One last drink and ten more cigarettes after everyone else has gone, I'm often blacked out, my body slumped over barstools like a discarded bag of trash until I stumble awake and make my way home.

I wake up in strangers' apartments, on the subway at the end of the F line; once, I pass out on the street. The next morning, on my way to work, I walk the most ashamed walks of shame. I've mapped the city's options for girls in my position; I know the Gap and the Urban Outfitters with the earliest opening hours, where I have the best shot at finding a cheap-enough, businessy enough top, where I can then change in the dressing room, freshen my makeup with spit on a tissue, pop a handful of Altoids while rushing to comb out nesty knots in the back of my hair. Some of the people who work in the stores begin to know me, smile when I'm the first customer to arrive, *Here again, girl? I see you, it's okay.* The truth about New York City is it won't clean you up, but it will never judge your mess.

I ride this business-boys-booze Tilt-A-Whirl without pause for two years. Then I meet James.

Surprising News

The night I meet James, I am meant to meet another man. My friend Sara, a former colleague, now a book editor who is older than I am and infinitely cool, has set it up. "He's like forty, recently divorced, a grownup, a bestselling novelist, I think you're going to like him," she says by way of enticement, an appeal to my success narcissism, my (and every other New Yorker's) high-achievers kink.

It's early June in Manhattan, a perfect just-summer night. I get out of work at 6:30, the weather showing off enough that I decide to walk the twenty-plus blocks from my new fact-checking job at *Glamour* magazine in Times Square to the Upper West Side, specifically to the classic-six apartment where a party's being held for the bestselling novelist Sara wants me to meet.

I need the walk, I need to decompress from a day of researching artificially engineered hair "bloopers," sex do's and don'ts ("according to men," but actually according to one *Glamour* editor who is not a man), Ashley Judd's beauty secrets provided by a publicist and not her secrets at all, and other assorted gendered journalism, which is what my current job is.

After *Talk* goes under, I have enough experience to become a freelance fact-checker, a job that in 2002, is in demand. There are no benefits, and I'm not writing anything yet, but I am adjacent to writing, and I recognize it as an opportunity—I'm getting paid to learn. In fact-checking, I see how reporters' raw copy comes in versus what ultimately gets published, what the editors change. I read through transcripts and track the rhythms of interviews. I re-report stories and discover common mistakes, identify what trips writers up. I'm demystifying the writing process and building up the confidence to do it on my own, even if I'm not ready yet.

The walk to the party takes around a half hour. By the time I arrive, things are in full swing. I'm wearing a red tube top with a white button-down unbuttoned and tied at the waist over it, oversize gold hoops, red lipstick, a messy bun, a pair of tight black polyester office pants with a flare at the bottom, and strappy black Steve Madden kitten-heel sandals. Everything is from Loehmann's or Daffy's or Marshalls. I'm lonely and damaged, but who has time for that? I look sexy. I know it.

I find the address and head into a tan brick building I remember as one of the famous ones, though I'm not sure; I'm not Manhattan enough in my bones to know. Across the street is Central Park, green and lush, a light breeze blowing through the tops of the trees. I climb the marble stairs and the doorman finds my name on the list, tells me where to go.

I take the elevator up. When the door opens I can hear the murmur of a book party, which, in 2002, all essentially look and sound the same: impressive location signaling impressive finances and/or impressive connections, bad wine, worse food, safe and staid fashion disguising generational wealth, socially strategic chatter, the same ten important book people talking about the same ten important books, too-tipsy assistants just shy of a fireable offense, intellectual one-upsmanship disguised as banter, playful-but-not-fun industry critiques—politics? war? that one *New Yorker* piece?—someone actually read that Pynchon book, someone actually met Pynchon, whispered gossip for people who pretend they're above gossip, all happening politely and at once, all on overlap. It's a fascinating study of a certain demographic, yet still somehow dull as fuck. I don't much enjoy these parties, but I want to be invited, would never not go when asked.

I see Sara across the room. She's tall, with a short Liza Minnelli haircut, wearing architectural Prada bought at the Barneys Warehouse Sale. Hard to miss. She's happy to see me, swans over, puts her arm around me, helps me get a drink. "Come on, I want you to meet Zach."

We walk into the living room, which is lined with tall windows with shutters tucked in, custom window treatments, window seats, the trim of which is done in the palest blue-gray. I spot a redheaded man in a tan linen suit in a conversation in the corner. We lock eyes long enough that we both smile before looking down and away, but he's not the man I'm there to meet.

The man I'm there for, the once-bestselling novelist with a new, not-bestselling book, is in the center of the room, holding court with a group of younger women, all wearing shift dresses, hanging on his words. Sara tugs me over, interrupts him, smiles widely, makes the introduction, *This is who she's told him about!* We shake hands and he holds mine too firmly, a finger grazes my wrist too tenderly, for too long. He's mostly bald on the top but has grown his salt-and-pepper hair long in the back, a follicular sculpture that seems attached to his highly manicured salt-and-pepper goatee. He's wearing a monkish white top and nineties-era Zubaz—flowy, multicolored, patterned pants that begin billowing at the waist and cinch in at the ankle and don't make a lot of sense in between. He's at least fifty-five, medium-tall with a medium build and clearly more than medium on the prowl.

I make small talk—*Your new book! How great*—then, realizing this is going nowhere, excuse myself. I head across the apartment to the black-and-white-checkered-floor kitchen, where there are no other guests, but there are cater waiters, which is the most comfortable place for me to be. I sit on the windowsill and ask one of them if it's okay to smoke; they don't know, but I start smoking out the window anyway. It's warm in the kitchen and I take off my white overshirt and I'm just in a tube top staring at the park, enjoying the breeze.

Within a few minutes, an extra-tan, middle-aged blond woman in a flouncy hippie-designer dress with flouncy hippie-socialite vibes appears in the kitchen. She saunters over and asks if she can bum a smoke and then we're talking about how she used to date someone in a famous jam band and somehow has jam-band money now and doesn't have to work anymore, which, she says, is a little sad and weird. She's spacy and probably on expensive drugs but is better than most of the people at the party and captivating enough that my anxiety is waning, and I might even be having a good time when suddenly, standing in front of me, is the redhead in the tan suit, come to join our kitchen party. I stare up at him and his skin is pale and his features are delicate; the almost-dusk light coming through the window is soft on his face. "Can I trouble you for a cigarette?" he says in the gentlest British accent, then, "Hi, I'm James."

I hand him a cigarette and a lighter and we start talking about the party and how the party is not fun and, at some point, jam-band lady suggests we all leave and go to this great bar she knows nearby and we are just buzzed enough and just intrigued enough by each other that we do.

The bar is not actually a bar but an opulent old-timey New York restaurant called Café des Artistes, where the 1981 film *My Dinner with Andre* was set, where, in 2002, the octogenarian Chanel-clad clientele dine on sturgeon schnitzel and steak tartare against a backdrop of wall-size Renoir-like murals of nubile wood nymphs. It's a grande dame, Manhattan-society haunt, exclusive and elegant in every way you fantasize a place like this to be. When we take our seats at the dark-wood-with-gilded-touches bar, I realize it's probably the most beautiful space I've ever seen.

We order drinks, and the tuxedo-clad bartender delivers snacks, not your typical bowl of finger-sweat peanuts, but a tower of tiny, delicate, hard-boiled quail eggs. James sits in the middle, seems at home in the space, engages with the other lady, his back to me. I start to feel self-conscious and underdressed, and also begin to worry about how much this is costing and how I'm going to pay. I start playing with the quail eggs. One of which accidentally rolls down the bar toward James, which he then, without turning around, rolls back to me. On we go like this, not talking to each other but flicking tiny spotted eggs across a classy bar until our drinks are finished. The social configuration is too strange for another round. James asks for the check, pays it, and we leave.

Outside, our jam-band-adjacent friend is clearly off-balance but says it's okay, she's a half a block from her house. James is headed home to Brooklyn, while I'm meeting friends on the Lower East Side. He offers to share a cab. In the ride downtown, I study his profile, his crisp white shirt, his tailored grownup suit. I don't know what to make of this polite, polished British man and I don't know if he knows what to make of me, so I stare over at him, flip down my tube top and say, "Do you want to make out or what?" and we do.

When the cab drops me off, my friends are smoking outside and there's traffic on the street, so my cab mate and I say an awkward, rushed goodbye. I don't give him my number and assume I'll never see him again, but the next day while I'm deep into checking the facts in a story about "the nosiest, sexiest, wildest things you're dying to know about men!" (actual coverline), an interoffice package arrives at the *Glamour* offices, a brown envelope sent from another magazine on another floor, addressed to me. Inside I find a single quail egg, a business card, and a note on letterhead, the essence of which is *That was fun, let's do it again.*

On our first date, we decide to meet on bikes in Brooklyn in the early evening and then maybe have a picnic or ride over to a bar. I arrive on my vintage cruiser in a vintage sundress, while James arrives wearing an oversize helmet, an oversize polo shirt, undersize bike shorts, and aqua socks, which he tells me are "quite handy for cycling, though I believe they are meant for the sea."

That night, I learn that he's an authentic oddball, a soft-spoken eccentric, easily embarrassed, adept at silent-film-style physical comedy, silly and quick to laugh. A classical pianist who also plays the cello, who loves player pianos and collects player piano rolls, a man wholly detached from pop culture, who nonperformatively doesn't listen to music made after 1955.

James lives in a two-room fourth-floor walk-up right near Atlantic Avenue in Brooklyn, with just enough space for a bed, a couch, a dining table, and his cello. He owns four robes—one silk!—which he calls "dressing gowns," and three pairs of slippers, one leather. He wears bespoke Italian cologne that smells of Mediterranean citrus, takes nightly baths, collects delicate, expensive bars of soap. We have few things in common except a sincere and immediate affection for the other. For a long time, longer than I imagine, this is enough.

The connection feels significant, so much so that, after our second date, I cease fucking around. When Gideon texts me to come over, I tell him I can't see him again. He asks *WHY* and then *Who is it?* and I won't tell him so he calls me at my freelance *Glamour* desk more than thirty times in a row the next day. When I finally relent, Gideon says he knows James and threatens to forward our most intimate correspondence and let James know what kind of girl I am. I beg him not to and he hangs up on me but doesn't follow through. We never talk again.

As for James, he's the first man I date who genuinely sees me and doesn't want to change what he sees. He's proud to be with me, takes me everywhere, introduces me to his friends and is enthusiastic to meet mine. He shows up when I'm in the emergency room with an anxiety-related stomach issue; doesn't care when, later that month, I get drunk and bored at a rooftop Soho House book party, strip down to my underwear, and dive into the not-on-swimming-hours pool. No one knows what to make of us, but it doesn't matter. We are quickly, intimately, spaciously in each other's corners; from the instant we meet, we have each other's backs. I admire him the way you do a particularly compelling outdoor sculpture, one that you never quite understand but cannot imagine as anything, anywhere else.

James is a junior editor at an important magazine, a fact he failed to mention the first night we met, a fact he treats like the least interesting thing about him. He grew up in proper academic English circles with proper academic English parents, and his relationship with ambition is earnest, un-American, mostly without ego, as close as you can get to pure. He works hard, but work has its place; his drive is not all-consuming like mine. He's charming and professionally generous, but not transactional or naïve. He can spot a charlatan or a shark, delights in and finds humor in the Americanness of it all, the game. He's not only unthreatened by my drive to succeed but desires little more than to see me get what I want.

I've just started pitching stories and manage to land a few assignments. When I get up the nerve to ask, James reads my drafts critically, honestly. I'd never shared my writing with anyone I'd dated before, but his feedback is gentle, kind, and direct. He shows me areas where I'm naturally skilled as a writer, encourages me to push myself to be more precise with language, allows me to believe I'm capable of more. When he's struggling with work, he asks my opinion. Sometimes I help him with editing, the first real editing I've ever done. I like doing it; I find it suits my obsessive, multitasking brain. James helps me see editing as accessible, a practical puzzle to be solved, rather than an elite, intimidating craft that's out of my reach.

We start seeing each other three or four nights a week. We cook together, plot out elaborate Ruth Reichl–sanctioned meals, laugh when we fail to achieve the desired results. We read the paper on Sundays, see films at the Film Forum, give each other time and space to work. He trusts me and I am trustworthy, he's steady with me and I am steady in return. For the first time, my life begins to feel safe and sane.

Into our first year of dating, James's parents want to meet me, and they're kind enough to pay for my plane ticket so we can fly to the U.K. without financial stress. I'm nervous to meet them, but I needn't be.

They're lovely, accomplished, curious, kind people, with a stone cottage in the English countryside, an old fluffy cat, and an overgrown fairyland garden where they keep bees. We sit around on soft sofas, drink tea; I read books while they tackle crossword puzzles. In the evenings, we take long walks through the wide-open, windy fields, which is the closest I've ever been to the Moors. One afternoon, James takes me on a tour of Oxford University, holds my hand as he leads me through the campus's impeccably manicured grounds. When I catch a glimpse of us in a window, I'm surprised by my own smiling reflection. I don't look—nor do I feel—out of place.

James's brother lives in London, and we visit him there before heading back to New York. We crash at his stylish Moroccan-themed flat, dine on curry, meet James's university friends in pubs. On this trip, James and I are genuinely, consistently happy. But when his brother drinks too much one night, looks me square in the eye, and says, "Oh, I get it—you're an aging party girl trying to make something of your life," the bubble bursts. I laugh it off, but inside I feel like social-climbing trash. I feel exposed.

———————————

In the two years we're together, both of our careers take off. James lands a promotion he wants. I make the jump out of fact-checking and, with his help on my edit test, into my first full-time magazine editor position. At *Time Out New York,* I edit, write, and report out a five-page section each week. The job doesn't pay a lot, but I make enough to move out of the four-bedroom Park Slope apartment/squat house I've been sharing with three roommates and into my own place, a one-bedroom on a bad street in a good Italian-American Brooklyn neighborhood, which feels like parts of Philly near where I grew up. I'm now anchored by a steady, age-appropriate job, a happy relationship, and a space of my own. New York begins to feel like home.

James and I travel together, the way young childless couples do. I'm giddy over every detail, in awe of every foreign-to-me train ride, every meal, every new town. We travel to a mountain resort in the Adirondacks, to a village in Ireland, to the coast of California, where he'll light a woodstove for us in a cabin in Big Sur. When he turns thirty, his friends throw a big party in London, and I fly in as a surprise. We have a good life; we support and respect each other. We are peers. It should be enough, but it's not enough, and around this time, I start getting itchy for more.

Officially, the more I want is to move in together, but that's not all I want. I've internalized the idea that the man with whom I'm spending all this sex time should be long-term partner material, that this pleasant ride we're on is insufficient without a clear and certain destination, a plan. More than anything, I want what this level of commitment signifies or I thought it signified at the time: that I'm good enough to be chosen, that it's okay to get comfortable in this life, that he won't pull the rug out from under me and leave.

James will not move in with me. The conversation is a hard stop. He's not ready, he says. He likes his apartment, he likes his independence, he likes things as they are. His resistance to change, his refusal to have a conversation about the future, sets off a fast-moving fire in my brain out to destroy everything around it, one I am unable to control or snuff out.

The truth is, I like things as they are too. But inside me is a hungry, terrified, security-craving goblin in the presence of whom I feel powerless; an ambitious monster who wants it all. I want the job, the bringing home of the bacon, the man to fry it up for, the offspring peeking out of my very own attaché case. I'm hard-charging toward a life I think I want, in a race to make something of myself, afraid that if I slow down even for a second, I might never be able to start up again. I'm afraid that James's refusal to move forward is proof of my deficiencies, my undesirability as a mate—that deep down, he knows I'm not partner material, that he's hip to my scam. That I'll never be good or smart enough for a guy like him.

This commitment issue was not unique to me, of course. On the day we turned thirty, a gun seemingly went off for most all of my straight female friends. Common wisdom—the magazines, books, movies; our mothers, sisters, mentors, friends—told us refusals from a partner to cohabit or promise marriage or reproduce meant noncommittal danger; that these were red flags, universal deal-breakers.

Despite the third-wave feminist bravado of our twenties, I remember few friends intentionally deciding to remain single once we moved into our thirties. I recall few thorough and honest self-examinations to determine if we were emotionally ready for marriage and the seemingly inevitable motherhood that came after, biological clock be damned. Instead, in our thirties, most of us in relationships who were *kinda-sorta* sure we might want the opportunity to be wives and mothers threw up our hands and accepted our biological lot; sat down in whatever romantic musical chairs seat we'd landed upon.

James and I were not fighters. We rarely argued. For better or worse, we handled disagreements with an awkward joke or a brief, direct conversation; not the chaotic all-hours conflicts modeled in my childhood, those that over the years I'd come to expect. I begin to convince myself that our quiet, steady relationship is not *real* love, that we are not passionate enough, that James doesn't truly *get* me and never will. I cannot stop thinking about all the things I think I want that he doesn't, all the ways I imagine he'll let me down, all the ways our relationship is doomed to fail.

I obsess and fixate, and one night, almost two years to the day we met, I break up with James over a cursed dinner in a not particularly good restaurant with embarrassingly floofy drinks and nonsensical urbanite-sculptor-meets-hunting-cabin decor. Afterward we walk back to his apartment, sit close together, cry, cry more. The next morning, I pack up the assorted things I've left at his place and leave. It's hard and it hurts, but I am proud of us. It was honest. We left things clean.

A few months later, I'm sitting at my desk at *Time Out* when I receive an email from James with the subject line "Surprising news," the main text of which explains politely, formally, that he finds himself engaged. He didn't want me to hear it from anyone else. She's English too, they play piano duets together. Do I remember her from his thirtieth birthday party? She was there. He thinks I'd like her. Maybe one day we'll all meet.

It's all surprising indeed.

Also a Writer

S oon after James and I break up, I start hanging out with an old friend, Alex. We'd met years earlier, at the internet start-up, which was both of our first jobs in New York. It's the same place I met Sara, and most every New Yorker I initially know, most everyone who'll be important to my life in the city while I'm there.

When we first meet, Alex is in his early twenties, sports spiked hair with blond tips, wears wrist sweatbands as a deliberate style choice. He's laid-back and quiet, a sensitive San Francisco boy, a young rock critic, but also a bit of a prodigy, considered by everyone we work with to be a talent and a find. Alex has a girlfriend who works in the office too. She and I are both assistants. Our jobs are sending faxes, transcribing interviews, making life easier for people like him.

We were all new to New York, and, despite our age difference, in the same life stage; aligned in our hopeful enthusiasm, beginning anew. Our days were a series of nonstop bearings-getting discoveries, our nascent friendships an emotional life raft, a hedge against the new-city overwhelm that lay just under the thrill.

They say geography is destiny. At this time, Alex and I not only work together but also happen to live in the same Brooklyn micro-neighborhood, share the same dowdy coffee shop, the same F train stop, the same nothing-special neighborhood bar. We have context for each other immediately in a way that anchors you to people, sharing neighborhood gossip and tips, and, if we're too drunk after a Manhattan work party—or feeling splurgy—cabs.

In the summer, Alex and his girlfriend invite me to the Coney Island Mermaid Parade. In the fall, we plan movie nights and watch Mariah Carey's *Glitter*, all cramped around someone's roommate's boxy TV. One night, the three of us go out dancing to a narrow, red-walled club in Fort Greene, everyone high-energy carousing until a fight breaks out and we have to leave. No one's ready to go home, so we escape to my apartment and stay up until sunrise listening to Joni Mitchell, smoking cigarettes and weed.

At dawn, I escort them back to their place wearing my going-out dress and an old pair of roller skates. Skate home alone as the sun comes up, wheeling carefully along the empty Brooklyn streets feeling surprisingly sturdy, like every decision I'd made up to this point led me to this moment, a moment when the city felt like it was mine.

Alex and I lose touch soon after the roller-skating night, float out of each other's lives as easily as we floated in. Then, in 2004, years past that first job, years since he and his girlfriend have broken up, the universe seems to push us together again. Suddenly we are running into each other everywhere—at random weeknight drinks, *Sopranos* viewing parties, in line for iced coffee, once, on the street. It's enough that it begins to feel like kismet, a series of awkward meet-cutes, the way movies tell us it's meant to be.

Our rekindled friendship is full of luck and serendipity, the kinds of magical, right-place, right-time events we'd all plan if we could. One night, we meet for what I think is a promotional Hudson River "booze cruise" only to discover it's actually a "blues cruise," a night on a boat with a group of hard-core middle-agers from Jersey; the most fun party, all of our fellow cruisers rocking out, the best. Another night we stumble stoned upon the closing of an art gallery, intrigued by the black-light-lit inside. The hosts are handing out smocks and paintbrushes at the door; it's free to the public—come in, come on, paint whatever you want on the walls—everyone grooving to nonannoying house music, the vibe fully alive. A few weeks after this we grab sushi at a cheap, nondescript sushi place and find ourselves at a table next to Laurie Anderson and Lou Reed. When we get out, it's raining, but there's a pedicab right in front to pick us up, as if it's been waiting just for us, the whole time.

We start meeting several times a week. We tell each other most every stupid thing about our days, the way best friends do. We talk about work, but it's not at the forefront. We are conversationally complementary, lit up by each other's brains, no topic off-limits, with a keen and earnest interest in the way the other thinks.

We talk about relationships, my breakup with James. Alex is newly single and says he's decided to play the field for a while, thinks maybe he'll enter his "asshole" phase. He's just turned twenty-seven. He's an unassuming, self-consciously erudite Greek man with a good heart and kind eyes. He'll never be an asshole, at least not intentionally, at least not in the way he thinks.

One night, he asks me to hang out early, but I can't. It's the night of the *Friends* finale, which I want to watch live. Instead, I ride my bike to meet him for a drink afterward. Once there, I cry into my third vodka tonic about the James engagement news, Ross and Rachel, the passage of time. Alex is a good listener, a supportive friend, the rare guy who can comfortably hold space for a woman crying in a bar and not feel the need to run or to make it right.

The bartender calls last call. We finish our drinks and Alex walks me around the corner to where I've locked my bike. We're in front of a brownstone, it's late and the street is empty, lit by the haze of a single streetlight. I look at him and somehow the air is changed between us, somehow I realize for the first time he's the perfect height. He leans in to kiss me and it's all the things you want a kiss to be. The kind of kiss that signals more than you imagined it would, the kind that feels like a guiding force.

From that night on, we're inseparable, even when we're apart. Alex is astonishingly funny and clever, his emails and texts a series of compact masterpieces rolling in one after another. I love lobbing the ball back, anticipating what comes next. We're telling our story in real time, a foreplay of ping-ponging characters, a private thrum we're both eager to establish and shape.

We commit seriously and fast—too drunk in love and often too drunk period to see what we're setting ourselves up for, ignoring the chasms between who we are as people and how we approach our lives. We can't imagine what life will look like when it's not built on just this kind of freedom, this blush of new love, on delayed adulthood's pleasures and delights.

We both work in New York media, we even started at the same place, but our approaches to our careers couldn't be farther afield. I'm strategic and unrelentingly ambitious, always pushing some professional boulder or another up a hill, pitching stories constantly, juggling two, three jobs at all times. And Alex is . . . not this way. He's chill, never chases a thing. He doesn't have to. He's now a staff writer at a high-profile men's magazine. The writing work comes to him.

It's important to say here that this person whom I love deeply is naturally, infuriatingly better than I am at the thing I most wanted to do. At the time, my brain did not know how to deal with this. I did not want Alex's talent and the way the world rewarded that talent to come between us, so I tried not to think about it. But deep down, it made me feel all sorts of things, sometimes awe and envy, but mostly discouragement and retreat.

Alex is a great writer; the kind whose sentences you remember long after you've read them, the kind whose drafts roll out maddeningly original, smart, well formed, and clean. He's the rare kind of writer who is special, who breaks through. I'd known this instinctively from reading him but didn't fully understand the extent until I started to see him through other people's eyes.

In the years we live together in New York, people—white men—

approach me often to tell me how great my boyfriend is at writing. Sometimes they refer to me by his last name: "_____'s girlfriend," or just "she's with _____." Wan hipsters in shawl cardigans corner me at parties, monopolize my time to discuss a piece of Alex's they've fact-checked, the profile on Jay-Z they just read, that one interview with Winona Ryder, *did you read what he wrote about Modest Mouse, blew my mind.* Then, if they manage to get around to me: "Oh, you're also a writer?"

I'm writing too, but it's not the same.

At *Time Out,* I'm working on stunty first-person gal-about-town stories, celebrity Q + As that top out at five hundred words. Each week, I edit and write my five-page section and I contribute to other parts of the magazine too. I never say no when someone needs quick copy; I fill in when other editors ask for help. Most nights, I'm in the office so late, the rats come out. Late enough that I can open one of the windows by my desk and light a cigarette without getting caught, blow the smoke toward the Hudson River, peer out over the city I love and want so much from, a city that's glowing with possibility, alive.

Into my first year at *Time Out,* I settle into New York in that satisfying way "real" New Yorkers, if they're lucky enough, do. The job pays little, but doing it well requires that I become a city insider, its greatest perk. In just a few months, my work provides a crash course on the five boroughs, a series of intimate glimpses of a New York most people never get to see. One week I'm interviewing a celebrity dentist in his cramped office on the top floor of the Chrysler Building. The next, I'm in the East Village studio of an underground painter who paints only when he's on LSD. The same month, I visit the all-burgundy Hell's Kitchen apartment and treatment space of a renowned sex therapist, revel when she spills off-the-record dirt about her well-known clientele. I'm assigned a "secret New York" story and find a way onto the High Line when it's just an abandoned elevated track, take a friend to stroll its overgrown-weeded blocks, discovering illegal residential gardens and makeshift art installations along the way.

I review far-flung restaurants in Brighton Beach, spas in Staten Island, zydeco shows downtown. When my friends in the news section can't find another female reporter who's the right height, I volunteer to try out for the Rockettes in Rockefeller Center, stand in line in a borrowed, too-tight leotard, balance on my dancer's shoes as I jot down details from the scene.

The job provides something I've never had before—access—and the access is exhilarating, brings forth the kinds of how-is-this-my-life stories I'll dine out on for years. I interview Donald Sutherland and he talks about the sex scene in *Don't Look Now* and, for longer than his publicist would like, why he never showed his "cock" on film.

> *Me (interrupting a long and boring DS rant about the*
> *Iraq war): I've noticed you show your ass a lot in movies,*
> *but you never show your cock.*
>
> *Donald Sutherland: An ass is one thing, but my cock is*
> *my cock. It's a distraction. You wouldn't look at my cock*
> *on screen and think,* That's the character's cock—you'd
> *only see it as my cock.*

Weeks after this, I'm one of only five journalists to show up to a private screening of Woody Harrelson's documentary about vegans. Afterward, he's generous enough to take the lot of us to a private table at Bungalow 8, where he's even more generous with his weed. A few months later, I attend the premiere of the third season of *The Wire*, manage an invite to the afterparty, and dance deep into the night with the cast, actors who are on the come up but as yet unfettered by fame, as open to experience and alive-feeling as I am, happier than any cast you've ever seen.

For all this, I'm paid $35,000 annually. Sometime in my second year, I manage to get them up to $37,500. I have a "real" job now, but I still make less than I did waiting tables. My rent alone costs nearly three weeks' pay. I am in serious debt; consistently, terrifyingly broke. In my little free time, I take side jobs writing for an in-house Target magazine no one's ever heard of and crafting special-advertising--section quizzes ("What's *your* faucet style?") for another publication called *Kitchens & Baths*.

I like reporting and I'm good at it. I have a knack for disrupting canned narratives, getting sources to open up. Though I'm not totally aware of it yet, I'm good at most parts of my job: generating ideas, identifying trends, and finding the hook of a story, the details that make people care. My copy is lively—not perfect, but clean, and it always arrives on time. Still, my pitches for well-paying stories at elite publications are regularly rejected, if they're responded to at all. I eventually manage to get one byline in *The New York Times* after pitching the same story about the new trend of gluten-free bakeries ten times. On the Wednesday morning when the story comes out, I head to our corner bodega early, buy up nearly every copy, excitedly share the accomplishment over watery-burnt coffee with my favorite deli guy.

Highs like this are rare. Like most of the writers I know, the door into "professional writer with livable wage" remains closed for me, no matter how hard I bang on it. My career, four years in, is still the grindiest grind. I steer a book proposal on the commercialization of optimism through more than a dozen revisions, make all the embarrassing cold calls to agents, sit through all the charm-assault lunches. When my proposal finally goes out to publishers, it's universally rejected. Editors tell my agent they like it, but it's too much of a risk, I'm not a big enough name. I write a second proposal for a book on female friendship. Again, no dice. Meanwhile, big-time editors reach out to Alex to write books, approach him with already crafted ideas. He shrugs at most all of it, rejects lucrative projects, blows off deadlines, still receives offers nonstop. There's a clear creative hierarchy to our relationship; it's not collaborative like I was with James. When I ask Alex to read my book proposal, he tells me he doesn't think it's a good idea.

"What will we do if I think it's bad?"

The response stings, but I justify it. Decide maybe he's right. I still want him (and everyone) to think I'm a cool girl. Tough. I love Alex and I know he loves me. I don't want to be jealous of him. I don't want to compete. I know enough about our business to know he'll win, but also we'll both lose. Still, the disparity between us nags at me. When he's out, I spy on his first-draft files, study the careful pacing of his sentences, the structure of his paragraphs, how he lands a story, wraps it all in a bow. I track these drafts against what's ultimately printed, scan to see if his editor improved upon the original, or broke Alex's (quite good) flow.

My ambition is naked and shameless. I'm a detective trying to crack the case of my own aspirations, fanatically searching for clues. Don't yet understand that beating this game will require more than my hardscrabble labor, that I can't win this one by force. At parties, I interrogate successful writers about their work, how they came up with ideas, who they pitched them to, how they landed a source. When a published-author pal is assigned an essay for *Vogue* and gets stuck in her writing, I volunteer to take an edit pass, spend a weekend carefully slicing out extraneous sentences, punching up verbs, flipping ideas. When another magazine friend is up for a prestigious job, I stay up all night to help with his edit test, wind up generating more than half of the ideas in the version he submits, never know if those ideas are why he lands the position, or if it's something else, something I still can't see.

Within a year of dating, Alex and I move in together, weaving our two independent lives into a tight tapestry of one. We paint the kitchen of our one-bedroom clementine orange, nab an old mirror at a stoop sale and hang it above the fireplaceless mantel, find a TV cart on the street. On Sundays, we get hangover chilaquiles from the Tex-Mex place on Fifth Avenue. On Wednesday nights, we watch *Lost*. We rent movies from a goth-hipster in blue-tinted glasses named Dave at the video store, have our first truly stupid fight over *Mulholland Drive*. In November, we huddle around a tiny black-and-white bar TV as Bush annihilates Kerry. In December, we drag a tree home from a vendor outside the hardware store, decorate it with assorted whimsical kitsch. Later that month, we meet each other's families. Alex's discerning mom likes my sense of style. My dad appreciates Alex's near-encyclopedic knowledge of seventies classic rock. The deli guy loves us; we're on a first-name basis with the barista down the street. When we're alone, our life is cozy and steady. We're a good match.

Outside this domestic bubble, however, are troubles, troubles we don't want to name. Not only am I secretly struggling with Alex's success and my own lack of it, I'm struggling to fit into our new social life too.

Though I'd managed to make a few friends since I'd moved to New York, the people I trust most I see in the smallest of groups, if not one-on-one. But Alex's friend group is different. They socialize in a pack. They're all established male writers and rock critics, a cult of big personalities, with big opinions to match. They share the same interests, go to the same bars each weekend, talk about the same things. When we're all out together, the group—which is less diverse in all ways than my own social circles—uniformly heterosexual, coupled up, white—often breaks up by gender. The men sit together and discuss their brand of man stuff; I'm relegated to the girls' table with their partners, like we're astronaut wives.

We talk about books and movies, but it's less riotous than the boys' conversation, more structured, polite. The chatter often falls to things like engagement rings—we're in our thirties, everyone's getting engaged—real estate, that chair from Design Within Reach one of them regrets buying in white. We talk about our jobs, but even though many of the women are also writers and editors, the way I want to talk about work feels too aggressive, off-putting, crass. One night one of the women calls me "such a careerist," with a laugh that suggests it's not actually funny, before delicately lifting her glass of white wine and moving to the other end of the bar.

These women are all smart and foundationally educated in a way I'm not. They have deep cultural reference points I don't have, which makes me feel self-conscious, but it's more than that. I'm out of step. I'd spent much of my twenties in survival mode, cleaning out fryolators, living under the thumb of an alcoholic husband, scraping to get by. Most of the people we know in New York spent that same period in liberal arts colleges and cosmopolitan cities sorting themselves out, making frivolous age-appropriate mistakes, building friendships and social networks, learning from peers in real time.

Truth was, since Beth, I'd had few truly close female friends. I made acquaintances easily but never learned to maintain friendships with any consistency. I was up for the drunken good times but felt wary of platonic intimacy, didn't love being soberly seen. For most of my twenties, I was a transitory outsider, just passing through. Whenever I left restaurant jobs and cities, I left the friendships be-hind too.

I overcompensate by trying to control the social narrative, by throwing elaborate parties I plan for weeks—themed sit-down dinners, Friendsgivings, New Year's Eve blowouts so packed you can't see the floor. They're big media parties we become known for, fun for all. Still, I often slip out in the middle of hosting because I'm too overwhelmed, light cigarette after cigarette on the stoop, like I'm back to being hos-pitality staff on a break. I'm firmly planted in this new life, but I'm still rough around the edges. I wear fifty-dollar red lipstick pilfered from work and have five-hundred-dollar highlights in my hair I get for free because I need to "try" them for my job, but under it all, I'm still the same prickly girl from Philly; compulsively shit-starting and direct, not fit for polite society, far from everyone's cup of tea.

We like to imagine ourselves the heroes of our own stories, the vic-tims at least. It's harder to see when we behave as villains ourselves. I feel trapped by the obligation of our social life, resent how Alex pushes it on me, how he thinks it will look weird if I'm the girlfriend who never shows up. I don't know how to talk about this. I'm afraid of being a bummer or—worse—a burden. When I express my discomfort, Alex doesn't want to hear it. He's actively annoyed, shuts me down. Instead of asserting my needs, I act out.

In just one year, we attend twelve weddings, and I'm overserved and over-raucous at most all of them, give unsolicited speeches, dance performatively hard and fall on my face, get caught smoking enough pot in a banquet room in Ohio we may still be wanted by the Cleveland police. I'm sloppy and ornery at bridal showers; pick fights with Alex over rooftop rosés, at hundred-dollar birthday brunches, at someone's fancy country house in Vermont. Is it boredom? Self-contempt? Class issues? A combination of the three? I can't keep track. Being part of a group like this exposes something in me neither of us really knew: I'd spent so long cultivating a professional persona, I no longer understood how to be a person outside of work, if I ever did.

My own friendships are now, almost without exception, colleagues or former colleagues. Our conversations mostly revolve around work and getting ahead. That—and partying—is what I think I have to offer, and I have a chip on my shoulder about it. It isn't just the engagement rings and the timid conversation, I resent the women we know for being "normal" in a way I think I'll never be, for being raised right, for moving through the world we live in with ease.

A year or so after we get together, Alex and I head out to dinner with a couple from the group. They are both writers, too. The husband is successful, bestselling, well compensated, well known. His wife writes about the same things he does, though she's made less of a mark, leans on her husband's name to get jobs. Once, when he writes a big feature for an even bigger magazine, the editor asks him to suggest a writer for the accompanying sidebar and he sends them her way. When the piece comes out, her name is stamped on its servicey 250-word listicle, the publishing scraps. *Anything* for a byline, I think. *Where's her fucking pride?* I'm not tender enough with myself to even imagine what it would be like to be lent this kind of professional generosity, to question if it bothers me more that this woman took the scraps or that my own partner would never offer them at all.

After we've ordered, the woman and I retreat to the ladies' room. She's just finished telling me about an apartment she and her husband bid on but lost to Matt Damon when she starts talking about a novel she abandoned after losing the only draft. The story sounds like a truth stretch, if not an utter lie. Still, she seems genuinely sad about it, says she doesn't think she'll ever write another novel again. "It's all so maddening really, this writing stuff," she explains.

In her voice I sense vulnerability, a prompt that makes me think we can drop the phony social veneer. What I say next is an attempt to bond, but I'm also courting danger. I've developed a bad habit of sprinkling a near-imperceptible bit of chaos into conversations like this, subtle, easily deniable strikes that make me feel quietly dominant or at least less inferior around these smart, cultured people than I often do. "I know, it's weird," I say. "I have a hard time writing because Alex is so much better and more successful than me. Sometimes I feel like I should just give up. I can't *imagine* what it must feel like for you."

It's evident from her face that she doesn't think this about herself or at least pretends that she doesn't. Her expression is momentarily hard in a way that reveals, for one second, a less polite person, a little bit wild, maybe more like me—but then quickly snaps back to a soft-nice face and she says chirpily, "I don't feel that way at all," smiles a weird smile, throws her paper towel in the trash, and exits through the bathroom door.

Years later, when I'm struggling to sort out what to write about, a close friend suggests, "Why don't you write about how Alex is a better and more successful writer than you? That would be interesting." I've never told my friend I feel this way, didn't know he knew. I hate hearing it out loud. Years after that, when I've got more than a decade of accomplishments under my belt, a new colleague introduces me to a client we're pitching as "Alex _____'s wife," as if this makes our project more appealing, as if my association with him is central to my value.

In these earlyish days of my career, I am not secure enough to handle being the "also a writer" in our relationship. When I think of Alex's couple friends, I'm jealous of both the men's success and the ease with which the women enjoy the spoils. But I'm equally appalled by what I see as their polite female surrender, the ceding of the professional floor, the already evident inequity in their relationships. My mother all over again.

I'm years away from being able to unpack what any of this means, so instead I default to survival mode again, start thinking career strategy, my next move. I like my job at *Time Out,* but the reality is I can't afford to keep it. I can't stomach staying in a less-empowered financial position than Alex, using his money to buy my own clothes, needing him to help pay my half of our rent. I'll be damned before I set myself in a heteronormative domestic trap. I've done this to myself, of course. By creating a life so singularly focused on "making it," by surrounding myself solely with those who do what I do at a level above what I'm doing, I've painted myself into a professional corner that's incestuous and suffocating and perspective destroying, with little room to breathe or grow.

I look around at my career options. There are few women working at well-paying places where you get to write about things that are not celebrity sightings or hair don'ts. The women I know who make it at those publications are often one of the few females, if not the only female, in the room. One friend I know breaks through at a men's magazine and thrives, but thriving requires flirting heavily with her married male boss, their relationship just at the edge of an affair. From the stories she relays about edit meetings, I gather she embodies a cool-girl persona, in on the tit jokes and the body shaming, throwing other women over in order to survive.

I don't have what it takes to be a freelancer. I have hustle, sure, but lack an immediately recognizable pedigree, a cache of funds or parental subsidy to make it through the lean times. I consider quitting media altogether—*maybe I'll go back and become a teacher after all, maybe even teach abroad, maybe we'll leave the city*—but I'm too committed to a lifestyle I can't afford and too enmeshed in a professional identity I use as an emotional shield to earnestly entertain anything else.

Turns out, I don't have to. Around the time I start thinking about all this, an unexpected door opens. For the first time in my life, I don't have to fight for my next job; instead I'm offered an easy escape hatch.

Sassiest Thirty-Two-Year-Old in America

What I'm about to tell you is the only true fairy tale of my life. This is the one where, as an angry, insecure girl of sixteen I come across a magazine that changes my life, shapes my tastes, and defines the person I think I can be and how, more than a decade later, one of the people who made that magazine seeks me out and wants to work with me.

The first night Kim France and I spend any significant time together is during the New York City blackout in 2003. By then, I've known of her for years. Back in the day, I read every word of the *Sassy* features she wrote and edited. I knew her *Sassy* nickname, her favorite bands, how she liked to dress.

When we meet, I'm actually already working for Kim, though I'm fairly sure she's not aware of this. I'm a freelance fact-checker at *Lucky*, a wildly successful magazine about shopping, which Kim founded a few years after *Sassy* folded. The *Lucky* fact-checkers work in a literal closet, a narrow hall space where four and, sometimes, five people share two long desks. None of the senior editors comes to the fact-checking closet unless they specifically need a fact checked, and even then, they go to our supervisor, a woman with an actual cubicle who does little but look at shoes all day online. Since Kim is the editor in chief, she has no reason to visit fact-checking plebes stuffed into a closet. As a result, I rarely see her at the office.

On the night of the blackout, I walk the four hundred sweaty miles from Times Square through Manhattan and across the Brooklyn Bridge with approximately 4 million strangers, many of whom are also sweating through their polyester work slacks and cultivating oozing blisters above their cheap Aldo soles. By the time I arrive at my apartment, the city is dark and creepy, and the sketchy playground across the street—where no one has ever played, unless you consider drug deals playing—feels sketchier than usual. My couple friends who care for me in a way established, stable couples sometimes adopt a feral adult human stray, text and say, "Come over here to Kim France's house, we have food and drinks!" My friends happen to be friends with Kim, more specifically, with Kim's husband. The offer is as intimidating as it is intriguing, but I'm just the type of person who wants to see how much weirder one of the weirdest nights I've ever experienced can get.

Before heading over, I place a battery-operated radio—the one my dad insisted I buy one time, the same time I refused his offer to walk around the city with a stun gun (*It'll be good, babe! You just zap it and it'll make anyone coming for you piss themselves*)—into my bike basket, duct-tape a flashlight to the front of it, and ride the ten blocks while listening to live NPR, fully pleased with my own scrappy-survivalist skills. It's dead-middle August, Son of Sam weather, the air muggy and still. When I arrive at Kim's, everyone's on her rooftop deck and no one hears the bell. I let myself in through the front door and cautiously climb the many stairs until I awkwardly spill out onto the roof and find them there.

"Hi, sorry, I don't know if you know me, but I work for you," I say by way of introduction. My voice is shaky, my whole body soaked with sweat. Kim is cool and removed under the best of circumstances, but on this night, she and her husband seem like they're arguing. She's visibly annoyed. Without bothering with niceties, she continues rolling and lighting a joint, passes it to me, and suddenly I'm stoned on a roof in a blackout in New York City at the home of my boss who is also an idol and I don't know what this means or how to be.

A few months after the blackout night, I see Kim again, but this time we're in her office. She's firing me. I missed the correct price of a new moisturizer by Revlon, a major advertiser, had it ten dollars under selling cost, and it went to print this way. It's my third mistake like this, which in this world, is akin to a crime. Kim breaks the news herself, says she likes me, tells me she *could* give me a break and overrule my supervisor's decision, but she doesn't think I really want this job, such as it is. She's right. I hate checking prices on skincare products and belts all day, hate the constant game of phone tag with publicists to sort out the availability of skirts, despise researching whether I've got the right name of the right shade of this month's chosen lip gloss.

Beyond a few big sites, online shopping isn't really a thing yet, and *Lucky* has a strict rule that we have to tell readers exactly where to buy anything we feature, to the point of including phone numbers to brick-and-mortar stores. No other magazine does this. It's a huge boon to retailers and a huge pain in the ass for me. Smaller designers often don't make enough of whatever jacket we've featured to handle the volume of orders we're about to send their way; they're thrilled for the placement but worried they'll let people down. It's complicated and emotional. Each page of the magazine requires at least fifteen calls. I check the facts on forty pages a month. The work is harder than when I fact-checked stories about unsolved murders at *Talk*.

Post *Lucky* firing, I assume I'm through with Condé Nast magazines for good. I think this because when I was a fact-checker, I'd met with not one but three of the company's HR reps for informational interviews, met with them enough that I became a "you again?" pest. All three explained that my growth prospects in the industry, and especially at this company, were not promising. Freelance fact-checkers like me rarely became staff writers or editors, they explained, then carefully laid out how higher-ups considered the kind of "research" and "reporting" I did to be distinct skills and, therefore, a different track. That's what they said. What I heard was something different.

Early 2000s Condé Nast was, as the films you've seen suggest, an elite, powerful, global-culture-arbitering snob factory where Image. Was. Everything. Female editors in particular served as immaculately groomed human marquees, walking advertisements for the company ethos. Even the company's HR people were known icons, written about in media columns. It didn't matter what these HR icons told me. What I heard was they weren't going to let just any hoi polloi, like fact-checkers they kept in a literal closet, join their exclusive media club.

However, one winter afternoon just as I'm getting antsy in my second year at *Time Out,* Kim's assistant calls. She sets up a lunch for us at DB Bistro Moderne, a then-famous restaurant located by Bryant Park, a block away from Condé Nast. When we arrive, Kim orders the restaurant's signature dish, a six-inch-high ground-beef burger stuffed with other kinds of beef, like short ribs, and also foie gras and also truffles and maybe gold—a burger that has been written up in *New York* magazine and costs a hundred dollars and which is impossible to eat. The spectacle and distraction of this burger takes up our entire meal.

It's early March, some days winter, some days spring. Kim's dressed in a complicated metallic dress with a shrunken leather blazer over it; fine jewelry hanging about her wrists and torso, even finer leather boots on her feet. I am wearing a sheer yellow polyester blouse from Forever 21, purple jeans I bought on clearance at Urban Outfitters, and high-top suede Wallabees. Kim has an account at the restaurant, a concept that I thought existed only on TV. When we're finished, she casually charges the meal to it. Afterward we stand outside and she fishes through her giant bag for a cigarette and then a lighter. I flash her mine and give her a light. I still don't know why she's invited me to lunch when she says, blowing a plume of smoke, "Hey, so I'm going to hire you. I've seen what you're doing at *Time Out* and want you to come back to *Lucky* as an editor." It's not a question.

"Wow, that's so flattering," I tell her, "and, God, you're amazing, but I don't think *Lucky*'s right for me." It's not a negotiating ploy, I'm not smooth enough to front. The truth is, as much as I admire Kim, *Lucky* doesn't align with any of my longer-form writing goals and, while I like clothes, I already know the allure of capital F fashion vibrates at a frequency I'll never hear.

I look over to gauge her reaction. She's leaning against the wall of the restaurant, ever so slightly disheveled in a way I find endearing, so authentically herself it's disarming. She stares at me directly for the first time of the day, sizes me up. Then, in a kind of singsong voice: "I'm going to make you an offer you can't refuse."

A week later, Kim calls with the offer: a staff editor position with a salary of $70,000 a year, nearly double what I was making, with full Condé Nast benefits, which are famously generous, including not just the fanciest health insurance I'll ever have, but things like full 401(k) matches, free lunch, and even, should you need them, legal fees. I don't know that I should negotiate her up, have little sense that this salary is tens of thousands of dollars less than what other *Lucky* editors at this level make. I don't know that to those who are savvier or come from more, this salary is paltry, a joke. I'm thirty-two, I've never made this much money in my life. The role is newly created for me, will bridge all departments. No one can explain exactly what the job will entail, but I'm drawn to it for the financial upgrade and the adjacency to Kim. I can't pass on the opportunity to learn what she has to teach me, whatever it is. I say yes.

The week before I start, Kim sends her driver to pick me up at the *Time Out* offices in the late evening, just as I'm getting out of work. It's snowing outside when the black Town Car pulls up and I slide into the plush backseat, careful not to bring in snow or street dirt. We drive along the West Side Highway and the suit-clad driver is silent. The car is peaceful, smells clean. For something we've all been conditioned to covet, luxury is among life's most fleeting joys; on fourth, fifth go-arounds, even the most lavish experiences become "normal" disturbingly fast. After this night, I'll ride in enough private cars that I'll no longer always sit back and notice. But tonight, chauffeured alone through the late-winter snow, watching the New York skyline pass by the car's tinted windows, I feel special. I feel what it is to be successful—and rich.

Like the conversation in our initial lunch meeting, the details about the night ahead of me are vague. I'm nervous about how it will go, worried I'll screw it all up. The driver takes me to Kim's new apartment near Washington Square Park. She's single now, lives in a spacious, art-filled, two-bedroom with parquet wood floors, a sunken living room, a soft brown-leather sectional sofa, and her aging shitzu, Weetzie Bat. The doorman rings me up. Kim's expecting me. We're going to hang out, just us. When I arrive at her floor, she greets me at the door with a casual "Hey," like it's totally normal I'm here. We get Thai takeout and pick at it and then Kim rolls several joints and we smoke them. She's at ease while she does this, talks to me like we're friends. It feels like we are.

Over the course of the evening, she gives me the lay of the *Lucky* land and I'm grateful. I sense this is not what everyone else gets, like we're gaming the system somehow, even if I don't know why. She tells me about the editors I'll be working with, the writers I'll be editing, where the problems are as she sees them, what needs to change. The situation probably should make me wary, but the events of my life thus far have led me to function best in off-grid spaces, made it so I'm more at ease with an unconventional boss like Kim than I'd be with a polished corporate type. Plus, she's Kim France! When she stops our conversation suddenly, jumps up, and asks if I'd like to see her *Sassy* archives, I honestly cannot believe my luck.

We look through Kim's *Sassy* boxes for at least an hour, and if I'm honest I could've looked for hours more. She's got all the old magazines, transcripts of her interviews, fan letters, Sassiest Girl in America submissions she liked but that didn't quite make the cut. I tell her I tried to be Sassiest Girl in America three years in a row, she says she

wished she knew me then. I leave that night knowing whatever happens in this job—and I already sense a lot will happen—it will all have
been worth it for this.

Because after that first night? The fairy tale all but ends. It is immediately evident the day I walk through *Lucky*'s frosted-glass doors that
I've made a mistake. The problem, and it is a big problem, is twofold.

*1. I'm not, and have never been, rich and don't under-
stand rich-people shit.*

2. Most everyone I work with does.

Lucky's *technically* a fashion magazine, but it's really more of a
style catalog, or a "mag-a-log," which is how it was referred to at the
time, to Kim's unending dismay. It set out to be accessible and "real"-
girl cool—closer in tone to *Sassy* than to, say, *Vogue*—but it was still
part of Condé Nast, a company that in 2005, still required that, before
starting their jobs, its female editors in chief undergo a high-end, head-
to-toe image makeover, including a visit to a diet doctor to trim them
down. When I arrive, *Lucky* magazine may be run by Kim France, but
it still played by Condé Nast rules.

Before *Lucky*, I was no stranger to shopping. I'd worked retail in high
school, and I certainly knew my way around a mall. I'd never cared
about labels, but throw me in a T.J.Maxx with a hundred dollars and
I'd come out with two good "of-the-moment" outfits, including shoes.
I was resourceful not only because I had to be but because I thought
it was fun. I dressed in clothes I liked and I dressed for myself, and
I mostly found a lot of joy in all of it. This, and the fact that I could
describe things imaginatively, should have made me a good fit for Kim's
magazine. But I was not.

Within days, I'm lost at the job. I don't know that Lancôme is not luxurious and should never be referred to as luxurious. I repeatedly mispronounce Comme des Garçons. I don't get that a $150 dress is a "budget" dress until after a fellow editor tells me matter-of-factly that you can't buy a decent dress for less than $500. After an office poll to calculate the "average" number of jeans in an "average" woman's closet, I'm shocked that most of my co-workers answered a dozen or more. My answer is two, one of which I got off the "free" table, part of a promotion sent to announce the launch of a new line of eco-friendly denim. I wear the jeans often, often enough that a fashion editor notices and decides they're my thing. Like *Sassy* before it, *Lucky* regularly features its editors as models in the magazine, often with a defining personal trait. I'm introduced in the next month's issue as "new staff editor/ eco-girl Jennifer Romolini" while modeling a stiff hemp-fabric top and the free jeans. Next to my awkward smile someone's typed up a quote about how I'm "really into the coral reefs." Print the legend, I guess.

To be fair, the work is mostly as smart as it can be. Kim's a former rock critic and she brings an edgy, rebellious spirit to the magazine, as does creative director (and *Sassy* alum) Andrea Linett and legendary beauty director Jean Godfrey-June. The three have a banned word list that tops out at over one hundred, will damn any of us to hell if we try to deploy schlocky women's mag phrases like "luscious locks." Each month, Kim goes through every page of the magazine with a red pen, calling out descriptions that are off the mark.

"You're better than this," she scrawls next to a lazy caption about sandals.

"Don't insult the reader, JR!" she replies when I suggest a pair of black pants is better than all other black pants you own.

"NO!!!" when we've used whatever word or phrase she hates that month, including "girly," "genius," "vibe," "guru," "bling," "jokey references to Martha Stewart," and, her least favorite, food references (*This delicious print . . .*) used to describe a nonfood item.

Could Kim and Andrea and Jean write the entire magazine themselves? Yes. They're all true creatives with vision, rare in an industry filled with well-heeled paper pushers. Do they need all of us? Not really. But we're in the last golden years of print publishing. Bulky mastheads are still symbols of clout; every task that could be accomplished by two is overseen by ten.

This means editors have time to fixate on the inane, to compare and despair, to neurotically consider their lot. In particular, there are a few born-rich, status-hungry white ladies playing a different game than the rest of us, poisoning the neroli-oil-scented well. These women hold the office hostage with tantrums about everything from first-class travel schedules to not getting for free that season's designer bubble skirt, a skirt they'll wear once, if ever, but that's not the point. They need to be important enough to get it for nothing at all.

As a person who is money-dumb, who delights in burning and sharing whatever wealth I've ever gained, I'm stunned by the cheapness. Senior staff demand not just bubble skirts but everything—their "corset" belts, their push-up bras, their three-hundred-dollar foreskin face creams—be delivered to them gratis, even though they can more than afford to pay. One morning I overhear an editor with a literal million-dollar painting hanging in her office casually explain how she steals coffee pods from the break room kitchen because her nanny likes them, this being the same nanny she chastises for taking off for Diwali. While complaining about her Indian nanny, she points over at my friend, an editor who's also Indian, and says, "Oh, *you* know." Another wealthy, *Mayflower*-white editor notoriously stiffs delivery drivers. Yet another tasks a team of assistants with making sure all of her plastic surgery procedures are comped, reprimanding and shaming them if they don't.

And it's not just the cheapness. There's a "someone else will clean it up" entitlement that's pervasive not just at *Lucky* but throughout the entire company, an attitude I find almost physically intolerable, behavior that makes me seethe. I see it in the cafeteria, at the "Asian Station," where women shriek "NO OIL!" at the tall-hatted stir-fry chef, rejecting bowls of limp red peppers and seared broccoli stalks during the lunch rush because they believe they've been tainted with fat. Or at the salad bar, where sharp-shouldered editors hold up the line to liberate hard-boiled egg whites from their less appealing hard-boiled yolks, leaving behind mounds of unappetizing yellow crumbs on counters and even the floor, no thought to whoever might come after them or who will wipe up their mess. And I see it especially in the unholy condition of the ladies' room, in the display of lazy, unsanitary habits that mark the shared space.

Who leaves a used pad on the floor?

It's maybe important to say here that I don't hate rich people. But I've also always felt uncomfortable in the bubbles created by wealth. In New York, the rich women I know obsess over things like how their multimillion-dollar brownstone lacks the original details of another friend's multimillion-dollar brownstone, which makes it just not as good. Or how one friend bought the same Stella McCartney dress as the other, even though *she knew I'd had it first.* Over drinks, a friend who has $47,000 in her "play money" bank account rants about how her husband is in mutual funds when the *real* money is in some other funds. I have one Manhattan-born, boarding-schooled pal explain the obscene amount of money she believes I need if I want to live a "decent" life, if I want to "properly" furnish a Brooklyn apartment, let alone buy a country house and furnish that too. One woman, a woman I'm close enough with to be a bridesmaid in her wedding, nitpicks at my appearance disapprovingly, tells me my blazers are ill-fitting, my jewelry looks cheap. When she enters my apartment for the first time, she says, "Is that a giant plastic sofa? *Ew.*" in reference to my pleather couch. It's all lighthearted—*I was joking, come on.* But it also sucks.

It's easy to get caught up in all of this, to train yourself to perpetually covet in just this way. The path from contented rube to status goblin is short. One day you're an oblivious normie thinking your normie stuff and normie life are great, then someone comes along and calls your couch plastic and—depending on the health of your ego—you feel withered, *less than*. You feel ashamed. Consumption, then, becomes solely about avoiding this shame, about appearances, about what some unimaginative jerks believe you should do, be, own. It's stupid high school behavior forever, the cycle, once you've succumbed to it, harder and harder to escape.

There's a type of person who, no matter if they grew up in financial lack or financial abundance, is particularly susceptible to this pressure. But the truth is we're all at least a little vulnerable to defining our success on other people's terms, to being lured and lulled into buying things we don't like or need, to taking jobs and projects we don't want, just to create an idea of who we are and perform it for others, never uncovering what we truly want for ourselves.

One afternoon one of the wealthiest women in the *Lucky* office and I are walking to a meeting together, making the smallest of small talk. We're in the middle of production for the February/Valentine's Day issue, the perfumed office halls narrowed by racks of lingerie, an elongated rainbow of bras and corsets and panties, labeled for upcoming shoots.

"UMMMM," the editor says, pausing to take hold of a bright purple garter set, "can you imagine?

"Oh my god, *who* would wear this?" she says, gasping when we pass a series of hot-pink thongs.

"I don't know," I reply, shrugging. "Me? I think it's kind of hot."

She flushes as deep purple as the garter when I say this, looks down at the floor, doesn't say another word. It's a rare glimpse of vulnerability, a surprise to us both. We're the same age, both in relationships. But she seems much older than I am, so stiff and buttoned up. She talks about her partner all the time, shows off the fancy jewelry he buys her, name-drops the fancy friends they know. But I sense from her full-body reaction to these mildly sleazy panties that there's not much by way of life's great free joys—fucking—in her life, and if there is, it's not much fun.

And this was the thing about most of the rich women I knew. I understood even in the moment that their limited beliefs about what makes a good life were largely hindrances to happiness, sad-boring jails. That these rich-people rules were bred into them, that they'd been criticized and compared in ways I never had, heard and felt pressures I never would. To paraphrase Joan Didion, the dream had taught these dreamers how to live. I was happy to dream of other things.

This is not to say I wasn't also a striver. I'm desperate to do a "good" job at *Lucky*, to have my goodness and hard work validated. Ultimately, I'm desperate to ascend.

Bad "Cultural" Fit

Psychologists say children who endure abuse search for faults in their own behavior to rationalize what's happened to them. Self-blame serves as a kind of protection, providing the child with a sense of safety and control. If they are bad, the thinking goes, then they brought the pain upon themselves. If they brought it upon themselves, then they alone have the power to fix it. Being "bad" becomes foundational to the child's identity, a quality mitigated only by overcompensating with what we think of as "good."

Carrying this pathology beyond childhood, abused children often transform into perfectionist, high-achieving adults. Professional success—and its accompanying accolades and external validation—becomes a space to hide within. It telegraphs to the world how they are now good.

I never feel like I'm good enough at *Lucky*. I fail to consider that the job may not be right for me, that there's nothing wrong with not caring about Goyard bags, that I'm perfectly fine as the Marshalls shopping yokel I am. Instead of starting down a path toward self-acceptance—or even acknowledging that such a path exists—I adapt and contort to become what the place needs. I make every editorial task Sisyphean, am teeth-grittingly anxious over captions about jeans, easily agitated and tightly wound. I purchase a fashion dictionary and fanatically study fashion terms until I can tell cigarette tailoring from stovepipe. I acquire the world's largest thesaurus and compulsively write and rewrite even the smallest assignments I receive.

Each morning, a senior editor walks through the office scouting for the website's "outfit of the day" (OOTD) girl, points a finger at the chosen one, *You! Cute!* Recognizing this as office currency, I start obsessing over what I wear to work. I follow trends we're covering in the magazine and spend hours on eBay tracking vintage dupes on the cheap. I compile an impressive collection of stacked-heel Frye boots, cap-toe Ferragamo pumps, sixties trench coats, seventies secretary dresses, a particularly good coiled snake belt. I wake up hours earlier than I need to to style myself, creating elaborate hairstyles to go with my elaborate outfits. All of which would be fun, pleasurable even, if it wasn't in service of my professional ambition, if I didn't feel a chest-clenching pressure to get it right.

One day in the office, a day when I've perhaps taken the costuming too far, a senior colleague looks over at me during a meeting and says, "It's hard to make a pretty girl ugly, Jenn, but somehow today you've managed." It's a cinematic-level bitchy comment, but I take the note. After a few months, I've assembled enough of a wardrobe and the know-how to pull it together that I manage to be the OOTD girl several times over. I rarely wear the same outfit twice.

While I may often feel isolated at *Lucky,* I'm not alone. I've bonded with a handful of colleagues who are, for a variety of reasons, similarly outside the rich-white-girl fold. Together we're a tight-knit group of misfits and underdogs, an us-versus-them office underground, our own aligned crew. We hang out on weekends, eat lunch together on weekdays, defend each other in meetings, put each other up for plum assignments, pitch in when a member's work piles too high.

At this time, I also begin managing, though it's not exactly official and there's not much by way of training or oversight. Outside the hierarchy of mastheads, magazines at this time don't follow org charts. Nor do they operate with formal "leadership" of any kind. Consistent, constructive feedback is nonexistent; employee development is not part of the culture. No one even really knows who reports to whom.

Still, even within this environment, leadership comes surprisingly naturally to me. I may not know how to pronounce "Balmain," but I excel at "big picture" thinking and minimizing chaos, at knowing how to balance workloads across teams, at recognizing who's good at what. Like my dad in his own business, I derive satisfaction from supporting and protecting the "good kids." I mentor eager young editors desperate for a shot, spend off-the-clock hours teaching caption writing to those who share my "hustle till you make it" worldview. My approach to management is generous but no-bullshit. I hold our work to the highest standard. And I make enemies of those who don't.

Eventually I'm tasked with editing a junior staffer who's popular in the office and well connected in publishing circles, but who I quickly discover half-asses most everything she's assigned. This woman is a strategic fabulist whose animated pitches sound spot-on in senior-staff-attended idea meetings. But the stories she subsequently files fall apart under any editorial scrutiny; they often involve products readers can't buy, sometimes because they don't even exist. Her sloppy reporting slows down production and takes up too much of my time, but it's not just that. The errors create problems for the people in the copy and fact-checking and art departments, more messes someone else has to clean up. This editor's a mover and shaker, on a nonstop charm offensive with anyone she thinks can give her a leg up. But her charm is lost on me.

You don't have to be a traumatized person from the fuck-around-and-find-out Northeast working class to feel intolerant of falseness. But an early childhood spent tracking the behavior of erratic adults has made me hypervigilant to facts-don't-line-up stories, extra-sensitive to false moves and outright lies. I have an overdeveloped bullshit detector—attuned to other people's bullshit, though not always to my own—but it's not just that. I personalize other people's bullshitting and viscerally react to it, consider it an insult to my intelligence, an attack. I'm quick to annoyance, blunt, and I don't back down from a fight. All of which was fine in Philly when I was fighting to get orders up in a dinner rush and screaming "No, fuck *YOU*" back at macho chefs. And it might be okay, admirable even, in this environment if I were a man, but it's a *serious* liability since I'm not.

Each story holds many truths. Women of my generation entered an inequitable workforce under the cultural pressure to race to and ruthlessly claim the few seats available at the table as our own. As a result, we grew up—no matter how privileged we actually were—internalizing scarcity. We learned to compete rather than collaborate, to view female peers as rivals for male attention and threats to our professional ascent. Like most women working at this time, the junior editor and I are tangled up in a broken system. In a winner-take-all climate like Condé Nast and, especially, in the absence of healthy managerial mitigation, we become little more than pecking-order hens engaged in our own version of a cockfight.

Because of what and where I came from, I lock in to the duel. Instead of sending the editor's pages to the research department, I begin fact-checking them myself first. I start tracking her mistakes, meticulously documenting every error I see. When I find discrepancies, I call her out directly. I ask her to find new sources, rewrite copy, resubmit ideas. I'm on a vigilante quest for justice that's above my pay grade: *I'm going to get this bitch to do her job.*

One Thursday afternoon, after finding the junior editor's "finished" section unprintable the night before it's supposed to go to print, I see that she's left early. I send an email asking that she return to the office to fix her mistakes. She emails back from her BlackBerry like I'm a nuisance, tells me it would be *impossible* to rectify this as she's on her way to . . . Saint-Tropez.

I don't report the behavior to our bosses. I'm not a snitch. Instead, I fix the problems in her section, re-report two of the stories in the eleventh hour, save the publishing day. For the next week, I stew about the situation while sorting out a fifteen-page denim guide, while describing three-thousand-dollar necklaces and trying to find a way to make objectively ugly shoes from a major advertiser seem actually cute.

After a few days, I start to relax. I imagine that the editor's last mistakes were egregious enough that this dumb work war will soon be over. She'll feel bad—or at least scared for her job—realize I haven't ratted her out, and want to resolve the situation with me when she's back.

However, when the editor returns, her first order of business is to print out the email I'd sent, an email that contained the word "unacceptable" and also, if memory serves, the phrase "what in the actual fuck." She marches this email to our immediate boss with the confidence of a person who's free of the guilt and shame that dictate everything I do, someone who—right or wrong, it matters little—knows how to get her way. Once inside our boss's office, the junior editor explains how "scary" I am, how upsetting my email was to receive, how my criticism made her cry.

I'm called in later to give my side of the story, but it's clear my side doesn't matter. I'm confrontational in a world where people don't confront, a street fighter in a ladies' auxiliary club. I've already lost. I receive a stern warning for this managerial overstep and am told if I want to keep my job, my behavior needs to change. Though she's not the one who delivers the message, Kim signs off on the reprimand. I'm crushed.

The scolding hits me hard. I rage-cry about it all day—in the office bathroom, on the train after work, at home chopping kale. I'm furious that someone is getting away with something, but more than that, I'm humiliated that I got in trouble. I can't make it make sense. I work as hard as, if not harder than, almost anyone else in the office. I put effort into looking and acting the part at the job, but no matter how I bend, I can't make myself fit.

The issue is coming up more and more: I expect work to be a meritocracy. I demand that someone listen when it is not.

———————————

Once, when I was a kid, my parents accidentally left me at a rest stop. It's a story I've told before, a story my mom hates. They were young when it happened, barely legal drinking age. I was four. We were on a summer road trip sharing several cars with a big group of their friends. They'd stopped at a rest stop and, in the commotion of piling back into the cars, my dad thought I was with my mom, while my mom thought I was with him. Without checking, they all drove off. They were only a few miles down the road when they realized what had happened, my mom tells me. She says I was alone for twenty minutes, maybe less. It felt much longer than this.

I remember looking around, not knowing what to do. I remember worrying if I moved from the spot where they'd left me they wouldn't be able to find me. So I stayed close. I wandered to a nearby tree with a good view of the parking lot, sat down against it in the summer's heat, dirt dusting my calves and falling into my plastic sandals, sweat beading on my upper lip. The rest stop smelled of truck exhaust, gasoline, and damp grass. It was eerily quiet and still. I was too young to conjure specific danger, unclear on what to fear. I watched the parking lot blankly, a four-year-old waiting as if on a police stakeout, steeling myself for whatever might happen next. This stakeout feeling became foundational; a sensation I've carried my entire life.

Growing up, I knew my parents loved me. And I was aware, from an early age, that they'd both kill to protect me, that they were uniquely strong and tough. But emotional safety is hard to parse, more complex and nuanced than it seems. My parents bought crayons and Barbies, built bikes and desks. I was loved and sheltered and fed. I was also abandoned, emotionally and sometimes physically. And I often felt like an afterthought or, worse, an obstacle to my parents living their lives.

Do most children sense they're a hindrance? To this day I feel—

and even in the moment I felt—compassion for my parents. We all know what it is to make a mistake, to do the wrong thing when you meant to do right. As a kid, I often felt the need to protect my parents from the burden of parenting, of me and my endless needs. From a young age, I attempted to meet those needs myself.

Into adulthood, however, my sense of safety distorts, the machine initially built all wrong, the calibrations off. I self-destruct when it's clear I should self-protect. I'm easily agitated and reactive, see danger where there's nothing to fear. Like a dazed and wounded animal, I attack at the slightest prod, the gentlest poke. My fight response stuck in overdrive, my central nervous system always on guard, my adrenaline dialed all the way up.

One afternoon in July, I'm in trouble at *Lucky* again, but this time it's worse. It's midweek, right before the Fourth. We're working on the big September issue, the thickest of the year. It's the month when women's magazines famously triple in size for fall fashion—a month at *Lucky* when there's more than enough work to go around.

Most of the staff, and all of the bosses, have already left for the holiday, long gone on summer sojourns to Europe, the Hamptons, Mustique. It's supposed to be a company-sanctioned half day, but one of the remaining editors wants the junior employees to stay to move more pages to senior-staff inboxes, even though they'll bottleneck there until the bosses return the following week. By 5:00, I hear friends in the copy department on the phone, canceling plans with their families. By 6:00, I ask if we can go and she says, "One more hour." At 7:00, I head to her office and explain I'm going home and I am telling anyone working on my pages to go home. She should too.

"You can't do that. We have a schedule with deadlines, it's important."

"If it was so important, more important people would be here to deal with it."

"Jenn, I'm not giving you permission to go."

"What are you going to do? Physically detain me? *Fuck. That.* And fuck off. You know this is bullshit."

I'm standing in her doorway when I say this. A key detail. When the HR report finally comes through, the editor calls me "threatening." The HR rep says I blocked an exit, making an employee feel "unsafe." It's my second warning. One more and I'm gone.

In the early days, I'm out of sync like this in all parts of my job at *Lucky,* what HR people often call a bad "cultural" fit. I'm unhappy, but I'm too stubborn to admit defeat. Plus, I respect Kim enough to want to stick it out, feel I owe her for giving me an opportunity when no one else would.

The truth is, Kim's struggling too. When I come to *Lucky,* she's the media world's newest darling, riding high on the magazine's success, profiled in *The New York Times* and elsewhere, her street style captured in *Vogue.* Like most all coveted jobs that seem great from the outside, a position like Kim's is an all-consuming stress prison once you're in it. It's starting to take a toll.

By the time we're working together, Kim is physically and emotionally unwell. And sensing and eventually confirming that she was unwell brought forth a kind of fierce loyalty in me that, because of my few female friendships at this point, I was not quite sure I had. Between us, there was kinship, a connection I couldn't explain and could not make sense of but knew was there. Our working relationship was flawed and difficult, but for better or for worse, my loyalty never waned.

In the time that I am at *Lucky,* Kim will go through the worst period of her life. She'll survive breast cancer, which I'll know about, and a mental health crisis, which I'll suspect but not confirm until she leaves abruptly one day for a month of treatment, the same month *Lucky's* executive editor is on her multiweek honeymoon, the month when I, a rube who knows next to nothing about fashion, am sort of put in charge of a magazine about fashion. It's sitcom-level high jinks, a month when I huddle with my best office friend R over pages of the magazine, try not to repeat the same adjectives in a ten-page story about a "month of outfits" created out of the same five items of clothing, rearranged and laid out in panels like a graphic novel. We finally nail it, but it's a test of our psychic strength.

"Is this look Lauren Hutton–inspired?"

"Wait, do you mean Lauren Bacall?"

"Is it slinky or silky or sophisticated or . . ."

"I don't fucking know!"

Before Kim leaves, before I start getting in trouble, she and I briefly become friends in the kind of thrilling, unsustainable, dialed-in way women sometimes get to become friends. A way a boss and an employee should never be friends, like we're planting a flag for some future us down the road. During the day, we chain-smoke cigarettes and trade gossip in her office-adjacent private bathroom until the space is dense with smoke. She invites me and a few senior staffers to her birthday party—held at some fancy design person's all-white apartment, the main décor of which is a black ceramic rat on a mantel, encased in glass. At the party, we'll both get anxious at the same time, signal to each other to leave, retreat to her apartment, smoke pot, and then return, laughing and stupid, pulling it together before we walk back through the door.

Once on a Friday afternoon, she asks me to go away with her for the weekend. She's rented a house in the Hamptons and no one else is going with her this weekend or maybe this one famous old-man writer is going, she doesn't know. This is how she is in these days: manic, impetuous, vague. I'll say yes, of course, because I am nothing but a woman with mom issues looking to please a female authority figure, but also because inside I'm still a sixteen-year-old girl and this is a dream.

We drive out in Kim's two-seater convertible, the car she chose when the company offered her a car. She asks if I want to listen to Led Zeppelin and FUCK YES I WANT TO LISTEN TO LED ZEPPELIN. The breeze is blowing and the music is blaring and Kim is driving fast. I've got Weetzie Bat on my lap. The dog needs to be fed a bottle cap of water every twenty minutes or she'll die or get sick, I'm not sure, but I follow instructions and water the dog and rock out to "Tangerine" while Long Island passes us by out the windows on a warm summer's night, the music so loud in my ears it temporarily shuts down my brain.

Soon after our trip, Kim becomes alienated from most of her friends because they're worried about her and she's not listening to their worries. Soon after that she'll fight with her family over whether she should go away and where she'll go away to. Eventually one day she just won't be there in the office and it will all be weird and hush-hush and opportunistic Marni-clad vultures will start circling and jockeying to take over but somehow I'm the one who's handed a stack of layouts and entrusted with editing and finessing that month's unfinished work.

I'll call Kim twice at the hospital. The first time I leave her a voice-mail and tell her that I want her to take care of herself, that she's a good person, that it will be okay. The second time we'll talk live, her voice hoarse and soft, to discuss her editor's letter, which she's written from the hospital. I don't want her to run it—it's too personal, too tender, too much for where we are. She won't listen to me and I'll talk to the managing editor and I'll try to have it stopped but I can't. It's what she wants, and we go to press this way. Printing it—and the fact that we called overalls "surprisingly sexy"—is one of my great regrets.

When Kim returns, it's all different. Her office door is closed more often now: no office cigarettes, no breaks, the inner circle tightened. At my annual review, I'm passed over for the promotion I want. The executive editor, who I deal with mostly now, who I covered for during her honeymoon, and then again for her maternity leave, tells me she *wishes* they could trust me with more responsibility. "But," she says, wincing, sucking saliva through her teeth, "you're just not *there*."

I'll respond to this shutout in the only way I understand to do anything, which is to throw my whole body into getting what I think I want. I become an "I'll Show You" human battering ram. I work constantly and maniacally, make myself a force to be reckoned with at a company I don't care about, fight for promotion to a role that is surely not right for me by quiet, unrelenting siege.

I monitor office politics and stay one step ahead. I learn to (at least somewhat) curb my rage. I'm never in trouble again. I start managing more writers, grabbing control of more sections. I edit new website columns and pitch and write a daily blog about eBay shopping. When another staffer leaves, I land the coveted celebrity cover stories, one of the few features in the magazine that comes with a byline. I head to the photo shoots, where I'm allotted twenty minutes to elicit a two-page spread's worth of thoughts on fashion and beauty faves from mid-aughts stars like Mandy Moore, Eva Mendes, Keri Russell, and Hilary Duff.

It's a simple, straightforward assignment that each month, without fail, becomes a begging/pleading scavenger hunt to hell. I need just nine shoppable items—makeup, clothes, perfume, shoes—to fill out the layout and quotes for why the cover subject likes them. But the stars are reluctant to give up the goods. They have preferences, but they also have spokesmodel and ambassador deals, companies they've pledged allegiance to, their own lines to push. Most won't go on record about a brand (even if they love it) unless they're paid to do so; many despise talking about style at all.

The interviews become a series of awkward interrogations, shatter any illusions I had about celebrity, and make me instantly, permanently wary of fame. I sit across from Avril Lavigne in an all-white Manhattan studio for an eye-stabbingly painful seventeen minutes in which she steadfastly refuses to provide answers beyond "accessories and shit," "belts maybe, I don't care," "the only clothes I like have skulls." I attempt to question Molly Sims in a studio-adjacent dressing room while she runs out the clock by ignoring me entirely, staring at herself in the makeup mirror, and meticulously plucking at her facial hair. I spend subsequent weeks fighting with publicists over which blush shade we can pretend their client wears, which fabricated "style inspirations" are best aligned with personal brands. I earn these publicists' respect for my persistence, for being a wheelin'-and-dealin' team player but also for calling out the game: "Come on, Claire, we just need *one fucking hair serum* so this doesn't look like a *total* Cover Girl ad!"

During this time, Kim and I rarely see each other, but she has few notes on my sections, and the ones she has are near-uniformly good. The next time I am up for a promotion, I get it—deputy editor—but without an accompanying salary increase, upon the announcement of which I raise a THIS IS RIDICULOUS protest loud enough for anyone who's listening to hear, but not loud enough for anything to change.

To the outside world, I'm already a success. *Lucky* is the first job I have that people think is a big deal. Friends and relatives I haven't heard from in years message me on Facebook to gush about the magazine, about that one lipstick story I was featured in, about how there was an old issue at their dentist's office and they saw my name. They chat me up online: *Did you really meet Heidi Klum? Do you get to keep the clothes? I always loved Liv Tyler, what's she like?*

It's the first job where the *idea* of what I do lies in stark contrast with the reality. It's the job where an outside narrative of my career and my life begins to form, where people start looking at me not as who I am but as what I do and—relatedly—what I can do for them. Acquaintances reach out, looking for access. A childhood friend pitches her new pet apparel business multiple times, even after I explain *Lucky* doesn't cover pets. An old high school boyfriend calls my extension at work to find out if his wife can send me samples from her hair accessory line. One of my mom's friends makes decoupage furniture she thinks "will be perfect for *Lucky*!" Someone else has a store that she's sure *needs* to be in one of our local guides. I feel bad saying no, but I can't say yes. Each interaction is awkward and uncomfortable, pushes me further from the person I used to be, distances me further from who and what I knew.

After three years at *Lucky,* I've changed. Professionally, with Kim's help, I'm a better writer and editor. And with my promotion, I finally have a résumé that can open some doors. But personally, I've become more cynical and guarded, more anxious than ever, constantly stressed. I'm concerned with different things now, particularly how things look, how *I* look, some of the Condé Nast snobbery rubbing off, how could it not?

I write every day for the *Lucky* website and I write in first person, selling trends to readers while simultaneously painting a picture of who I am and how I live. Every part of my life is up for grabs for inclusion in the daily blog, my motivation for even the smallest life choices increasingly contrived. I choose parties and movies and trips in accordance with what will make the best copy, steer conversations to dialogue I can use later, locations that will make the best scenes. I'd moved to New York to live a full life, but my life and my work are entirely blurred now. My world becomes increasingly shallow and small.

One afternoon I head to the office of an integrative medicine doctor I'd interviewed when I was at *Time Out.* This time I'm here for treatment. Mainly for ongoing gastrointestinal issues, my embarrassing IBS, the fact that I can eat fewer and fewer foods without experiencing duress, my body never not settling some kind of score. The doctor and I'd hit it off the first time we met. It was for a story about how to build your immune system on a budget; he'd had good tips. Since then, he's kept in touch, pitched me his new vitamin line for placement in *Lucky,* which I've dutifully passed along. The day of my appointment is the first time I've seen him in years.

"You don't look well," he says bluntly as he examines me, not holding back. "What happened? Last time I saw you, you were buoyant, happy. Now your chi is so low."

I'm skeptical—*who can see chi?*—but I also sense he's right. I'm stagnating. I quickly decide a new job will fix it. The pages I currently edit at *Lucky* require approval from seven editors. Even the web stories must be signed off by five. I want more autonomy, I want to climb the next rung on the ladder, to have more control. Blogging feels immediate, the writing more spontaneous, fresh. When I'm recruited for a job at a big tech company with an offer of a 30 percent salary increase to write a fashion and beauty blog, I take it even though the company seems like—and will turn out to be—toxic pandemonium, a mismanaged mess.

One of my last full days in the *Lucky* office is a Friday, a day when most of the senior staff work from home. For some reason, Kim is there, making the office rounds. At this point, I've worked for her for four years. I know her well enough to notice she looks unwell, but no longer well enough to directly ask. I walk to the managing editor's office and inquire, "Is Kim okay?" Ten minutes later the managing editor calls and tells me, *Actually, not really,* then: *Would you mind helping her get home?*

Turns out, Kim has a mega migraine, the blinding kind. She gets a lot of them during these years, keeps her office door closed so she can lie down on the sofa in between meetings with the lights dim. It's lunchtime. Kim's assistant has ordered her a vat of chicken soup in a tall plastic container, which we're taking to go. The soup is hot and leaking, sloshing out of its container and into a clear plastic bag that's knotted at the top and looks like it should contain something more fun, like a pet fish. The assistant hands me the bag and I hold it by the knot, out and away from my body. Kim exits her office wrapped in a dark-colored cashmere blanket, which covers her head like an Italian widow in mourning's veil. I take her by the arm and together with the sloshing soup bag and the blanket veil we walk out of the office to the elevator.

We make it down the elevator without incident, a feat if you know Condé Nast, and out to Kim's car, the driver waiting. She answers three work calls on the ride downtown, all of them about business, all of them tense. It's 2008, magazine publishing's best days gasping to an end. Soon McKinsey's corporate-mess cleaners will come through and clean the egregious excess out of this opulent house. Soon there will be no first-class flights, no wardrobe allowances, no personal drivers, no private cars.

When we reach Kim's apartment, she kicks off her shoes, grabs a ratty old, oversize cardigan, throws it on over her Zero + Maria Cornejo dress. Weetzie Bat is still alive, but struggling. Kim scoops her up as I place the soup in the kitchen, see the take-out containers and newspapers and unopened mail strewn around, see the sadness in her house. She's standing by the door with the dog in her arms, waiting for me to leave. She looks smaller than I think of her, frail. My imminent departure from *Lucky* hangs in the air.

"Don't try to be in charge, it's not worth it," she says as we say goodbye. "It's really just not any fun."

It's a generous warning. I dismiss it out of hand.

Nonrecognition Aggression

The cats arrive two years before the baby does.

I first spot the good cat in the window of a yellow school bus that's been renovated into a traveling cat shelter and is now called the Cattywagon. I'm on my way back from buying gluten-free bread from an overpriced health food store that sells nondelicious foods to people who want to punish themselves in the name of performative health. The bread is for dipping into a tomato-based seafood stew whose ingredients my sister and I had spent the entire day procuring for a dish we'll later prepare for dinner party guests.

The cat is a gray tabby, the best kind of kitten. We lock eyes through the window. She's serving a look both forlorn and discerning—the exact look you want from a cat.

I'd been pining for a pet. After leaving *Lucky*, I feel an urge to domesticate, to nurture something outside myself, to dedicate my extracurricular life to a world beyond boozing in bars. I grow tomatoes on the fire escape. I prepare and can pickles from the four cucumbers that grow in the windowsill pot. I attempt to learn how to knit.

By now, Alex and I are both in our mid-thirties, solidly middle career, with middle-career salaries. After six months of round-the-clock work at the tech company, I impress my bosses enough that I'm promoted from blogger to editor, with an accompanying raise. We live in a spacious floor-through apartment on a prime block near Prospect Park, with ample light and tin-ceiling tiles. It's rent-controlled, which makes our salaries go further. There's finally a bit of extra money coming in. It's all *nearly* perfect. Clearly time to ramp up the stakes. Time for a pet.

Back at the Cattywagon, the good cat's stare is intense enough that I walk inside the bus as if summoned. The good cat shares its cage with a cat-mate, a tiny but fierce-looking calico, a runt who's ferociously batting a stuffed turtle while simultaneously hanging from the side of the crate, upside down, like a murderous aerialist.

"Is the tabby available for adoption?" my sister and I ask the gray-haired hippie/bus driver/cat foster mom, who's wearing a handwritten name tag that says "Enid" with a picture of a cat drawn next to it.

"Yeah, but she comes with the calico. They're bonded sisters, they come as a set."

"What if we just want one?"

"You can't have just one."

I snap a pic of the two cats and text it to Alex on my BlackBerry, which renders them distorted anime. "kittens needs saving! temporary foster! ok?"

I don't wait for an answer.

"We'll take them."

Enid gives me an application to fill out and a paper to sign. My sister holds the pretentious bread, and I take the bonded cat sisters, who we'll soon discover are not really sisters but, more important, are not actually bonded. I carry them the ten blocks home in their portable crate, juggling them with a heavy bag, which contains the stuffed turtle, kibble samples, a miniature litter box, and a bag of fine-dust cat litter that's already sprung a leak.

I do not consider that Alex may be angry about this, or if I do, I don't care. I don't consider how he and I are different, how he's less impulsive than I am, needs time to carefully consider decisions like this. I've been pushing for a cat for months. I want a pet as a trial run for having a baby, though I don't tell him this. I want him to see how fun it is to take care of something. I am a woman with thirty-five years on this patriarchal planet; my eggs are in decline, the world tells me, my womb in fossilizing retreat. There's only so much more time. Alex and I have been together for four of my prime baby years and *we should've already had a baby!* is the story I'm telling myself. I don't give much thought to if we're ready to do this or not, if Alex is the person I should do this with or not. I'm too busy chasing a narrow idea of the ideal life: marriage, motherhood, professional reputation, outward success. I don't pause to ask questions. Instead, I get cats.

Six months after the Cattywagon, Alex and I get married in City Hall. We decide one night over mediocre nachos and serviceable margaritas in a Mexican restaurant down the street from where we live. I meet him there after attending the *Project Runway* season finale at New York Fashion Week, where my tech company credentials meant I was seated, for reasons still unclear to me, in the front row, near Bradley Whitford from *The West Wing*. When I arrive to meet Alex for a late dinner, I'm ravenous and overdressed. He's been out drinking with his friends. He looks at me mid–nachos bite and says, "I want you to be my wife." In response, I ask if he is drunk and tell him he should take the weekend to be sure, but then we attend two New York media weddings over the weekend because we are on a continuous thirties matrimony tour and I am too excited about this maybe-engagement and tell everyone we know we're engaged.

Within three weeks, we've booked a dinner for thirty of our closest friends and family at the Rainbow Room and an entire Brooklyn bar we love for a party after. I get an off-the-rack white minidress and he gets a suit and we both get shoes fancier than any shoes we've ever owned before. I buy us a couple of thin gold bands and we get a marriage license and send an email inviting all the people we know to the bar and fewer people to the restaurant. Exactly a month after Nacho Night, we stand in front of a dark-stained particleboard podium and get married by a no-nonsense lady judge from the Bronx. In the few existing pictures from this day, our teeth shine and our eyes sparkle. We look like two people in love. We are. When my mother arrives at the courthouse, she pulls me aside and whispers, "Wow, you look so much happier than you did on your first wedding day." I am.

I want to say Alex and I worked out our children/no children conflict before this, that the years of late-night talks and fights before we married when I told him no kids was a relationship ender mean we're now on the same page about our future. That Alex is ready to be a dad or I'm okay with not being a mom. But the truth is we get married in a hurry and just stop talking about it until one night after we're married we drink a lot of wine at a rented beach house and I get pregnant.

The doctor had *just* told me it would take months at my age. That I had an insecure cervix and might not be able to carry to term. She said I was of advanced maternal age with a history of miscarriage and I'd be lucky to get pregnant in half a year and that, even then, the pregnancy might not take. She was a tell-it-like-it-is doctor who sugar-coated nothing and delivered news with an "expect the worst, hope for the best" spin.

At the beach house the morning after, I tell Alex this, say it's highly unlikely I'm pregnant, even though I already excitedly sense that I am. Two weeks later, when I find out for sure, he says, "You lied to me!" It's a joke and also not at all a joke, and we go out to celebrate. He drinks three martinis and I have a glass of seltzer and we talk about baby names, but mostly we are both scared, though about different things. He's afraid a baby will cause irreparable harm to our careers, our relationship, and our lives together. I'm afraid that no matter how much he accepts fatherhood, he'll never forgive me for forcing him into it.

As pregnancies go, I have an easy one, and work my job at the tech company until my due date. The day after, I experience false labor and Alex takes the day off and we pace around the apartment and wait. The next day he goes back to work and I'm utterly lost without my own job to distract me from my life so I make a pineapple upside-down cake and eat it out of the pan while standing by a window spying at the neighbors with backyards. Will we ever be the neighbors with back-yards? Where will our kid play? What if I forget to make the kid lunch? What do kids eat? I check and recheck the infant supply drawer: dia-pers, diaper cream, doll-size nail clippers, a weird cone thing I've been told you use to suction snot.

Two days later, after a desperate call, my sister arrives. She walks with me all over Brooklyn. She swings with me on swings. She takes me to the movies and afterward, I have a beer. On the fifth day, she researches "foods to induce labor" and makes eggplant Parmesan. I go into labor that night.

The baby comes five days late in six hours with nine pushes. In labor I squeeze Alex's hand so tight it turns purple and clench my jaw so hard that I lose the crown on a back tooth. I also lose multiple liters of blood. There's talk of a transfusion but the "expect the worst, hope for the best" doctor says I should be fine even if the delivery room looks like a scene from *Evil Dead II*. When they wheel us away from the horror-movie room I am white as the sheet they've used to tie the baby to my body. "I can hold my baby just fine," I tell the nurse before we depart. "New mothers are unpredictable," she replies in a lighthearted tone that's also firm.

The chair arrives two days after the baby does.

The chair is contained in a six-foot-by-four-foot cardboard box and, on the unseasonably hazy-humid May afternoon after we bring the baby home, this box is carried out of a dented van by two men, dragged the six steps up our stoop, and dumped on its side in front of our building's front door. After the drop, one of the men gives the doorbell a courtesy ring, then they both jump back into the dented van and drive away before we even realize the enormous chair in the even bigger cardboard box is now blocking the building's only means of egress.

I'd known the chair would be a problem. I'd ordered it—a pale gray "glider" with a high back, lumbar support, and ergonomic arm height designed for "the most comfortable late-night feedings!" that would blend perfectly with the nursery's woodland-creatures theme— because I was afraid I'd be a bad mom and I thought the chair would help me be a better one. I ordered it after the unnecessarily high-design crib, the homemade baby food maker I'd never use, the stroller that cost more than my first car. I was an advanced-maternal-age pregnant woman of some means living in a capitalist society that convinced mothers these were the things they and their unborn fetuses needed to survive and thrive. I registered at Buy Buy Baby for the rest, the sleep sacks and the burp cloths, the My Brest Friend pillow the internet explains is essential if I want my breasts to stay my friends. I registered using a spreadsheet another mom had meticulously organized, thinking of every possible need and sharing widely among my circle of friends, a pregnant gang of doomsday preppers, except the doomsday was birth, and we could never be prepared.

I ordered the chair at a discount from a site whose dubious shipping system made the discount not worth the cost. I ordered it under the six-months-pregnant bouncy bloom, the good hormones kicking in, hair goddess thick, an air of unstoppable optimism all around me. I was healthy and happy, and, best of all, prepared. What could go wrong?

Well, this. Alex's reluctance about fatherhood put me in a tough spot; at least, that's the way it felt at the time. I'd long heard his laments about how babies ruined people's lives, made them uncool. I knew he thought motherhood would change me and us, and I was determined to be the exception to this rule, to prove him wrong. I wanted to make it look easy, *be* easy for him.

I wanted things to stay the same for him, but I secretly couldn't wait to change and transform. I saw motherhood as a chance to become a different, better, more sober, consistent person; saw it as the opportunity for a deep, essential, and primal homecoming. I thought we could compartmentalize our experiences: I could protect Alex from the worst of it and, in the process, preserve the longest and happiest relationship I'd ever had. I entered into this make-it-easy-for-the-man martyrdom voluntarily, reflexively, like it was the most natural way to be—even when it meant moving a hundred-pound chair by myself two days after giving birth.

From the moment the chair is dumped on our stoop, Alex is angry about it. At first he blames the movers, then he blames New York, then he blames me. "What the fuck were you thinking? Why do we even need this chair?"

The chair begins blocking the stoop at 3:30 P.M. Soon our neighbors will come home, soon they will understandably want to enter their homes.

I nurse the baby on the couch, I change the baby's diaper, I apply the stubby-belly-button salve to the belly-button stub, I put the baby in a fresh onesie and a sleep suit so there's no chance of asphyxiation from a blanket, even if the blanket is organic muslin, light as air. I place the baby stomach down, in the empty designy crib atop the world's tautest sheet. I turn on the white noise machine and the baby monitor. Then I walk to the kitchen, grab our largest butcher knife, and head down the stairs. I manage to push our building's front door open enough to slide my spongy maternity-pants-clad body out sideways and begin hacking at the thick cardboard box with the giant knife as if it is the *Revenant* bear and I must attack it to death in order to sleep inside its body. I cut down one side, then another, slicing and stabbing and goring angrily, my fury lodging seeds of resentment toward my husband that will bloom and grow and stay.

The cardboard is triple-ply, corrugated on the inside, held together with thick, heavy staples. By the time I free the expensive, unnecessary chair from the box, I'm sweating all over. There's a small gash on my hand, another one on the chair's arm. I release the chair from the cardboard and watch as all four sides of the box fall down around it, a magician's trick. I push it away from the front of the building's door, open the door and, with all my body's force, move the chair inside, ripping my fresh perineum stitches as I go.

The chair is now safely out of the way of the front door of the apartment building, maneuvered into a nook in the first-floor vestibule, where it remains until I find two Russian men whose Craigslist ad claims they can "move anything!" to carry it over their heads and up over an old banister and safely into the nursery with the mural of a forest and the stuffed animals and the poster of a baby deer.

That evening, I will bleed more than I've ever bled before. I'll ignore the pain of my thrashed vulva and focus instead on the pain of breast feeding through nipple blisters due to the baby's bad latch, the one the doula/the internet/all my "football" holds can't seem to fix. Later, when my husband asks if I'd like to watch *Breaking Bad,* I'll say yes even though I really mean no.

Nonrecognition aggression occurs when one domestic animal is uncharacteristically aggressive toward a companion animal after a period of separation. The problem is usually caused by unfamiliar pheromones that are most often released during moments of stress. These pheromones signal danger to the other animal or animals that live in the home, causing them to become aggressive.

A few days after the chair arrives, when the baby is five days old, Alex leaves to attend an off-site retreat for the fancy magazine where he works, which is held at a two-thousand-dollar-a-night resort on a beach in the Hamptons. Before he leaves, he takes the good cat, the tabby, to the vet for a checkup, and when she returns, she's wearing a cone and not only looks weird but also smells weird to the demon calico, who decides quickly that the punishment for a weird smell is death. When she's not actively trying to bite the tabby's throat, the calico howls and growls and makes ungodly sounds that sound like a ghost if a ghost wished everyone in their home dead. We call the vet to report this attempted cat homicide, but he just laughs and says, "Oh, hahaha, that's just nonrecognition aggression! Hahaha, it will pass in a few days."

Alex is gone for three nights. I am left alone with a five-day-old baby, bleeding nipples, a bleeding vagina, a tabby cat in a cone, and a calico out for unfamiliar blood. I tell my husband I'll be fine. I *am* fine, in fact. I'm talented at suffering. Look how strong I am!

We live in a railroad apartment with pocket doors that separate the rooms. I bring Cone Cat into our bedroom with the baby. Murder Cat spends the night trying to pry open the pocket doors, hissing, howling, pushing her white paw inside. The baby wakes up four times. The bed is wet with breast milk, blood, and, later, tears. When my husband calls the next day, I tell him everything is under control.

I'm a survivor, I'm surviving.

See?

Though I have three months maternity leave, I start taking work calls after the first week, as soon as Alex returns from his trip. I pretend to be aghast at this intrusion, but in truth I welcome it. I schedule check-ins while I am nursing and while I am sterilizing bottles and scrubbing breast pump parts. I want to hear gossip, I want to be needed for advice. The person I've chosen to cover my maternity leave is not incompetent but also not good, a strategic placeholder planted so everyone will miss me, so I will be needed, to showcase my comparative value. I don't think of how it would feel to be a placeholder, to be set up to fail or at best muddle through. In truth, I'm terrified of being replaced. I'm terrified they'll discover I'm not indispensable, that it's better without me.

I miss the noise of work, the chaos, the drama, the chatter. I do not yet know how to be quiet and still. Being alone with a new baby is all quiet stillness, more boring than anyone says. I am afraid of being alone with the baby, but I can't admit this so I make more pineapple upside-down cakes and a complicated recipe from *Cook's Illustrated* that involves sugaring pork fat. I redecorate the apartment and invite two of our friends I like best over for pork dinner and pineapple upside-down cake.

In the next few months, even after I return to work, I take on 90 percent of the childcare and 80 percent of the domestic work and when people tell me I'm so lucky that my husband does laundry and changes diapers, when they stare at him dreamily while he wears the baby in the baby carrier like they didn't know a man could do such things, like he is a dog playing the saxophone, a switch flips. I see only red. I become a nonrecognition aggression murder cat, out for blood. Everything he does is wrong and bad, everything I do is right and good.

"Why are you expecting your partner to live up to an outdated idea of masculinity?" an old therapist I haven't seen for years asks when I head in for an emergency session two weeks after I've given birth, nursing the baby under a blanket as we talk. I've complained that he's not fixing anything, that I wish he was handier around the house. I'm beginning to see the inefficiencies of our partnership, the problems in a system built for fun. "So what if he can't fix things? You believe your husband is not hypermasculine like your father, but what I've always heard from you is this is largely a good thing."

On the subway home, I begin to think of the traditional roles of masculinity and femininity. They'd always seemed so boring and restrictive, but when they're removed there's no clear delineation of how to balance all the adult tasks, no map to follow. My husband is not expected to bring home the bigger paycheck, or fix the kitchen sink. But I am largely, through biology, still trapped in the role of primary childcare provider. I also bring home the bigger paycheck and am the only one interested in fixing the kitchen sink. In this uncharted terrain we are meant to operate as equals—I can do anything he can do—which somehow, in our equation anyway, means I do everything.

It does not occur to me to say, "Can you help me with this?" I don't feel like I can ask him to take on more. Early fatherhood is a shock to him. He wasn't ready. Was I? It doesn't matter. I am protecting him in a way I'll never protect myself. I want him to sleep when I don't sleep, eat when I am not eating. I am at the beginning stages of becoming a woman I hate.

While on maternity leave, I take the baby on hours-long walks through Brooklyn, from the bridge to Sunset Park to the Gowanus Canal, ambling in a postpartum haze. Once I forget to look before crossing the street and a driver almost hits us, screams out the window, "Watch where you're going, lady! You have a *fucking baby!*"

I eat lunch alone in cafés, the baby strapped to my chest, drop crumbs atop the baby's downy head. I fall asleep during the day while breast-feeding, the baby's and my hearts beating each against the other; sob quietly in the middle of the night as I try and fail to rock the baby to sleep. It is the most intimate of times, nothing like it, the purest, most intense love. The most alone I have ever been.

My boss, the editor in chief of the site I work for within the tech company, announces her departure the day I return from maternity leave. I decide to go for her job, and I land it. With the promise of my new salary and benefits, Alex goes freelance, a decision we do not think out or discuss enough. He's also fully immersed in—and struggling with—writing a book, a struggle I have little compassion for and instead resent. While Alex wrestles with writer's block and emotionally checks out, I'm all-systems-go filling in the adult-living gaps.

In the fall, right before Thanksgiving—which we're hosting—he decides he needs a week away to fully focus and find the book's spine. I want to support him, so I agree. He absconds to a friend's cabin in upstate New York, leaving me alone to not only work and care for a baby but order the turkey, borrow the folding chairs, change the litter-boxes, clean the house in preparation for parental scrutiny, tuck away the messiest bits of our lives.

Three days before the holiday, with the baby on my hip and a to-do list in my hand, I break our agreed upon no-contact rule to call and alert him that *actually* his mother is arriving earlier than he'd told me, tomorrow instead of the following day. I'm exasperated, bubbling with rage. I can't hide it. It's obvious that I'm keeping score of every ball he drops and leaves me to pick up. More and more, our relationship is reduced to these petty domestic equations, my deepening bitterness math.

"Why are you calling me about this?" he asks, incredulous. He was *right* in the middle of writing, he says, his voice tight. He'd *finally* found some flow. "I fucked up, okay? You don't have to rub my face in it. What do you expect me to do?"

Looking back, I still don't know the answer. Why *did* I call him? What exactly was I hoping to achieve? Was it just to have him bear witness to my struggle? Or was I unconsciously too jealous of his work to leave him be?

We snipe at each other for the next twenty minutes, until I eventually slam down the phone. A year later, when Alex fails to turn in his book, he'll blame it on this conversation and others like it. If only I'd granted him uninterrupted work time, the project could have succeeded. Without me and my burdensome needs, he could've thrived.

For the first year of the baby's life, my weekday routine is parsed out into fifteen-minute increments—nurse shower nurse daycare drop-off subway office subway nurse bath nurse bed answer emails sleep for four hours begin again. When I'm away from the baby for too long, my breasts leak, no matter how I try to pump them dry. At the office, I'm often racing to the bathroom before meetings, quickly stuffing my bra with toilet paper so it doesn't drip.

Once, during a week when I forget to pick up the baby after work and arrive home to an empty apartment only to race the two subway stops back, late to daycare, our baby is the last one there; the same week my post-pregnancy hair begins to fall out and my post-pregnancy body remains unfamiliar enough that I'm still wearing maternity pants to work; I look through Alex's digital camera. He's been out with former co-workers. He's still drinking and smoking, carousing, attending events, his life less fractured than mine. There are pictures of revelry, close-up shots of cocktails, group selfies, contrasting shoes against a bar floor, an ironic cash register sign. There is also a series of five artistically shot photos of him. Smiling, blurry, handsome, at ease. Happy.

When he comes home later that night I ask about the pictures. I attempt to be subtle, but I am incapable of subtlety, so the words come out stabby, strange: "I looked at your camera. Who took those pictures of you last night?"

"Oh, I don't know. We were all passing around the camera. Maybe Steve."

"Steve took this picture? Really? Steve who came to Thanksgiving wearing dirty sweatpants?"

"Oh, right. I guess that was Jane. Why?"

"I don't know. These look like the pictures you take of someone you love."

I don't have the right words to tell him that I wish I was going out, I wish we were socializing together, I wish I felt at home in my body, I wish my tits weren't rocks, I wish I wasn't tired all the time, that I'm worried he'll leave me, that I know I've stopped being fun and am afraid I'll never find fun again. That I'm so overwhelmed and anxious, a curtain has dropped over my brain, that I've begun thinking dark thoughts. That I'm already sure I'm fucking this all up. That I don't recognize him, that I don't recognize myself.

"What are you saying? You're acting crazy."

What is marriage if not a thousand abandonments and a thousand returns, until, one day, maybe you don't. I am not ready for such realities. I know there are women whose Awakenings cause them to walk into rivers with pockets full of rocks. I know I do not feel safe with the people who are supposed to care for me and that I am increasingly incapable of caring for myself. But I don't have time for therapy, I don't seek treatment for my depression. I do not address the inequities in my marriage. Instead, I work.

In the winter after the baby's born, Alex and I lose our rent-controlled apartment when the landlord unexpectedly sells the building. We eventually find a place several subway stops deeper into Brooklyn, but our new rent is more than double what we had paid. One morning, rushing to the office while lugging a heavy laptop and my even heavier breast pump, I slip and fall near the subway stairs, shattering my right elbow, requiring emergency surgery to rebuild the joint. Two metal plates and three bolts later I'm left with a stiff robot arm, a year of physical therapy, and out-of-pocket medical bills topping out over $20K. We'd already drained our savings for the move. Alex makes less as a freelancer than he thought he would, a fraction of what he once did. Daycare costs more than a week's pay.

Now the walls are closing in. Now I'm driven by fear. My new position is high-pressure with a steep corporate learning curve. Doing it well requires my entire brain. Whatever creative dreams I had for myself now seem indulgent, frivolous, out of place. Attending to my mental health feels selfish and inconvenient, against every working-class doctrine I know.

It's an immense privilege to consider work as anything beyond basic survival. A life dedicated to creating art of any kind is, for most of us, precarious and unsustainable. A modern-day marriage of two artists is as financially sturdy as sand. I knew intellectually that I wanted to be a mother more than I needed to be a writer. I just hadn't calculated that I'd land in the role of primary provider and be faced with such a stark either-or choice. Nor had I anticipated the grief I'd feel when I realize that, short of some unforeseen fiscal miracle, I won't get both.

My blue-collar pragmatism quickly overrides all these flights of fancy. I stuff the bad feelings down. I set a goal to succeed as an executive at the tech company no matter what it takes, to create the kind of stability and security our family had yet to see and I myself had never known. As for most people, my labor becomes, once again, not about a "calling" but a means of getting by. A high-stakes game I need to win.

Corporate Barbie

I f I had a tendency toward workaholism before, my years at the tech company send it into overdrive. With increasing unrest at home, I become determined to succeed at work, to win every professional pie-eating contest, even if the prize is simply more corporate pie.

The tech company I work for was once a nimble, innovative, web 1.0 pioneer. But by the time I arrive in the 2000s, it's more than a decade old, essentially *geriatric* in internet years. A revolving door of CEOs fail to usher in a unifying or forward-looking company vision; they offer only scattered strategies, stale ideas. Employee morale is low. Overwrought HR "culture" initiatives rely heavily on retro company merch giveaways, nostalgia for what once was.

It's impossible to overstate how disorienting it is to operate inside a past-its-prime Fortune 500 wasteland like this, to climb to the multilayered upper echelons and stare into the hideously inefficient belly of such a beast. Success here requires not talent per se but hypervigilance: the ability to identify and eradicate obstacles with a sniper's precision; to machete your way through nonsensical systems; to turn work into an all-consuming war. All qualities that, at this moment in my life, I happen to have in spades.

My battles at the tech company begin early in my tenure. It's been months and, though I've been verbally promised a promotion, I still haven't *officially* landed my former boss's job. Instead, since returning from maternity leave, I've endured a series of high-level interviews with executives who don't know me or my work, along with a formal review of my résumé and a rigorous background check. Additionally, I'm required to submit to a 360-degree "internal evaluation," in which each of my colleagues is privately grilled regarding my current job performance, areas where I need to improve, and my potential for growth. All of it feels needlessly complicated and even invasive. Searching for other opportunities while I'm still leaking breast milk seems worse.

I'm already doing the bulk of the job for no extra pay, and have been for weeks. When I mention this to the "interim" vice president I now report to, she tells me to be patient, that I'm new to this department, these things take time. She's a rah-rah company evangelist, a woman in her forties who wore a bunny onesie to work on Halloween and maintains a bowl of candy on her desk year round. She presents a warm, huggy office-mom image. Under the artifice, I sense she's cold and slippery as an eel.

"How do *you* imagine the company should handle hiring for an *E4*?" she asks when I offer the slightest "is all this really necessary" protest. In practice, the job I'm going for is not much different than the one I already have. But the new position is *technically*, in corporate parlance, a level "E4:L2" (at least that's how I remember it. As likely: The CAPTCHA that makes up Elon Musk's kid's name or R2-D2). Whatever the label, this level is considered a bigger HR deal. Hence, the rigmarole.

"Should I tell the CEO?" Bunny-Onesie continues. "'You know, Jenn seems like a nice gal, let's just give her the job'?" Then, her tone as serious as if they're staffing for the CIA: "That doesn't seem like an especially responsible way to do business, does it?"

She delivers this last line with the kind of smug, grownup-in-the-room energy I'll encounter often during these years, a patronizing reminder that I'm out of place here, that, with my lack of an MBA, I'm a stowaway in this business with a capital "B." It's also foreshadowing: the tech company is a sluggish corporate tank operating at a centenarian tortoise pace. Every personnel change involves an arduous process like this one. No move can be made without cutting through reams of red tape.

A month after this conversation, I discover I've passed my E4:L2 review not by an announcement or a sunny "congrats!" email but when I receive invites to twenty-seven new meetings and I notice there's more cash in that week's pay. Once the promotion becomes official, the "interim" vice president is no longer my boss. I'm assigned instead to a senior vice president (SVP) I've never met who works three thousand miles away. When I email to introduce myself, I'm told by his assistant that he doesn't have time for regular check-ins, though they're going to "try."

In these first weeks as E4:L2, I'm essentially on my own in the tech company's Manhattan office, a dull gray cubicle farm with as much natural light as a submarine. My closest colleagues are in Northern California; the bloggers I manage work from home. I'm still doing all the work of my original job—my new manager's assistant explains there's no "head count" to "backfill" my previous role—but now that I've leveled up, I'm also expected to represent my department in multiple daily meetings, to formally communicate our "wins and worries" to senior teams. I have little context for business etiquette at this level. My only professional experience is in restaurants and publishing. Compared to this, Condé Nast was a rave.

I attend mandatory "Stand Up" meetings where I don't stand up but instead sit in gunmetal-hued Aeron chairs around boat-size conference-room tables and flush with heart-thumping anxiety awaiting my turn to speak. I pretend to absorb dreary stats sheets. I guess at the definition of "ROI." I characterize obvious opportunities as "low-hanging fruit." If I don't hear what I want the first time from a stake-holder, I put a pin in it. I learn we can always circle back, take the conversation offline. If there's a pain point, we'll take another deep dive.

In the 2010s, Silicon Valley loves a "disrupter," but I quickly discover what this translates to in real life is literally just *interrupting,* raising your hand in the middle of Mitch's overworked PowerPoint and blurting out, "Wait, why are we doing [terrible/expensive idea]? Who's this initiative actually *for?*" It's the Tom Hanks in *Big* tactic—so simple, it could be executed by a kid—and I begin to implement it as often as I can. It earns me a reputation as a shit starter and a maverick, which translates well in these white-collar rooms of mostly white-collared men, particularly because it's unexpected from a "creative type" and, more important, a girl.

The part of the company I run is the "lifestyle" section, a resourced-starved, understaffed afterthought of the "News" division, the unloved stepsister of better-funded and more-well-respected categories like Finance and Sports, which are run by men. I oversee a team of highly capable female writers and editors who cover fashion, beauty, fitness, recipes, parenting, pets, and PG-13-rated sex for an audience that's less edgy-cool coastal elite than it is down-home cozy, a *USA Today* for the digital age, all low-budget cooking and cleaning hacks and detailed reporting on Kate Middleton's lipstick shade.

It's a site I wouldn't necessarily read myself, but I understand the assignment. Unlike my last job, where I often struggled to find the right tone, my editorial vision for the tech company's lifestyle site is confident and clear. Having grown up working class in a house where *People* magazine was the primary news source, I'm near-preternaturally skilled at a job that entails getting inside the minds of mainstream audiences and knowing what makes them tick and—*most important*—click.

In addition to meetings and managing the day-to-day operations of our site, I'm in charge of an open-blogging, user-generated-content (UGC) platform, a project of which my bosses are especially proud. They boast about its utility in board meetings, rave to advertisers about how it bolsters "community" and "engagement," how it's all happy midwestern moms sharing their happy-mom tips. It is not. Even with our team's nonstop screening and moderation efforts, it's less populated by wholesome homemaking tricks than by racism, homophobia, and many, many, *many* sneaky user-generated dick pics.

The work never stops coming. I put in sixty-hour weeks. There's always a fire to extinguish, an ego to soothe, an errant dong to delete. In these early months, I relish most any work challenge. The productivity gives me purpose, clearly orders and arranges my days. I show up overprepared to every meeting. I carefully map out editorial goals. I fight for more resources for my team, mostly in vain.

I frequently field unsolicited feedback from top-tier male executives, which is often a nuisance, if not a total waste of my time. One afternoon, a senior male executive calls me "hot pants" in the office kitchen, a comment on the red trousers I wore earlier that week. Another morning, an SVP pulls me aside to talk about the number of mothers I've hired: *Is your ENTIRE staff pregnant?* The same day a high-up guy from marketing suggests that what the site I run *really* needs is more "nip-slips." I smile politely and ignore them. I tap into a well of competitiveness, a Sun Tzu–level of discipline I didn't know I had.

In every strategic, interpersonal way I initially failed at *Lucky,* I triumph in corporate life. The secret to my success is always-on mania, though at this time you'd probably characterize it as "passion" for what I do. If I'm not at my desk, I'm on my BlackBerry. When I'm out, I regularly interrupt friends' stories and life updates to hold up an index finger—*Just one second, I really need to address this*—and tap out emails, disregarding any damage I've caused to conversational flow. I never slow down long enough to consider how little I'm giving to my friendships, how uncomfortable it must be to sit with someone so checked out. Staying on top of my work is my top priority; doing so makes me feel responsible and important, a sensation I relish. I'm no longer the messy unreliable fuckup I felt like in my twenties, I think, but a sturdier person; respectable, established, moored.

I'm not only a distracted friend. Outside childcare duties, I'm barely present at home. After the baby's bath and bedtime routines, when Alex and I finally sit down to eat takeout, I often spend the meal refreshing my inbox rather than asking about his day. Later, I pull out my laptop and check traffic numbers while we're supposed to be watching *Game of Thrones.* Instead of reaching for him in bed, I lie awake with my back turned, proactively identifying and solving problems at the office in my head. Priding myself on my diligence, how little escapes my gaze.

In a capitalist society, onerous work is often as satisfying as it is depleting. We've been conditioned from a young age to find pleasure in accomplishment's rigors and strains. It feels natural to view my overwork as noble, to settle into that foundational groove of the brain. In these first high-achieving months, I revel in the rush of my own competence, but the accompanying stress means it's at the expense of the health of my central nervous system. Threats to my job real and imagined keep my amygdala firing throughout my days. Goals at the company I work for remain in flux; it's hard to predict which way to march. I survive multiple rounds of layoffs and I'm assured my department is not a future target, but my position never feels quite safe. The job provides my family's healthcare and our livelihood. By definition, I'm dependent on it. Keeping me motivated to work harder, to do as much as I can with less, is an institutional feature not a bug.

Within a few months, I'm visible enough within the company that someone from in-house PR asks if they can start pitching me out as a "lifestyle expert," explaining it will be good for my career to be more "high profile," an ambassador for the brand. Plus, she whispers conspiratorially, "it doesn't hurt to get this kind of attention around here."

I want the attention. As an E4:L2, I'm now caught up in an "employee retention"/stock reward plan with elaborate vesting rules, one that promises thousands in bonus money, but only if you maintain a high performance and remain at the company for several years, an incentive program as complex as any Ponzi scheme. Because my ambition is currently wrapped up in fiscal gain, because I've decided that what's wrong with my marriage is money—if Alex and I only had more of it I'm *sure* we'll resent each other less—I am quickly conditioned through this intermittent Pavlovian financial reinforcement to do even more to excel. I don't think about the fact that with each step further into this world, I'm recognizing myself less. That with all the strategizing and jargon parroting, I'm transforming into a kind of Corporate Barbie, not just toeing, but guzzling down the company line. Or that, with the finishing school makeover I'm about to sign up for, this transformation will be all but complete.

I say yes to the in-house PR team and I'm enrolled in media training, which is held in a fake studio in midtown in a building where you can purchase a gyro, a gold watch, and learn tai chi. Over the course of two days, my trainer-coach, Elaine, a handsome curly-haired brunette in red glasses who I feel sure I've seen on *CSI*, introduces me to each of the different types of TV appearances I may be called upon to do. I'm filmed sitting behind a fake anchor's desk like I'm a guest on a talk show and asked fake talk-show questions. I'm recorded standing next to a table topped with random props like Frisbees and sunblock and asked to describe each item succinctly, taught how to gesture at them but not block them with my hands. I'm instructed on the most photogenic way to sit on a high stool with no back, how to speak *to* the camera but not directly *into* it, how to answer the question you want to answer, instead of the one you're asked. Afterward, Elaine plays back the tapes and we analyze my responses, how convincing I am, how authoritative I look and sound.

"Oh boy, you fidget too much," Elaine says in a faint Queens accent. "And your smile's too big. You're showing too many teeth! . . . You see that? It's distracting when you talk with your hands." Elaine advises me to wear color on TV but never pattern; to always appear enthusiastic but, more important, calm and smooth. And it's not just a smooth demeanor I'm meant to project; this rule extends to my hair ("Never, ever go on without a blowout!") and my body, too. I still don't fit into my prebaby clothes and, while I haven't necessarily considered this a problem, Elaine does: "Spanx are a godsend for TV," she tells me, staring at the fleshy lumps stretching against my viscose trousers. I wish I could disappear into her too-high stool. "Did you know you can wear two pair at once? Even three?" I wonder what she says to her male trainees, but I don't bother to ask.

Soon after my time with Elaine, I start serving as a tech company spokesperson, spouting corporate talking points in satellite radio tours and on live local newscasts, becoming a regular "what's trending now" expert on something called BetterTV. I leave the house at 4:00 A.M. to make an appearance on the *Today* show, my stomach snug in doubled-up shapewear while I discuss parents' back-to-school tips. Afterward, I head straight to the office to edit parenting stories, moderate the few UGC mom blogs that offer mom tips, a reminder that I haven't spent quality time with my own offspring in days. One morning, when discussing sex and dating trends on-air with Hoda and Kathie Lee, I momentarily blank on a question when I realize I myself have not had sex in weeks. I can't remember when Alex and I even last hung out outside of the couch. In front of a camera, I promote what it is to have a healthy "lifestyle." Behind it, I barely have a life.

For *The Wall Street Journal,* I'm photographed wearing an indie-designer blouse, five-inch stilettos, and a tweed pencil skirt so tight it restricts my gait. The photos are for a feature about how tech companies are becoming more glamorous, how "work wear" now goes beyond the hoodie, how we're as stylish as our legacy-media peers.

In these pictures, I'm slathered in makeup, my hair in an Elaine-approved blowout, my false eyelashes applied by someone else. The accompanying story reads, "Ms. Romolini aims for a look that is both pretty and powerful." Then: "'I manage a lot of people and I'm in a lot of high-profile meetings,' she said. 'I want to make sure I can walk into any room, but at the same time I don't want to take myself too seriously or take fashion too seriously.'"

The quotes are just another careful calculation, a strategic part of the act. I don't feel pretty or even particularly powerful. I lack anything close to this portrayed insouciance. The truth is I'm taking all of this *dead seriously*. I thought about that outfit I couldn't walk a step in for weeks.

I keep performing. I don slim blazers. I run meetings. I present decks. I don't have impostor syndrome so much as impersonator awareness. I'd never pictured this kind of life for myself. I can't believe this is me. Still, the people who know me best seem unfazed by my new business persona. More, they're pleased with my success. Now that I'm a manager, I talk to my dad about my work often. Unlike my writing, he understands the fundamentals of running a business, identifies with my stress. I'll take any excuse to connect with and feel closer to him, to receive his approval for my decisions, for us to relate. My mom says she's worried I'm working too much, but I can tell she's equally proud. She enjoys the bragging rights of my TV appearances, calls to tell me her friend saw me on Anderson Cooper's new daytime talk show and you know what? He thought it was her in a blond wig.

The best part of my job is, by far, managing writers. Unlike many of my corporate peers, I understand what goes into writing and editing, and I'm keenly aware of my staff's challenges, what motivates someone to do this kind of job well. As a result, I don't look at their work as commodified, disposable "content production" but as something of value that requires skill. I shower praise for particularly well-crafted sentences. I delight in clever headlines. I dedicate a large portion of each month to group brainstorming and collaborating, challenge writers to be creative and inventive, push editors to elevate dull language, to make the daily slog of stories as smart as we can. I miss my own writing, but there's zero time for it. I decide training others will do. I neglect corporate duties to vet story pitches. Even when I'm overwhelmed with other work, I roll up my sleeves to help a writer who seems particularly stuck. For this effort, I earn the staff's trust and respect. The highest reward a boss can get.

When positions open up, I fill them with hardworking misfits and weirdos, down-on-their-luck single moms, reporters whose talent I sense has been undervalued elsewhere, women I see something in, women who need a break like I once did. I'm generous with salaries and fight to bump up bonuses, a stealthy Robin Hood on an inside job to rob the corporate pot. I tell new hires to never accept the first HR offer, sneakily reveal the specific number they should ask for, what I think they can score. When I find out I have an employee "entertainment" budget, I spend every last dollar hosting elaborate team dinners, running up the bill at New York institutions like the Russian Tea Room and Sammy's Roumanian steak house (RIP), where we get so drunk on icy vodka, we dance the polka, all on the company dime. Despite the occasional managerial misstep (mistakes I'll torment myself over in the moment and regret for years), I'm mostly a compassionate and intuitive leader. I'm skilled at zeroing in on employees' strengths and working around their weaknesses, at making the interpersonal puzzle pieces fit.

Into my second year as E4:L2, the company hires a new CEO (the fourth since I've been there). This man will soon be fired in an embarrassing public scandal, but before he is, he manages to order and execute another reorganization of our division, with more layoffs.

This is bad news for the group of elite news journalists who were hired a year earlier on someone's media relevancy/prestige whim and then given nothing to do. But it's actually *good* news for my team, our HR rep explains. "Lifestyle is performing so well!" he says, his voice sugary. "We're bringing in an *experienced* general manager to bolster your success." This new person will oversee me and my department, take all the pesky E5 and E6 business dealings off my plate. It's not a "demotion," HR guy explains enthusiastically when I express concern, but an "extra layer of support." I'm skeptical. *Another* senior executive? The company is already so top heavy, it's a wonder we haven't toppled over and collapsed.

Even a broken clock is right twice a day. In some miracle of fate, this HR decision is actually correct. My new boss, Jessica, is a hard-charging, jokes-cracking, commuter-flats-wearing, no-bullshit-tolerating dynamo I can't help but admire and feel aligned with right out of the gate. Jessica has a double MBA and global executive experience and possesses all the business polish I lack. She speaks the suits' language and commands their respect in an impressive way I can't, at least not yet, though she's eager to show me how.

In our first week working together, Jessica observes me running hot in a contentious meeting, arguing with a colleague I not so subtly can't stand. She calls right after, her tone friendly but firm. "Listen, between us chickens, I too think Chad should eat a dick. But if you want them to listen to you, Romolini, you've got to slow your roll. A little sugar in these situations goes a long way."

The feedback is reasonable, her delivery kind. But I can barely sit through the critique. For overachievers, having a manager you respect and admire is often a double-edged sword, something akin to a curse. Jessica will turn out to be the best boss I'll ever have. I'm cowed by her competent, calming presence. I'll do anything to avoid her criticism, to exceed her expectations and, in turn, receive her praise. With Jessica as my boss, I feel even more pressure to succeed: I can't tolerate letting her down. In these first weeks, she sets a series of stretch goals

I cannot imagine meeting. But I don't tell her this. Instead, I throw myself further into the job. By working even more hours, I meet each and every one.

With two of us now pushing, the boulder moves faster up the hill. Jessica works intercompany systems to our advantage. She fights and wins budget battles, captures more head count, justifies more sales and marketing resources. She lands high-profile distribution deals and multimillion-dollar ad campaigns. The site starts regularly reaching 50 million readers a month. Within six months, we're bringing in $42 million a year. Depending on the week, we're either the most popular or the second most popular digital destination for women not just in the United States but in the world. Though my corporate skin may still feel foreign, I'm starting to get comfortable in it. We're winning, and the winning feels good.

I spend my days in a busy Manhattan office surrounded by people, overloaded with responsibilities, my brain cluttered with a series of never-ending tasks. Alex works from home alone in a small, window-less "office" in our scantly furnished apartment deep in Brooklyn surrounded by boxes we have yet to unpack. He's increasingly iso-lated, rarely spends time with another adult besides me. He's given up on his book, though he hasn't told me this yet. He's also strug-gling to generate consistent freelance work and bring home consist-ent pay. He's never encountered failure like this, never had to fight his way out of a corner in the ways I have; this dip in his success trajectory is entirely new. He personalizes every rejection, chastises himself for every minor mistake, is frequently mired in shame. I sym-pathize, but I struggle to understand. I find his lack of industry terri-fying, his cynical outlook intolerable. Though he never asks directly, it's clear what he needs when I get home is extra tenderness, a pres-ent and patient ear. What he needs from me is a lot. I have so little to give.

We start avoiding more subjects—his work; my work; the back taxes he owes, which I've just discovered; the apartment we currently live in, which he hates; why we no longer ever see friends. Even with the money I'm making, we've known for months that we need more to maintain a life in Brooklyn, to pay for preschool, to keep the fridge stocked with organic fruit, to save. I still love New York as much as I always have. But it's becoming increasingly hard to justify living here, or to know if we still belong in this city where we met and fell in love. We've changed so much.

One Sunday in late January we treat ourselves to brunch at Bubby's in DUMBO and, afterward, decide to stroll the new Brooklyn Bridge Park. It's a clear, sunny winter's day, crisp and cold but warm enough to be comfortable in the right clothes. Our snowsuit-clad toddler races a safe distance ahead of us. We walk behind, holding hands, for the moment at least, close. When we arrive at the new carousel, we discover it's not open yet. I scoop the baby up instinctively, bring our attention toward the river, point out bridges, identify the ships. The distraction works, a meltdown over the unavailable ride narrowly avoided. We're quiet for a minute, enjoying this small parenting triumph. The baby occasionally punctuates our silence: "Boat!" "Boat!"

"Hey, so about the L.A. thing," Alex says, restarting a conversation we've been batting around for weeks, a move he's wanted for months. He's wearing the big black parka we bought on sale together and a blue wool hat we've shared for years, unsure if it was originally his or mine. When I was pregnant, he let his thick, black beard grow in, and it suits him; he hasn't shaved since.

The baby starts squirming. Alex holds out his arms and wordlessly instigates a transfer, hugs the baby close, twirls and dramatically bounces up and down, is met with giggles, delight. Despite his initial fears about fatherhood, he's an attentive dad, a natural caretaker. And he's trying harder to stay on top of things at home while I'm out working my big important job, even though I often bitch about how nothing's done right. Just the week before, I dropped everything to train down to DC with other tech company executives to record an interview with Michelle Obama at the White House, an opportunity too good to pass up. Doing so left Alex at home on deadline with zero childcare and an eighteen-month-old with the flu. When I returned, I corrected him for using Tylenol instead of Advil to bring down the baby's fever, scolded him for not heeding the pediatrician's advice. The micromanaging is a form of control, a long-embedded trauma response, a way to stave off the nonstop guilt I feel for not being there, for not being a perfect mom. I haven't connected any of this yet.

"I've been thinking," he says now, steeling himself against the wind. "We should consider the L.A. thing. There are a lot of reasons it makes sense."

He's been offered a job in Los Angeles at a just-launched men's website everyone's excited about, a job where he'll be on staff again. It's a job he wants, with a secure salary we need. I'm unsure if it's the right move, but he's all in, selling hard. People we know recently moved to L.A. and they love it, he reminds me. *We have friends out there, with kids.* Our Brooklyn apartment is too expensive and it's never felt like home, he says, building his case. L.A. is so much cheaper than New York; there, we can afford to rent an entire house.

We're at the river's edge now. Spread out behind Alex is the city I love and fought to be a part of, iconic skyscrapers I've worked and reported stories in, the familiar bridges and streets I've walked and run and ridden along countless times, places where I've built the most con-sequential parts of my adult life.

I stare at Alex's face and then at the baby's. They've always looked so much alike. They share the same expression now, two sets of wind-swept winter cheeks, identical brown eyes squinting in the sun.

I'm thirty-eight, but the truth is I don't know myself, at least not well enough to confidently assert what I want. Alex and I have been together for seven years, but for all our interdependence, we don't understand how to be adult partners, lack the pragmatism required to collaborate on big life decisions like these. When you don't have a specific outcome in mind, you may as well roll the dice. Though I never imagined living in California, I get caught up in Alex's enthusiasm, this uncharacteristic burst of optimism and hope. Maybe this is just what our family needs, I think, a fresh start.

Pulling a Geographic

"P ulling" or "doing" "a geographic" is a term used by those in recovery circles to describe moving to a new location with the hope of leaving one's problems in the old one, discarding toxic habits and tendencies on a past-you curb, along with that futon you bought in 2002. While a new environment may *occasionally* jump-start an addict's recovery process, it's more often than not a false promise, a last-ditch bargaining chip when you've got few cards left to play.

When we think about life-annihilating addiction, most of us imagine a problematic relationship with drugs and/or alcohol, maybe gambling, food, or getting it on. However, since at least the 1990s, more and more research shows that many of us become chronically addicted to work, engaging with our careers in ways that devastate both our physical and our mental health.

According to the Workaholics Anonymous handbook, those with a predisposition to overwork often grow up in chaotic homes. In adulthood, hyperfocus on their careers creates a sense of control in their lives, allowing them to disassociate from painful memories, from grief, from a poor or weak sense of self. These types of workaholics unconsciously, repeatedly seek out chaotic workplaces in order to maintain a high level of stress that's familiar from childhood, to keep their brains in an activated state. In these cases, workaholism becomes a *physical* addiction to stress hormones like adrenaline. It may also be something called a *process* addiction, as sufferers become addicted to the routines and rituals of working, and find themselves lost when and if they stop.

Like many addictions, workaholism is cumulative: over time, sufferers become dependent on the fleeting, drug-like euphoria that comes from accomplishment; the positive, secure, confident feelings—absent in the rest of their lives—that come with a pat on the back from a boss or a good performance review. Over-immersion in work acts as a kind of antianxiety, a controlled space to fully submerge in and calm an unquiet mind. Workaholics like these develop a dependency on their own competence, an outsize need to be efficient, productive, to do things "right."

Understanding and identifying workaholism in the United States is complicated by the fact that our country's unifying ethos—late-stage capitalism—teaches us to exalt the labor of moneymaking and to calculate our worth based on our productivity, to conflate happiness with success. This capitalist conditioning begins nearly as soon as we are sentient. Certainly by the time we reach school age, most Americans have learned that a sure way to be liked and even loved is to achieve.

Add to this the grim cult of overwork popularized in the 2010s, an omnipresent #hustleharder social media culture, and the onslaught of a #girlboss ethos that blurred the lines between life and work and positioned the performance of entrepreneurship and an impressive at-work identity as fundamental to a successful life. Add to that the holier-than-thou virtues of a Protestant work ethic pushed on Americans for centuries, and it often feels like if you're not giving work everything you've got—even if you know the physical, emotional, and social toll it takes—you're a loser. For survivors of trauma, those whose foundational feelings of unworthiness create a chasm that can never quite be filled, this dysfunctional relationship with work is often even more complex, harder to identify, and extraordinarily difficult to disentangle from.

With more success, there's more depth to bury internal

wounds. Wounds that, no matter how hard we push, no external accomplishment—or geographic change—can possibly heal.

I'm living in California and my mother and I are on the phone fighting. She's mad because she wants to come and stay with us, to see her grandchild, but I've told her it's a bad time, which it is. It's a sunny early morning in Los Angeles in late May, already hot. I'm driving down Wilshire Boulevard in my newly leased Prius, having just renewed my license for the first time in years.

Alex and I have been in L.A. for two months. We managed to pull off the move just weeks after our day by the river, breaking our Brooklyn lease and throwing too much money at a team of movers who packed and transported our belongings with the delicacy of fugitives on the lam. When I told my bosses about Alex's new job, they agreed to my relocation so long as I work out of the Los Angeles office and am prepared to travel to other offices whenever asked. The tech company's L.A. flagship is located in a sterile corporate complex on the west side of the city. I live fourteen miles away, on the east side, a rookie Angeleno mistake. Each day, no matter how early I leave, I must decide between sitting on the hot, dusty freeway in traffic that moves one mile every ten minutes or driving the "back roads," guided by GPS, making wild four-lane left turns through the City of Angels and trying not to crash.

I am now fifty minutes into my ninety-minute commute. Through the car's Bluetooth speaker my mother has been pushing against my decision about her visit the entire way.

"I'm your mother, how can you say there's a bad time for me to come?"

"I'm your mother. I just want to stay on your couch for *two* nights."

"I'm your mother and I live three thousand miles away."

She repeats the fact that we are biologically related again and again, as if the words mean something different in repetition, as if in repetition, she'll get her way. It doesn't matter what I say, she can't hear me. Even when I was a kid, her agenda always usurped my needs. I know she loves me, but she seems to actively choose not to listen to or understand me. It's been like this since we were singing in the kitchen in Southwest Philly, since I lied about my report cards, since the times in adolescence when she slapped my face to make me shut my mouth. For as far back as I can remember, I've felt intolerably unheard and unseen in my mother's presence, too difficult and unlovable to be listened to and understood, emotionally on my own. I don't yet have words for these feelings, I won't uncover even the concept of "boundaries" for years. But with the move west and more distance, something's shifted. A crack's formed, shedding a sliver of light on areas of my psyche I'd intentionally kept dark. Since our move to Los Angeles, I've started having violent recurrent dreams about my mother. I wake up shaking. The pain suddenly feels more acute.

The truth is my mother feels abandoned by me too. This conversation is nothing new. Into her second glass of red wine on our last visit, she cornered me by the dishwasher and began sobbing: "I just feel so rejected by you!" It's not just the move, it's the years of missed baby showers and communions, the cousins' weddings I'm invited to but never attend, how infrequently I've visited my grandmother in the home. I've made different choices than my mother did, chose a path outside of the tight-knit fabric of our family, failed to heed that obligatory pull. When I was growing up, she and my dad had opportunities to leave—to California, to Massachusetts, to places further away—and chose not to pursue them.

Instead, they took care of their grandparents, then their parents. Bought them new clothes and paid for their haircuts, cleaned their homes, picked them up for diner breakfasts and family dinners, did the caretaking even when they didn't want to, even when they resented it, even when it felt like too much. My teen parents grew up to be adults of immense integrity who built their lives around a sense of duty, concerned more with the physical welfare of others than with overcoming their own psychic wounds. They put down roots and watched them grow, stayed in the same place and stayed friends with people they'd known since they were in their teens.

The choices I've made were possible, in part, because of the financial independence my parents achieved: they simply never needed me the way their families needed them. This is what we think of as progress, of course, even if in practice it doesn't always feel that way. My life is not necessarily happier for making different choices. Into my thirties and forties, my adulthood is unsettled, lacking community, my identity fragmented. Still, my life, such as it is, is my own.

Through the car's speakers my mother's voice becomes louder and tighter; I can hear the familiar vocal tics, how close she is to tipping over into tears or rage, or both. At home, I have a willful two-year-old and a husband who is increasingly, sinkingly depressed, our geographic doing little to improve his mental health. At his new job, he writes a popular weekly column that's ostensibly about football, but it's mostly a reflection on his life in Los Angeles, about us. It's the best and most intimate work he's ever done. If you read between the lines, you see that it's the most mournful too.

Since the move, we rarely see each other. I leave the house at 6:00 A.M. and rush every night to get back home for bedtime, then work more. I clean the floors and the toilet because Alex won't. I book the doctor's appointments and look up the swim lessons, research the preschools and order the new crib sheets, make sure the daycare cubby is always stocked with sunblock and an extra pair of pants, am called frequently when it's not. My family's survival depends on my keeping it all together, and I am barely keeping any of it together.

The tension with my mother is ramping up, in this conversation, and in our lives.

"Mom, I just don't feel safe with you right now," I tell her, my voice cracking.

"How do you think that makes me feel?"

I can't consider this. I can barely consider my own feelings, let alone hers.

————————————

By the time we arrive in Los Angeles, my good boss, Jessica, is long gone, having resigned abruptly months before for a better job. For days after hearing the news of her resignation, I cry whenever I'm in private, bereft. Before she leaves, Jessica secures me a stock package as a reward for the hard work we did together. It's a generous and thoughtful parting gift, though I can't cash any of it in for years.

After Jessica leaves, HR tells me they're considering putting me in charge. Maybe I can even level up to an E5 or E6 this time, which would qualify me for an assistant, which in all these years of working in senior roles I've never had. *Let's see how you do,* the HR rep says. But the promise is torn away as quickly as a Charlie Brown football, my gullibility and misplaced trust as shameful and thick-headed, the company's commitment to my career growth an ongoing trick.

Instead, when I arrive in L.A., I'm assigned a new boss. Bob is a golf-tan man with a heavily whitened smile who'd made his name in New York finance and loves to discuss: his Hollywood Hills home, his DVD collection, his Porsche. Bob likes me well enough, but what he likes best is giving me all of his work. I now oversee not just the lifestyle site but three others, including the online home of a famously "nice" celebrity who is, offscreen—according to her beleaguered staff—a Gollum who's impossible to please. I rarely edit anymore. I don't have time. I'm now in charge of a team of thirty-five people, ten of whom directly report to me.

Bob doesn't have kids. His leadership style is that of a man who spends his nonwork time collecting expensive Bordeaux, reading nose-hair clipper reviews, and watching *Die Hard with a Vengeance* on repeat. His expectations and demands are free of consideration for parental obligation. Like many men, he has the luxury to behave as if children raise themselves. Under Bob, my expanded role requires that I'm continually on the move.

One week, I'm called to Vegas to speak to advertisers about global digital strategy. The next, I'm sent to the London office to train the U.K. team. I travel cross-country for mandatory "check-ins" with the New York staff. I slip into pointy-toed heels to fly up and attend high-level meetings at the company's Northern California flagship, meet vice presidents at their stand-up desks, hold court in meetings alongside the company's overconfident CEOs.

I'm adaptable and adventurous enough to derive a bit of pleasure from all this jetting around, even if it's rushed. And I remain grounded enough to feel grateful for an opportunity to see the world on someone else's dime. Still, the schedule—plus the late-night hotel wine I knock back to put me to sleep and the extra iced coffees I nurse all day to keep me awake—begins to take a toll. I don't know it yet, but I've developed a gastric ulcer, have started guzzling Pepto wherever I am, my workaholism now as cliché as an eighties stockbroker dad's.

The travel takes a toll on my marriage too, puts extra pressure on Alex to hold things down at home when he's already struggling himself. My absence keeps us from establishing family routines, a life for ourselves where we live now. We skip the get-to-know-you parent social at the new preschool after I miss a flight. I turn down an invitation to a neighbor's May Day potluck because I'll be out of town. We say no to enough catch-up drinks requests from the few people we know in L.A. that eventually they stop asking. Instead of putting in the effort required to build a community here, nearly all my energy remains in service of my job.

Four years in and I'm still a rising star at the tech company. The pressure is high to beat my last quarter's performance and then do it again every quarter after that. Every hour of my weekday time is now accounted for, eaten up by meetings that appear on my calendar like kudzu, meetings I attend by phone sometimes long into the night. I deliver better results and manage a stronger team than most every male executive at my level. My performance reviews are uniformly high. Still, one afternoon an assistant shares a file that shows I earn at least $100,000 less than each of my male peers, some making $150K to $175K more, a fact that makes me feel both stupid and incensed. I thought I was at least competitively compensated. I'd been told there was no more money whenever I requested a raise. The Charlie Brown football again.

I bring the disparity to Bob, who briefly looks up from his favorite work activity (stalking his enemies on LinkedIn) to tell me there's nothing he can do. When I bring the issue to HR, I'm offered more stock, which I take though I'm increasingly convinced none of it will amount to more than corporate dust. The company is in bad shape. The latest CEO is bringing in nonstop press coverage that paints us as even more of a clown-car operation, a bumbling joke.

This new CEO is a young, pretty, wealthy, thin, *female* Silicon Valley star, a tech-world unicorn the industry can't stop gossiping about, a woman who cultivates a basic rich-lady-with-a-stylist wardrobe, which, coming out of a world of fleece vests, is remarkable enough to land her in *Vogue*. She's the focus of countless columns on the corporate gender gap, a fixture in essays about work-life balance, the merits of her appointment hotly debated in newspaper op-eds. *A LADY! Running a company! AND she's a new mom? What does it all mean?!* Inside the company, and away from the breathless glass-ceiling intrigue (or glass cliff, depending on who you read), this CEO often appears over her skis, falters in important meetings, earns an internal reputation as a person who's careless with power, contemptuous toward employees, and occasionally, outright cruel.

The first time we meet is on one of my trips to Northern California. It's a Thursday afternoon, I'm just offstage after giving a company-wide presentation about a new editorial initiative, one my team and I had spent weeks preparing, a presentation I was so nervous to deliver I'd dry-heaved in a nearby ladies' room just before going on. The stage is in the corporate cafeteria on the company's main "campus." It's a cavernous room that seats thousands, garishly decorated to look like a fifties diner if they had diners in space. I'm still shaking from the performance anxiety, my J. Crew stretch-twill suit damp with sweat. As I weave through the space diner on my way out to the airport to catch a flight back to L.A., I feel a tap on my shoulder.

"Jenn!"

It's Jim, a colleague from corporate finance I've known for years and like.

"Great job on the talk! Did you know _____ is here?" He drops the CEO's name with fanboy reverence, as if he's said *Beyoncé*. "She just saw you speak. You two should really meet!"

Jim guides me back through the astro-themed eatery. We pass tables piled with baskets of beet chips, slim fridges stocked with upscale seltzer and blueberries, a frozen yogurt machine with an elaborate accompanying sundae station that's attracted a crowd. When we finally reach the CEO, she's standing in a corner surrounded by men in bland button-downs. She's a petite woman in a loud-patterned, wide-skirted, tea-length designer dress that's swallowing her frame a bit; out of a place in this otherworldly geek dreamscape or, at least, impossible to miss.

When we're introduced, the CEO holds out her soft, small hand and I shake it. She responds with a chortle, a glimmer of recognition. Apparently, she knows who I am.

"Oh my god, you run the lifestyle site, don't you?" she says, pulling her hand back, still chuckling. "Did you know Anna Wintour told me our lifestyle site is *hideous*? No, wait! She actually said it's *grotesque*. She can't *bear* to look at it! Frankly, neither can I!"

The young, pretty, wealthy, female CEO in the expensive Nordstrom-personal-shopper dress blurts out these sentences gleefully. It's as if she couldn't wait to tell someone, like what she's communicated is a most charming anecdote or, at least, news I can use. I smile and nod in response, give a little fake laugh even though my face betrays me, burns as if I've been slapped. I'm not impressed by this woman, or really even intimidated by her title. But none of that matters. The weird trick of power is, whether you respect it or not, it can always tear you down.

It's not just the CEO's social foibles that are causing strife. She's recently instituted a series of "Let Them Eat Cake!" employee initiatives that have the entire global workforce up in arms. The worst is a staff rating system she's designed to wipe out a large percentage of our teams without calling it a layoff, a word she forbids us to use (we're told to say "remix" instead). It's a devious policy whereby managers rank each of their employees on a scale from 1 to 5 and then, when you add and divide the numbers, the final average must be within a small percentage of the number 3. If it isn't, you must re-rank the employees until it is. Each fiscal quarter, a certain percentage of your employees *must* be high-performing 5s, and that same percentage must be low-performing 1s.

There are zero loopholes, no exceptions will be made. You are not allowed to rate all of your employees 3s to make things equal; you cannot argue with HR that you manage a rock-star team of 4s and 5s. Even if everyone who works for you is doing a great or at least serviceable job, this new policy forces you to claim otherwise. If an employee receives a low score over subsequent quarters or more than once in the same year, they are automatically "transitioned out." More plainly: fired, with cause.

The system will ultimately result in hundreds of firings, a mass layoff under any name. Since the terminations are considered performance-based, the company is not required to offer severance packages. Those who are fired won't receive a dime. The policy saves the company hundreds of thousands, if not millions, of dollars. It remains the most cynical and sadistic cost-cutting method I've ever seen.

The CEO calls a mandatory meeting to discuss the system, which (no surprise) no one likes. We're asked to submit questions and concerns and told that this is where they'll be addressed. But the CEO, who's earning $900,000 *a week* to do her job, arrives with a different agenda. Instead of answering questions or even placating us with inspiring lip service, she sits down and stares into a camera that's telecasting this meeting to employees worldwide. Then, smiling a wide smile, she holds up a copy of the 1946 children's book *Bobbie Had a Nickel*. She's a thirty-seven-year-old multimillionaire responsible for the fiscal fate of thousands. Without explanation, she repositions herself in a corporate-office chair on a stage in a fake diner in Northern California and proceeds to read *Bobbie Had a Nickel* aloud to a global team of thirteen thousand adults.

Bobbie had a nickel all his very own. Should he buy some candy or an ice cream cone?

Should he buy a bubble pipe? Or a boat of wood?

Bobbie sat and wondered, Bobbie sat and thought. What would be the NICEST thing a nickel ever bought?

I'll never know. I close my laptop before she finishes. I've seen enough.

We become who we pretend to be goes the old Vonnegut adage, so we must be careful about who we pretend to be. At work, I put up a stink about the CEO's ranking system to anyone who will listen, scream at Bob behind closed doors that I'm not going to do it, that this is unjust garbage, that I'll simply refuse. Lying about my employees' job performance goes against everything I say I stand for, far outside my moral code. But I don't quit over it. I don't even threaten to leave. Instead, I implement the policy. I make it work like I always have, even though I know by carrying the CEO's filth water, I'm part of the problem. I'm aware I'm crossing a serious ethical line.

The longer I stay at the tech company, the more my priorities skew. I can't stomach my behavior, but I can't stop either. I have only a year before my biggest stock package vests; at this point, it could amount to enough money to buy us a house. I'm desperate to hold on. We've been in Los Angeles for months and I haven't made any new friends.

I'm barely keeping up with anyone from home. My mother's still calling, I'm still putting off her visit. Outside of Alex, the closest people in my life are now almost without exception my co-workers. More accurately, my closest friends are my employees, who like me but—let's be honest—are also paid to talk to me.

With the new ranking protocol, things are increasingly strained. One staff reporter I hired and respect calls on a Monday afternoon and resigns without notice, tells me it's her last day. "Jenn, you know I'm better than this," she says. I'd rotated her into the low-performing 1 position that quarter, though she didn't deserve it (the problem being, no one did). The reporter's exit leaves a major hole in the team's daily production, one we scramble to fill. Company drama like this is escalating, feels all-consuming. It's becoming harder and harder to relate to anyone outside the cult of where I work.

On the weekends, in the afternoons, while the baby naps across the hall, I lie down on our old bed, which is too big for our new bedroom in the dark little bungalow Alex chose for us because I was too busy working to come on the trip. I stare blankly at our new bedroom ceiling for hours, feeling numb.

Our room is right next to an avocado tree so big and so close that its roots threaten to subsume the house. At night, the avocados (a non-delicious variety, we're disappointed to find) fall off their branches with a thud that scares away the wild-eyed possums that frequent our new backyard but does not faze the rats, who we hear feasting on the fruit while we're trying to sleep. Between the rats, the nightmares about my mother, and my guilt over the ranking policy, I'm sleeping less and less.

At night, when the rats finish feasting, I watch them scurry up and along the wires that keep our house connected to other houses just like ours—a tidy row of bungalows with sprays of golden yarrow and bright fuchsia bougainvillea blooming out front. The plants attract a kaleidoscope of butterflies that fly beneath the stories-tall palm trees that sway high above us in the perpetually blue sky. Inside, the house we rent is small and shadowy, crawling with brown spiders and red-eyed termites, and flanked by rats. But outside, it's a visual paradise, a *Truman Show*–perfect block so pretty it looks fake. Our front yard is even enclosed by a white-picket fence. I've recently set up a sprinkler in an effort to keep the jasmine plants alive and, in the late evenings, we turn it on and let the baby run through the spray. When the light shines on the water's dome, it makes rainbows. Sometimes Alex joins, and I imagine we must look so happy, smiling at neighbors as they stroll by, watching as the sun goes down and the few clouds above us turn cotton-candy pink.

Moving always brings forth a kind of disorienting emptiness. It's beautiful here, but I'm too displaced to enjoy it. I blame the move for our problems, transfer my despair to Los Angeles as an idea, to the city's unfamiliar quirks, lean into its unfair clichés (The traffic? The *worst*! The people? Just *too nice*!). The truth is simply that this beautiful city does not feel like mine. I miss New York, but it's not just New York. It's the entire Northeast American coast. It's the smells of winter, the trees, the gruff confrontations, the beaches and boardwalks at the Jersey Shore, the ways people I grew up around connect, the coffee from the chain of convenience stores that exist only at home, the comfort in knowing that—even if I didn't see them—my oldest friends were an hour's train or car ride away. I feel a throbbing homesickness, a lack of center or belonging, a profound loneliness that's been gnawing at me since long before we even left. Maybe even more than New York, I miss myself.

One Saturday night in the fall, friends from Brooklyn are in town. We have dinner at an outdoor restaurant that serves upscale charcuterie and smells of woodsmoke. We order three bottles of wine. After dinner, we head back to our house, send the babysitter home. Alex and our friend N's husband sit inside, while N and I step out onto the back porch by the avocado tree so I can smoke. I've picked up the habit again, which I've mostly hidden from Alex. Though sometimes, like now, I'm defiant about it. *I'm going to smoke. I don't care if you like it.*

N and I are old friends, since before I even knew Alex. We are old drinkers too, and we are drunk. As we talk, I ash my cigarette into a potted succulent; she notices but doesn't frown.

"We never use this porch," I say. "I don't think we've been out here for months." I'm embarrassed by the mess, the dirt.

I tell her how unhappy I am, how we never should've moved, how much my job sucks here, how Alex isn't happier and neither am I.

What about the hiking? What about the beach? she says. *What about this yard? Come on, there has to be something you like.*

N has a baby, N has a partner, N lives in a good apartment and has a good, and also stressful, job. She is a strong, stoic, sturdy type, not one to mince words, rarely cries. She looks out over the Los Angeles night, into the twinkling lights and the silhouetted palms. The air smells like Los Angeles always does, like fire, eucalyptus, and sage. For a moment, I see the situation through another person's eyes. My cute, smart husband chatting up hers; a healthy, happy toddler fast asleep inside. The night air and the breeze and the porch and the street are all undeniably pleasant, the entire scene just inarguably *nice*.

"You know it's not worse for you, right," she says, staring at me in a way that suggests empathy but also shut-the-fuck-up tough love. "We all feel like this. None of us thought it would be this way." She gestures inside the house to her partner, who's sitting in our new tweed midcentury chair and holding an Aperol spritz. "It's not what any of us thought it would be, but it's good enough. At some point you have to accept that it's good and it's enough."

We drink more and talk more, drink, talk, drink, talk. Later that night, N will walk over to my chair and hug me on the dusty, dirty porch while I sit and sob into her belly, feeling her warmth and her heartbeat, hugging her tight. The avocados will fall around us. *Thump, thump, thump.* I'll hold on to my good, solid friend too tight and for too long, as if awaiting a chemical transfer of her peace.

Is this good? Is it enough?

Will anything ever be?

Into our second year in Los Angeles, I muster all my hustle to lift the persistent cloud that's hanging over my family, to slap a bright coat of paint on top of the ugly blemishes in our lives. It's an avoidant coping strategy requiring cash, a bit of which we have for the first time.

Neither Alex nor I understand how to be smart or intentional with this new bit of money. When we were growing up, our parents never modeled fiscal responsibility, only contradictory fear and subsequent indulgence. There's no personal finance sketch in *Free to Be . . . You & Me*. We were both English majors, "bad at math" kids. In high school, I failed algebra *three* times. To this day, I don't believe either of us could properly read a spreadsheet or explain the meaning of "401(k)."

In these years when I start earning more than we need for basic survival, I'm out of my comfort zone, completely lost. I look at our bank accounts and do not understand what the numbers mean beyond "Hey, we can afford things we couldn't afford before" and "Oh, there's extra to spend." The fact of having money at all makes me overwhelmed and anxious, my fiscal ignorance an ongoing source of shame. I'd lived with some degree of financial terror for most of my life; it was the mode I operated best in, a worn-in stress blankie, all I'd ever known. To address what kept me from having a healthy relationship with money would be to open up avenues into my personhood I wasn't ready to walk down. To take care of my money would be to take care of myself, to resolve that I deserve to feel safe. At this point in my life, I'd sooner burn our cash in a backyard fire than enter into that kind of self-reflective space.

Instead of saving or thinking about our future, Alex and I overuse our salaries to throw cash at every problem, pay big to make any inconvenience small. We invest in expensive extended-hours childcare. We hire a team of people to clean. We purchase a second car, a more comfortable couch, a bigger, thinner TV. We don't seek treatment for Alex's depression (when I suggest it, he vehemently declines) or therapy to address the issues in our marriage. Instead, we commit to rewarding our adult efforts with childlike "treats": trendy two-hundred-dollar sweatshirts, overpriced haircuts, expensive takeout, upscale vacations to Hawaii and Paris, a twenty-five-dollar-an-hour babysitter at least one night per week. We begin touring our new city's restaurants and bars, the hottest places we read about in *Los Angeles* magazine, no menu cost too high, living large and tipping big, though we often bicker through bites of gourmet deviled eggs and smoked-trout salads, between sips of exotic cocktails made from liquor the waiter tells us originated in Greece.

I find us a new L.A. house a few blocks away that is sunnier than our current house, another geographic, the rent thousands more. We decide no amount of tech stock money is worth how working there makes me feel, leaving behind a substantial nest egg. It's not money-smart, it's emotional desperation: I try to get a sunny new job to go with the sunny new house in this sunny new city, and I hope it will all make us sunnier too.

FempowHERment

I n 2014, the world of women's media deems me important enough that an official person reaches out about me giving an official speech on an official stage, a thing she calls a "keynote." We're early in the era of women's professional conferences, Leaning In but not yet Leaning Over, influencers still baking in the internet's womb. We're ushering in the era of pink-pussy-hat feminism, the tide high for wealthy white women anointed as life experts commanding stages at career development conferences with earnest-pun names that combine a female pronoun with a noun that connotes take-chargeness. While I'm sure there are people delivering meaningful speeches commensurate with their fees in 2014, there are also a whole lot of charlatans spouting bootstrapy, work-as-salvation American Dream advice that, with rare exceptions, disguises the truth, which is "rich husband/ generational wealth provided this American Dream."

These conferences become the source code of #hustleharder culture, the origin story for the burnout epidemic that's soon to come. I'm not saying I'm any better than these women at this time, but when the email offer comes, I do not know what a keynote speech is, but I do know the entire enterprise smells of a scam.

When I call the conference organizers to request more information, they tell me they've been watching my career and it's "inspiring." When I ask what they want me to talk about, they say, "Just be inspiring." They're not offering cash to craft and perform this inspiring twenty-minute speech, but they are offering a free trip to Rhode Island. As it turns out, I am a person enticed by minimal flattery and a free trip to Rhode Island. Plus, my bosses want me to do it; they believe it will be beneficial to the brand.

In terms of my "inspiring" work: At this point I'm the new vice president of content of a website for young women that is part owned by a popular actress who is both beautiful and charming, and also politically neutral and nonthreatening enough to be widely adored. All of which bodes well for the viability of the place where I have just started working, a start-up that, like all start-ups, is not a real place at all but more a house that's in the process of being carefully staged for a someday buyer who everyone hopes will be distracted enough by this staging that they'll fail to check the water pressure in the sink.

Los Angeles versus New York clichés are among the most boring clichés, we can all agree. Still, work is different here, less straightforward; job expectations are less direct. I am offered my new position at the start-up one afternoon in a famous L.A. vegan restaurant that serves dishes with names like "I Am Serenity" and "I Am Inspired." When you order you have to say the dish's entire name and if you don't, if you mumble-order, say something like "I'll have the Whole," the server repeats back to you, "You're 'I Am Whole.'" When they drop off the food, it's "The 'I Am Whole'?" Both times it sounds like they're calling you an asshole, which is, frankly, a more honest exchange: "And you are the Ahole?" Yes, I am.

This trip to the vegan restaurant is *technically* my second interview for the start-up job; the first occurred a year prior, in this same restaurant (then, I was "Blessed"). The start-up now has a handful of new executives running it, some of whom are friends with the female celebrity founder. They're all in attendance for my second interview, for the optics, I suspect, to show me how serious they are, how important this interview will be. It's the first time we've all met. One of the executives arrives a half hour late, something I'd not encountered in a job interview before. She slips into a chair at the far end of the table, where she'll stare at her phone, text frantically and constantly, for nearly the entirety of the meal.

Despite the fact that these executives have shown up, or perhaps because of it, I'm not as sure about the job as I was a year before. If my time at the big tech company taught me anything, it's an ability to sniff out a dysfunctional workplace with the accuracy of those cancer-smelling dogs. They explain they can only pay me half of what I'm making now, less than I've made in years. I respond by saying that I love the brand but probably can't swing the money, using my own never-take-the-first-offer advice. In response, the executives start talking about equity like it's Christmas and equity is the year's most sought-after toy, which in 2014, it might be.

I'm trying to seem cool and up on their start-up jargon, but if I'm being honest, I don't really understand what they mean by "equity." I know it's a good thing, and when they say they're looking to sell the company within two years and they expect to race full throttle toward this goal and achieve it in a mere twenty-four months, at which time this imaginary equity will turn into actual money—a fire lights within me. It's as if I've been challenged to an irresistible, honor-defending duel. Although half of the people who will go on to become my bosses have yet to look up from their phones while interviewing me and there are other red flags galore, the minute I hear this, I know I'll probably take the job. At this point in my life, I cannot turn away from a challenge like this, even if I know it will require all of my time and energy.

But the start-up people don't know this, so they're trying to convince me. Our drinks come (we are Whole, Liberated, Aware, Joyful, and Glowing), and they tell me about the downtown Los Angeles office they're renting in one of the city's coolest buildings, which they know is just ten minutes from where I live; how we'll work in this office only four days a week, and how I'll get to hire a staff, whomever I want, and there will be free snacks. The young executives wax poetic about the potential for company merch. They talk about how they want to get tote bags made and pencils too, how they're looking into their own book imprint, where we can publish young authors. They want to build a podcast studio and maybe develop an app and *Jenn, come on, when will you get another chance like this?* The opportunity to *build something from the ground up—as full partners, together.*

They paint the most beautiful picture of work, such an office utopia that I almost believe it. If you told me that in eighteen months these nice start-up fairies would be slamming doors in my face and throwing office debris at each other while shriek-screaming and red-face crying, that we'd actually have to work seven days a week, and are in the office for five, not the promised four, and those days would be spent pointing at each other and me whenever anything went wrong like we are all Spidermans in the Spiderman meme circle, I for sure would not have believed that.

––––––––––

Our meeting's wrapping up and I have yet to commit. The executive who hasn't looked up from her phone suddenly looks directly at my face. She seems to have had enough of this conversation she's not participated in, decides it's time to seal the deal.

In her final pitch of why I should come work for the start-up, the executive who seems too young to have her title, and too inexperienced for most work at all, pulls a notepad out of her thousand-dollar bag, writes something down, rips the page off the pad, folds it in half, and passes it to me.

"That's a collector's item," she says, and then, gesturing to the notepad, "There were only fifty of these made."

I unfold the paper. It's white, lightweight, rectangle shaped, maybe five by seven. Embossed upon it is a pixelated photograph of a broad-smiling Kim Kardashian standing next to her second husband, Kris Humphries, who has his arm around her and is also smiling. It appears to be related to their wedding, exclusive swag from the event, a VIP gift.

On the bottom of the sheet of paper, right below Kim Kardashian's impossibly delicate waist, the executive has written the date we are meeting. She sees me staring and says, "Look at that again in a year from now. You're going to be so happy you work where you do."

Even today, I don't know if this is the dumbest thing to ever happen in a job interview or the most cunning, but it has the desired effect. As the executive intended, the secret Kardashian swag opens a portal in my brain, the part reserved for my most shameful feelings about class and belonging and wanting to know what's behind the most-exclusive first-class curtain, the part of me that still desperately wants to feel important, relevant, and cool. This executive has baited me with her greatest power—VIP access—and now I am certain that the job I was on the fence about just five minutes before must be mine.

I thank the group and get up to leave, tell them I have a lot to think about. I'm grabbing my bag when an executive with no experience executing anything asks where my dress is from. It's a vintage dress from the eighties I got for cheap on eBay back in the *Lucky* days, the designer not particularly well known. This executive recognizes the designer as one of her friend's favorites, she says, and then tells me that her friend has so many of this designer's dresses and then she says the first name of her friend, a famous person who is distinctly famous even by her first name, and now, even though I am near-sure most everything's she said is a lie, I guess we're off to the races.

I am fresh out of my thirties when I take the start-up job. I am a parent to a spiky, intense outlaw of a four-year-old whose neurodiversity is just beginning to make itself known. I'm married to a brilliant person I love and who loves me, but the love between us has failed to keep the hurt from mounting, the stacks of emotional needs long gone unmet. Our daily arguments about topics that don't matter (grocery preferences, cat litter, who paid the gas bill) eclipse arguments about those that do (the second baby I want that he doesn't, reckless overspending, sexual scarcity). As a result, our marriage is increasingly cold and strained. Still, when the topic of this new job comes up, Alex is enthusiastic, supportive. The role will cut hours out of my commute, giving me more time at home, and us more time to work things out. Plus, we both believe any job will be better than the tech company, the stress of which he's been absorbing for years.

Of course, how does one define "better"? Even casual Buddhists know "there" is rarely better than "here." Though I understood the start-up would be a different kind of workplace, the culture I enter into is a shock. There are no systems in place, no map to follow, no concrete understanding of who ultimately calls the shots. My multiple bosses give disparate daily direction. One wants us to make a lot of PowerPoints. One is obsessed with the bottom line. Another, accustomed to running things from her living room, seems surprised that work customarily has set hours. This boss arrives at the office around 2:00 P.M., if her fitness regimen allows. When it doesn't she arrives at 4:00 P.M. Bottom line boss insists on being cc'd on everything we do and needs to sign off on any decision we make but won't sign anything or make any important decisions when Mercury is retrograde. I learn to Google *Is mercury in retrograde?* A concept I did not fully understand before this job, at the beginning of every week.

Another boss comes to work around noon, engaging in the same routine after she arrives. First she takes a loop around, waves in the faces of those wearing headphones so people know she's there. After this, she sits on the couch in the middle of the office, the one that's located next to the bullpen of the five young (Smart! Wonderful!) reporters and editors I've hired, reporters and editors I attempt (and often fail) to protect from the chaos of the place. Once she's settled on the couch next to the young reporters and editors, the executive, who, again, is one of all of our bosses, pulls a mask that is officially known as an "ostrich pillow" over her head.

The ostrich pillow looks like a combination of a ski mask and a gray flannel duvet. It's quilted plus puffed out on all sides, has an oval hole in the front for the wearer's mouth and nose to peek out, and narrows at the neck. The name "ostrich" here is a misnomer: the mask's all-around quilting doubles the size of the wearer's head, more akin to wearing a gray-flannel ready-to-roast turkey over one's face or a space-suit helmet, rendered soft. Though it's made for sleeping on planes at any angle, its use here is to facilitate a Transcendental Meditation (TM) session on a sofa in the middle of a workplace during the work-day around lunch.

We're never told the preferred etiquette for what to do when this boss places the mask-pillow over her face while sitting on the sofa for an hour. No one knows if they're supposed to be quiet during these masked meditation sessions, when she appears as a silent turkey-headed ghoul. At some point I ask if we should stay silent during her meditations and the executive tells me that, *actually,* the noise from the office helps her concentrate. When we move to a larger office, we show this boss a proposed plan for her own meditation room, but she says that would make her so lonely and holds the second syllable a lit-tle longer than the first so you can tell that this statement is meant to be sad.

"This is the best way for me to do TM," she explains, fondling the crystals in the leather satchel around her neck while drinking water out a of bottle that also has crystals in it, a Los Angeles cliché beyond any Los Angeles cliché, a post–Los Angeles cliché. Clichés are cliché for a reason. This story happens to be true.

It's not just innocuous things like office hours and meditation eti-quette. The leadership style at the start-up is evasive, inconsistent, hard to predict. The bosses are half in the office, half out; half disen-gaged from company, half highly interested in what's going on. There's paranoia, accusations sprung seemingly without cause; distrust even when there's no display of disloyalty; explosive anger that's often misplaced. Some days the bosses get mad enough to throw things; one day someone throws a check at the company CFO. Some days the bosses come in crying about the D-list actors they're dating, other days they're focused on perceived social media slights. But mostly they're mad because they have plans to do things that don't involve working and working is getting in the way of these plans.

My bosses are close acquaintances with a number of truly famous and semifamous people, those with immense power and wealth, those who live life at an unfathomably different pace than regular working schlubs. When I begin long-term planning for the site, I'm told to keep in mind that the executives' schedules require flexibility, that they may need to pick up on a whim to a yacht in Greece one Monday; retreat without notice to a compound in Montana for weeks; drop everything to jet off to Costa Rica for a last-minute sloth-hugging/parasailing excursion, anywhere they may be needed to support a spiritual recentering, to nurture and actively celebrate others as they follow their bliss.

From day one on the job, it's clear my bosses don't like me, that I annoy them, that I'm too "businessy" and uptight for the way they wish work to be. They communicate this annoyance constantly, across platforms, their messages a series of erratic taunts and pleas. I receive no-caps, no-punctuation texts at 10:30 at night, texts that I believe to be commands and try to ascertain how to take action on but, by the time I think I understand what they want, a second text has arrived that is just emojis, a text that seems to negate the first. Sometimes I'll get a link to a story with no context, ostrich-head-pillow boss frustrated the following day when I don't know what she meant. On occasion, the team sends confidential company information via social media DM, but it's not a main account, it's a finsta account, so don't worry about that.

One Sunday night, Mercury Retrograde boss messages me over Instagram to announce that I should prepare to clear my calendar for the upcoming week. We have a high-profile visitor coming, she says, a person I need to meet. It's a globally famous female celebrity who's in an ongoing public feud with another globally famous female celebrity. Celebrity One is, apparently, now pissed enough that she wants to write an open letter exposing her side of their beef. Or, *actually*, my boss says, having offered up my services without my consent, she wants *me* to write the letter. The plan is that over the course of the next few days, I'll interview the celebrity and compose the story in her voice. Then, with the celebrity's final editorial approval, we'll publish it later in the week on our site.

"Just think of the *TRAFFIC*," Bottom Line boss says when I suggest the project sounds messy, that it's sure to ignite the online ire of the other celebrity's fans, that it's not the kind of attention we want. "Come on, Jenn. Don't be *stupid*. No editor would turn this story down."

I spend the next three days sitting across from a globally famous celebrity in the start-up's all-white conference room. Each day, she arrives wearing the same designer tracksuit (a strategic move to devalue paparazzi shots, she explains) and proceeds to snack on the same food (travel packets of almond butter, "the easiest protein"). On the first day, we discuss the details of the feud, which I've already read whiffs of in tabloids. She lays out her case. When I appear skeptical about her version of events, she hands me her phone.

We scroll through years of text exchanges between these famous and powerful women, most of them innocuous (if corny) salutations punctuated with pictures of homemade desserts. When we finally arrive at the inciting incident, it's brief and juvenile, bitchy, and clearly not the entirety of this tale. But the celebrity sitting before me is determined that I see things her way. She wants our letter to be a barn burner, a sprawling feminist manifesto, one that defines a move-ment, explains not only her side but her larger life philosophy, how she believes women should be.

I craft one letter for the celebrity, then another. She emails feed-back at 6:00 A.M., midnight, and three in the morning; calls me from the car on her way to, and then while she's on, a private plane. We can't agree on the definition of feminism or her relationship to it. She's sweet with me, and even a little self-conscious, but she's also too hurt and angry to be rational, feels trapped by an outside narra-tive she can't control, is hyperfocused on righting a perceived wrong. Though she doesn't say it, it's clear none of her handlers would green-light any part of this letter. That's why we're together. She's gone rogue.

By the end of the week, I've worked day and night, holding down the duties of my real job and writing and editing the celebrity's letter until we've finally drafted a version she likes. The end result is less a declaration of feminist power than a shallow screed of ax-to-grind pettiness. I dread running it, but my bosses can't wait. They call an emergency meeting to discuss the letter's social media rollout, decide which news outlet to give the big scoop to first, how we'll secure the site's infostructure so we can handle all the attention and not crash.

While my bosses and I plot publishing strategy, the celebrity heads out for the weekend on a last-minute jaunt to Burning Man. No one knows *exactly* what happened in the groovy Nevada desert, but by Monday, she's had a change of heart and calls the letter off. Upon receiving the news, my bosses are furious, crestfallen: *That story would've put us on the map.* One blames me for the loss, says I influ-enced the celebrity. The outcome is my fault because, she tells me, I was never "energetically on board."

But the celebrity seems pleased with her decision. A few days later, a three-foot-tall flower arrangement arrives, addressed to me. The flowers are exotic and unruly, over-the-top extravagant. The vessel they're held in is as wide as the surface of my desk. When I open the card, it reads:

> *From one good feminist to another, thanks for helping me heal.*
> *Xoxo,*
>
>   _____

After the letter debacle, I tried even harder to get a handle on the job, to gain clarity on what my bosses expect—*I am a people pleaser, desperate for validation, overachieving, please tell me how to please!* I tried in gentle no caps and in enthusiastic exclamation points and silly emailed GIFs and smiley emojis too. But in trying I somehow caused further offense, my style of trying deemed too direct.

My direct style will turn out to be the water in *The Wizard of Oz* that melts the witch except if water didn't melt witches but instead made them flustered and mad and caused them to refuse to answer emails or come into work because now "the vibes are bad." I'm bringing my bad vibes into a job where there is an actual poster on the wall that says, GOOD VIBES ONLY and would've surely been fired if I hadn't tripled the site's traffic in three months and relentlessly met every obnoxious objective the vibes-hating executives set out; if I wasn't starting work at 4:00 A.M. to publish the first stories of the day in order to beat the East Coast. If the house I was methodically, obsessively staging wasn't as successful, if outside investors weren't as smitten with the numbers I brought in, I would have certainly been cut loose at the first "Hey, I don't really understand . . ." squawk. I *could* have been set free.

But instead of bowing to the job's unmitigated chaos, I'm my father's daughter—I don't flinch. I'm my mother's daughter too. I refuse to back down. I'm a person who survived both of them, uniquely built to thrive in just this kind of toxic mess. To believe it's my fault if the job isn't working, my trauma narcissism such that I'm acceptable to myself only if I'm pleasing others, if I exceed expectations, if I win. I can't tolerate failure, let my family down, or even begin to examine the ideas about myself and my career I'd held for over a decade, too afraid of where pulling the yarn on that particular sweater might end.

After flirting with the condition for years, I'm a full-fledged work-aholic now and, like any person in the late stages of any addiction, I require more and more of the substance to deliver the high, even when I'm fairly sure rock bottom is close, the lows becoming nearly intolerably low. The success stakes at the start-up are the highest I'll ever experience; in the absence of an HR department, my employee protections are the most scarce. I've cut my salary significantly, am earning almost too-little money to live with the promise of a financial prize later, never more carrot-and-sticked. This is fine for the other executives with rich husbands, with financial cushions stacked higher than the Princess and the Pea's. But it's not okay for me, not for much longer. I left so much tech company stock money on the table to take this job. I can no longer afford to lose the game. As a result, I'm moving faster and faster, my obsessive work dominating even more of my headspace, nearly every waking second of my time.

I look at this impossible job as a riddle, a puzzle, the solution to which I am sure, if I work hard enough, I can find. I use every trick in my arsenal, every slippery tool for success I've learned to acquire what I need. At night I sit around gaming my bosses' personality quirks: strategizing conversation topics to make them like me more, construct-ing carefully chosen stylish-but-not-too-stylish outfits that may garner more respect.

At the same time, I never let up on the gas of the site's daily pro-duction, sorting out the best time to publish "John Stamos Visits the Full House House!" creating the perfect, most clickable headline for what this one twenty-two-year-old learned from *Gilmore Girls,* as told in GIFs. On weekends, I intently study the competition and later steal and implement everything I see that they're doing right. I personally post to our site's social media accounts around the clock: from the bathroom floor when I'm bathing my child, from the restaurants where I'm supposed to be out on a date with Alex, from bed when I can't sleep in the middle of the night. Each day I dig in deeper, strategize harder. Each day, I win a bit more.

The executives I work for tell investors, advertisers, and anyone else who will listen that what we make each day is a site focused on spreading sisterhood and pop-feminist joy, but like everyone trying to win the internet at this time, we're really building a factory for whatever trash the Facebook Trending Trash Heap wants to eat that day or whatever we've engineered that week in our Exploitative Personal Essay lab. I attempt to set some standards around what we publish and what we won't—no takedowns, no celebrity kids, no hair balls trapped inside human holes—but by 2014, the race to the internet's bottom has already begun in earnest and, despite my impressive title, I'm little more than dogsled racing with the other content dogs while the money people in their money sled cry, "MORE CLICKS! MUSH!"

But no one knows this. No one knows about the executives' tantrums and the vibes and dogsled racing; no one knows what a workaholic tweaker I am, how truly tweaked I've become. In the eyes of the outside world I have an "inspiring" job, I have it made. And, because diversity in 2014 means "all white men but we'll throw in a white lady," I get asked to show up to more conferences where I tell inspiring stories that inspire people, particularly women, to work more. I flatter myself into thinking that I am not the same as my lady-leader peers at these conferences. I am convinced I'm not as bad as the inspiring female entrepreneurs I share stages with, the business book "authors" I watch scream at and humiliate unpaid conference interns if they fail to procure copies of books these authors did not actually write, books they paid not only to have written for them but to buy their way onto bestseller lists, books they hold up at conferences and sign as if they personally toiled over the words and ideas within. I tell myself that the monstrous ambition of these women is different than my own monstrous ambition, and, in a small way, it is: Theirs is mainly for personal profit and mine is mostly for personal pain.

Still, like these women, I play up the fantasy of my professional life. For years, I publicly praise the female executives I work under and alongside, pretend they are leaders and visionaries they will never be. I am complicit in selling a narrow, convenient, overinflated narrative about women and work that I am beginning to know is—at least in my experience—a lie.

The 2010s were a socially sanctioned #bossbitch boot camp—*the future is fucking female; get out of the way, fellas, it's our time.* We were an army of marching, stomping Wonder Woman–posing power hoarders, a pantsuit-wearing overcorrection. Our leadership styles borrowing heavily from the systems of toxic masculinity that subjugated us for years, generations of greedy/selfish/ruthless white men, men we claimed to be better than, when many of us behaved just as badly (if not worse) when put in charge; men who—plot twist—were the ones investing in and pulling the strings on this girlbossian movement, exploiting and commodifying and profiting off our feminism, allowing us to believe we had control as they remained the big-money puppeteers. It's as if we believed that by removing the masculinity from our corner offices, we would remove the toxic too; as if the slickest scammers and underminers went only by a certain set of pronouns; as if cruelty and incompetence could be perpetrated by one gender alone.

I don't think my bosses set out to be the labor-exploiting diva-monsters they turned out to be. They were ignorant and ill formed, in over their heads, spoiled kids performing adult roles as entrepreneurs for big-money men, competing with and taking cues from the heavily filtered Instagram lives of other unqualified Cs in stylish C-suites, their business and management training gleaned from little more than hashtags and memes. Their inexperience, youth, and privilege all led to a pathetic kind of learned helplessness, a desperate need for attention and validation they did not earn, a grotesquely sheltered understanding of Planet Earth and the diverse people and experiences upon it, a failure of imagination that never allowed them to envision or create anything broader than selfish winner-take-all success. The winner, obviously, being them.

In my twelve years working in women's media, I encountered a series of leaders like this. These powerful women, all somehow uncomfortable in their boss skins; all shocked by and resentful of the often selfless work it takes to successfully boss. In my day-to-day work under these leaders, women who publicly spouted fempowerment platitudes slammed doors in my face, called me names, required that I eliminate the positions of employees on maternity leave ("Let's be honest, she's not going to offer us anything for months"), asked that I fire a young woman struggling with mental health because she was "bumming us out." One boss got violent, frequently kicked the back of my office chair when she was mad. I was called into and sat down in conference rooms by female executives who tried to convince me I was wrong about HR issues I was inconveniently right about, interrogating and berating me until I broke down and conceded. I was denied an earned and promised bonus, a bonus I needed, by a boss far wealthier than I will ever be, who didn't understand why I needed it. This boss claimed sisterhood, cried when confronted, told me she loved me, called me "bb."

Another boss who wanted every woman to find her voice set out an hourglass whenever our meetings began: "When I turn this over," she said, "this is how long you're allowed to talk." Her time was precious; *spit it out, why didn't you come to me with this sooner? if you can't explain yourself in three minutes you shouldn't get to explain.* At the tech company, I was summoned monthly to corporate "career development" sessions for female employees only, forced to watch that TED Talk on Power Posing and then forced to try it out in front of the group. I was rated by our vice president on whether I looked confident enough, if I looked like I "felt" it enough. The entire meeting was a spectacle, a charade: *this* is what will make us better at working, not fewer hours, not more boundaries around work, not better pay. It was tough love. It was hazing. It was a sorority I never wanted to pledge.

As foretold, my job at the start-up lasts exactly two years before the company is sold. I feel bad to leave my staff, so I stay months longer than I should. This extra time and effort are never acknowledged; instead, I walk in one afternoon after lunch to find my office gutted, its contents dumped haphazardly into the hall by another executive who apparently couldn't wait until I was officially gone to move into the space.

I make enough money in the start-up's sale to pay off Alex's and my debt and finally put away my life's first real savings, an immense accomplishment, a relief. And because of the prominence of my job, I'm able to sell a book, a career guide with a memoir hiding inside. Landing this book deal is a high point of my life. I'm thrilled to devote myself to sentences again, to the puzzle of my own work, even if the thrill is short-lived. I'm given a year to finish the book, but I eat up months of the contracted time working dutifully longer at the start-up than I should. After my last day in the start-up office, I race to meet my upcoming book deadline. I set punishingly high daily word-count goals. I write seven days a week.

When the book is finished, I make the editorial concessions my high-powered agent asks for and, as a result, the book I write turns out more inspiring than I feel (among the changes: he suggests cutting a chapter about crying in the office because it's "not relatable," and I do). At my agent's urging that I stay "relatable" and don't go "too dark," I keep selling a plucky, happy professional image, both in the keynote speeches I'm now performing regularly on conference stages and in what I'm writing on the page.

Even when I know I have more important things to say about work, I'm too motivated by fear to say them. I'm afraid to ask for an extension from the publisher, afraid to be a burden, a problem, to be "bad." I'm also worried that slowing down will mean losing my place in some imaginary race that exists only in my mind, forfeiting the steam of my career, all I've worked for down the tubes.

I'm recruited for and offered another job just as I turn in the manuscript—another website, more important, the title in the C-suite, among the highest you can get. It's a job big enough and aligned with people important enough it could change the trajectory of my life. It's an opportunity my agent tells me will help me sell more books, one several people I trust tell me I'd be "crazy" to turn down. I'm in zero shape to take on this job, a fact that I sense even then. After a decade of nonstop work with no significant break, I'm already running on fumes. But I take it because I know it looks good to the outside world and I cannot stop achieving. Because I haven't acquired coping mechanisms beyond the push of my own labor, because I falsely believe pushing myself like this has saved me from my worst impulses, that it's what gives me value, and will save me again.

On one of my last days at the start-up, I need to use one of the executive's offices in the morning before she comes in to make a phone call that requires a landline. I ask the other executives and they say it's fine if I use hers. The office is sleek and cute, exactly the office you'd want for the head of a company like this—bright feminine colors, retro floral patterns, designy chairs, nostalgic eighties childhood kitsch sprinkled about. This executive's been photographed in her office many times, empowering snapshots that accompany press pieces about our company's millennial-whispering, our prescient finger on the pulse of young women's media.

I post up at her desk a few minutes before my call to prep. I plug my computer into the nearest outlet and realize the outlet doesn't work. I try another; it doesn't work either. I turn on the lamp, no dice. When I go to use the phone, the receiver is dead. This is when I realize: There is no electricity in this office, anywhere. The office was nothing more than a set.

WART and All

A French test called the Work Addiction Risk Test (charmingly referred to as WART) is one of the few tools available to help mental health workers identify workaholism in their patients. First devised by Dr. Bryan, WART is built around five dimensions: compulsive tendencies, control, impaired communication and self-absorption, inability to delegate, and low levels of self-worth. The test offers twenty-five statements, and asks for a rating of each on a scale from 1 to 4, ranging from *never true* (1) to *always true* (4).

A sampling of those statements:

I prefer to do most things myself, rather than ask for help.
I find myself doing two or three things at one time, such as eating lunch, writing a memo, and talking on the telephone.
I overcommit myself by accepting more work than I can finish.
I feel guilty when I am not working on something.
Things just never seem to move fast enough or get done fast enough for me.
I find myself continuing to work after my co-workers have stopped.
I get angry when people do not meet my standards of perfection.
It is hard for me to relax when I am not working.
I get upset with myself for making even the smallest mistake.

I put more thought, time, and energy into my work than I do into my relationships.

When I took this test, just as my voice collapsed in 2017, I got 96 out of 100, a near-perfect score. When I took this test, I was near-perfect at working and not much else.

It's late summer 2017, I'm seven months into my new C-suite Holly-wood job and three months into the vocal glitching. After wrapping my book tour and running a half dozen meetings per day at my new job, plus giving a half dozen speeches and panel talks in the span of a few weeks, I've developed chronic laryngitis. My throat is tight, my neck throbs deep into the night. Speaking is entirely unpredictable; some-times I sound squeaky like a dolphin, sometimes husky and whispery, some mornings I can't talk at all. I'm scared but I'm also busy, over-booked, and annoyed by the inconvenience of having a body; I keep hoping the problem will just go away on its own. However, when what started in June continues into the fall, I can no longer deny it's time to find out what's wrong.

We're years into living in L.A. and I still don't have a doctor, so I head to a random primary care physician, who gives me the full work-up and, after finding nothing, suggests I'm just "stressed" but allows a specialist referral after I insist. He's horn-rimmed-glasses clad and sus-picious seeming, passes over a sheet from his prescription pad. On it is scrawled the name and number of Dr. Anca Barbu, a woman appar-ently famous in vocal surgery circles, something I didn't know was a thing. "If there's anything *really* wrong, you'll be in good hands. She trained in Boston," he says, then whispers, "*with the doctor who worked on Adele.*"

I've allotted a short window for my appointment at Dr. Barbu's

Beverly Hills office, carefully planned over lunch, a time when I know my boss is out of the office and won't come looking for me. I plan on racing back before I'm missed, before there's an emergency that's not really an emergency, more an ego craving or urgent whim.

At check-in, I apologize to the receptionist while explaining my hurry, but I needn't have worried. Dr. Barbu wants to get on with it too. She's not interested in an extended patient intake. We're not here to gab (the gabbing being the problem, after all). Instead, within moments of my arrival she instructs me to hop up on a red leather stool so my face is eye level with hers, a position so close and so intimate that under different circumstances, we might kiss. She wraps a paper bib around my neck, hands over a paper napkin, and tells me to stick out my tongue as she places the cord of a long, thin camera down my throat.

With my tongue held and the camera descending, I'm directed to make the sound "EEEEEEEE," clearly and without gagging, a task more awkward and humiliating than I initially understand.

"EEEEEE—" *Cough cough gag spit.*

"I can't get a clear picture unless you stay calm. Let's try again."

"EEEEEE—" *Choke choke drool gag.*

"Okay, close your eyes this time and think of something soothing."

I think of our good cat when she was just a kitten, of our child playing at the beach.

"EEEEEEEE . . ."

As she examines, Dr. Barbu clicks on the monitor, jots down notes, documenting what she sees. When we're finished with the tongue-camera exercise, she flips the monitor around and reveals what she's found.

"See here, there are at least two polyps, which means your vocal cords can't meet, which is why you're struggling to talk," she explains. She suggests the cause is likely a combination of factors, but mainly reckless overuse, comparing the amount of speaking I've done recently to a novice runner entering a marathon. The images of my vocal cords resemble blown-up female genitalia; the polyps are reddish purple and bulbous, like a particularly angry STD.

"My opinion is you need surgery," she says flatly, outlining the risks in case I oppose: The polyps will get bigger, they could burst, they could bleed; they'll build up scar tissue, paralyze the vocal cords. She says my voice could never return to its normal state.

"The earliest surgery appointment I have is in six weeks."

"There's no way to fix this any earlier?" I say, already calculating the cost of working a full-time job plus promoting my book at speaking gigs while sounding like a freaky sex dolphin for the next month and a half.

Until then, she'd like me to go on complete voice rest, which she stresses means not uttering a word. But if that's not realistic (which— *is this bitch crazy?*—it's clearly not), I'm to limit any speaking to fewer than three hours per day, in quiet rooms, at low volume. Post-surgery, I should prepare to remain completely silent for two weeks, and restrict talking for a few months after that.

"This is a good thing," she says, smiling, wrapping up. She expects I'll heal completely within the year.

On the way out, I begin to simultaneously sweat and cry. The diagnosis is better than I expected, the suggested treatment such a short sacrifice in a long, privileged life. But my brain is broken, so all I think is *How the hell am I supposed to stop talking and keep working?*

I'm totally fucked.

I head back to the office. I've been gone for ninety minutes, and there are dozens of messages awaiting my response. I cancel an appearance at a handbag store pop-up where I'm scheduled to speak on a subject like "owning it." I send another email canceling my participation in a panel discussion on something like "making it" that's set to include me, an Instagram poet, the female founder of a fitness phenomenon, and another Lady in Business. I receive swift replies. Both organizers seem annoyed, which I expected. I'm disappointed in myself for letting them down, and sad to lose the opportunities to promote my book.

I'm aware that I *should* heed the doctor's advice, but I honestly can't conceive of it. The high-profile project I've been hired to oversee is launching in the next few weeks. I'm required to pitch ideas and talk out strategy with my bosses daily, run multiple planning meetings, spout feedback on everything from stories to design, chat up anxious members of my team.

I have coffee with big-name writers I'm trying to woo into writing for me and realize the ambient noise is too loud for me to talk over. I talk over it anyway. I'm working against a deadline at high speed. I need to decelerate the train, but I don't. The team is counting on me, we've come so far, success is too important. The idea of not giving it my all, of missing even a small detail, of potentially living with a failure I could've prevented is unfathomable, completely out of character, not an option no matter how beat down I feel. I have a reputation to protect, a family to feed. I've been hired for a reason—there are expectations I must meet. In fact, I plan to exceed them, continue to go above and beyond, to control everything within my control. I work nights. I head into the office on weekends. I work and I talk and I work.

What's the point of stopping now? I whisper to Alex when he expresses concern. He's alarmed, but he's also recently been laid off, media's pivot to video striking once more. We're a one-income house again—mine—and we both know the stakes of my slowing down. My voice becomes ghostlike, a strange, haunting crackle. In a follow-up appointment, I "EEEEE" again, and the Boston-trained, Adele-adjacent surgeon shows me another screen reflecting my inflamed esophagus, the lumps angrier now, veiny as an alcoholic's nose.

"You've been talking, I see. The polyps are now bleeding. You need to talk less."

———————————————

Before I was old enough to voice an idea of who I was, one was voiced for me. I was a brat, a liar, a bitch, a sneak, *bad*. My teen parents— too young, too hurt, ill prepared for the task at hand—punched and pinched and pulled my body more times than my brain has memory for, more times than I can count. No family story is tidy. Like all parents, mine were inconsistent and imperfect. As the therapy trope goes, they did the best they could with the (limited) tools they had.

Still, speaking up in a house of chaos is a summoning. Contradict, and you could be slapped across the face. Fight back, and you might be kicked down the stairs. Crack wise, and you'll receive a black eye dark enough that you're out of school for a week. In childhood, abandoning my voice became a matter of accretion. Eventually, when told to do so enough, one learns to shut the fuck up.

I came into young adulthood hurt and hollerin', scream-screeching at rotten men and sleazy restaurant bosses, tempering my anxiety with as much nicotine smoke as possible, pouring enough alcohol down my throat to set it aflame, pushing my vocal cords as far as I could. Into my thirties and forties, my battered voice became a vehicle for success, an instrument to convince others to hire and retain and promote me, to let me rally teams and lead. It also allowed me to create and perform an identity, to hide from the world how awful I felt inside, how chronically unsafe and ashamed.

What does it mean to have value? What determines success? How do we know if we've failed? In the weeks leading up to my vocal cord surgery, I can't talk, so I'm forced to observe. I start noticing aspects of work I'd been moving too fast to see. I listen in on chaotic who-just-joined conference calls and become acutely attuned to the name-dropping, the undermining, the overwhelming callousness and interpersonal disregard. I sit in on conversations with famous, beloved gurus spouting impressive-sounding word scrambles that upon close read don't add up to much. I see how dismissive these beloved thought leaders are of junior staffers—how ungenerous they are, how rude.

In staff meetings, I smile obligingly at flaccid boss jokes and watch others do the same; nod along to unfocused plans and proposals that have little hope of coming true; bear witness to petty and cruel inter-employee squabbles no one's mediating, favor-currying and position-jockeying no one is discouraging, a great dance of winner-take-all dysfunction, none of it bringing out anyone's best. For the first time in a long time, I see the game as an observer, not a player. It looks vulgar, it feels sad. It makes my stomach turn.

I begin to realize what I have is not simply a surface problem but more a revolution from within. My brain is as sick as my voice. I let an all-caps tirade from a C in the C-suite go unanswered for hours longer than I should. I stop racing to coddle and capitulate. I don't have the vocal strength to cajole. What I'm feeling is new, and I'm afraid to give words to it. Though I don't know it yet, something is quaking inside me, the cracks that formed in our first days in Los Angeles now blowing open, wide. I am headed toward a beginning and an end.

Once the date of surgery is locked, I whisper-ask my boss if they'd prefer I come into the office during the two-week voice rest period or complete my work from home.

"Make sure your department is covered, but stay home," they reply. "I don't want a weird *mute* walking around."

On the day of surgery, before general anesthesia, I'm a shaky, anxious mess. A nurse pats my leg and covers me in an extra blanket. "You watch too many doctor shows," she says. "You'll be fine."

She's right. The surgery goes off without a hitch. Dr. Barbu finds and removes five polyps from the space where she initially thought there were two. I wake up groggy and sore, but relieved.

The next two weeks are silent, peaceful. It's October and there's a slight chill in the Los Angeles air. In the afternoons, I go to the grocery store. I pick my kid up early from school. I make dinner. I wipe down the countertops. I feed the cats. I sit close with Alex and watch bad, and good, TV. I go for slow, contemplative neighborhood walks.

I wander through the house carrying just-folded laundry and see how much I've neglected, every detail at home that I've missed. For the first time in decades, I am less concerned with earning a living than I am with earning my life back.

In our follow-up appointment, I speak to Dr. Barbu using my new voice for the first time. Like she'd warned me it might be in our pre-op discussions, it's different. Firmer, brighter. I sound younger than I did before; there's even a bit of a lilt. Comparing the before and after pictures, my vocal cords now appear fresh and smooth, a clean start. I worry about recurrence, but she assures me it's unlikely to happen.

"You understand your voice better now," she says, "and you know how to protect it." I thank her, getting a bit teary. To the surprise of both of us, we hug.

When I return to work the next day, it's the same stress theater, each character hitting their marks. I'll work there for six months more, but I'll never really be there, or anywhere, in the same way again.

Best Decision Ever Made for You

The knock comes at 3:51 on a Monday afternoon. I'm sitting at my desk in the windowless, fluorescent-lit office where I'd worked for more than a year at my second Hollywood job. Outside was all billowy palm trees and glittering blue skies, gleaming golf carts transporting important people to important places, a balcony where, according to the orientation tour guide, Rita Hayworth used to sunbathe in the nude. But inside things are not—and had never been, at least for me—especially bright.

For the longest time, my worst fear was that I'd grow up and never achieve "success" in the limited ways I understood it, never live among interesting people or have access to interesting things. I feared that my life would be a meaningless drudgery, a middle-class (if I was lucky) cliché. That I'd marry an incurious man, work an uninspiring job, become a prisoner to maintaining the lives of ungrateful children in a cookie-cutter, middle-of-nowhere home.

For a longer time than that I was sure I'd never be more than a lonely, hurt, angry, too-fragile kid who didn't understand how to be around other people in the world. I was afraid I'd never live outside what I'd known, that I'd live a small, insignificant life, disconnected, never feeling seen.

From that place of sorrow, I tailor-made a professional fairy tale for myself, an escape; devised a map for how to climb up and out of my station and into a new, shiny life. For two decades, I handed my life over to that fairy tale, to work. I understood America to be a game, and I wanted to win at it, take those winnings as far as I could. I believed a career was the only thing I could count on, the thing that would save me from the unreliable parts of life, what would save me from myself.

There are the stories of our lives and then there are the lives we are actually living. By the time the knock comes on the door of the Hollywood office where I've worked at a quote unquote dream job for the past fourteen months, I no longer understand the story of my life. What I increasingly do know is I am deeply, unsustainably unhappy inside it.

Before the knock came, it was a normal day. I'd held a morning staff meeting, answered endless emails, engaged in the all-day hum of meaningless Slack discourse (grumble grumble! joke! faint praise! donuts in the kitchen!—GIF—*sounds good!*), the pings and dings and dongs following me everywhere, even to the toilet, where I brought my phone. I'd scheduled a one-on-one with one of my five direct reports where we'd discussed goals; those they were meeting already, those they expected to meet soon. I'd put out a minor administrative fire that someone else was trying to make major. Later, I'd eaten an overpriced desk salad washed down with water from the watercooler out of a metal bottle that smelled faintly like swamp.

By 4:00 P.M., I am editing a story while frowning and wearing headphones, something I usually do on Mondays. Because of the headphones, I don't hear the knock at the door. But it grows louder, and louder still, until it is unmistakably not part of my editing playlist but a sound that demands attention.

Two of my colleagues, senior to me in longevity at the company, but not in title or experience, are standing outside. One is carrying a yellow folder. The other is carrying a chair. They look nervous and ask to come inside. My office is small, a charmless industrial closet, a worthy trade-off for the privilege of having a door.

The office comfortably accommodates only a desk and two chairs, one on each side, facing each other. The colleague carrying the additional chair struggles to squeeze it through the narrow doorway, banging it against the door and then the wall and then the door again, until landing it, at last, upon the ground, at an angle, and in such tight proximity to the chair of Colleague One, that when Colleague Two sits, they're touching knees.

"We've come to tell you that today is your last day. The company is going in another direction."

"You're firing me?" I said, my stomach dropping, my face flushing hot.

"We're going in a different direction." Colleague One ignores my question. I recognize the HR script, spot a glint of self-satisfaction in her eyes as she sticks to it. Colleague Two shakes his leg like he has to pee.

"Wait, you're seriously *firing* me? What did I do wrong?"

Colleague One ignores the question, as she's likely been coached to do. Colleague Two stares at the floor as intently as if it contains the Rosetta stone.

We've entered the point of the firing where things can get tricky. Emotions may fly, so it's most important for the firer to stay neutral, emotionless, flat no matter what. "So, we like to make little packets for people," Colleague One continues, firmly, pushing the yellow folder toward me. "You need to sign what's in this packet in the next twenty-one days—and waive the age thing."

"You mean the 'age *discrimination* thing' because I'm over forty?"

"Correct. If you don't sign this, you won't be eligible for severance." Colleague One pauses. She leans in and stares at me intently, eyes lit up like those of a game show host gesturing toward a prize. "We're offering you Two. Weeks. Severance."

Out of the corner of my eye, I notice movement. I look through the glass door of my office; a man I've never seen before, a large man, is standing just outside. I look back to Colleague One and ask if I can have until the end of the day to pack my stuff.

"No."

From the man outside, Colleague One retrieves and hands me a stack of unbuilt cardboard boxes. "You'll be leaving now," she says.

The staff—a team I'd hired and managed—is escorted to another part of the building by the colleagues. They all flee the floor as if part of a drill. Stationed by the front door of the empty workspace is a second brawny man. I'm guarded by the first.

My office doesn't have enough floor space to reconstruct the boxes, so I sit on the ground just outside the door. I fold, push, and maneuver one corrugated side into another, but nothing fits. I use scissors and tape and try to make the bottoms hold. When one cardboard sculpture is complete, I place a few books and papers inside it, satisfied. When I lift it up, everything falls out the bottom. It's the last straw.

I'm a forty-five-year-old woman with a C-suite title, the breadwinner of my family. I'm capable, competent, and respected, but I can't build this fucking box.

As I sit alone on the floor in my work slacks and my smart ankle boots in the hall outside my now-former office, a valve bursts. Something I've been holding in for longer than I know rushes out.

I begin to simultaneously shake and cry.

I cry because I've been humiliated and I'm deeply ashamed. I cry because I'm afraid. I cry because I know—even then, left alone on the floor with the unbuilt boxes—that this as-seen-on-TV firing is a thunderclap, and that even if I don't yet understand how, things will never be the same.

Within the hour, I've packed the boxes. I turn in my badge and am escorted outside the building by security, then allowed to make it alone the rest of the way to my car. Once inside the car, I call my friend Kristen, the calmest person I know, a person who, despite my best efforts, knows me. I'm sobbing, snotting, yelling, hysterical, deranged as I spit out the news. "Oh, honey," she says carefully, gingerly. "This is the best decision that's ever been made for you. I know it doesn't feel like it now, but you've just been set free."

Free As a Bird

If there's one thing you need to know about blue jays, it's that they're jerks. In fact, some birders on some birder sites go as far as to call them "airborne jerks of the highest order." The blue jay is eleven inches, three ounces of domination, aggression, and spite; a smart and socially complex animal, who's also greedy, rapacious. This is especially true of the females, who are territorial, who attack and decapitate their rivals, that is, when they're not feasting on their rivals' young. Blue jays—or their Southern California cousins, scrub jays, same bloodline, same bad attitude—are the undeniable "bullies" of the avian kingdom. One YouTube birder explains, rather admiringly, that they're "take charge, no-nonsense birds," while filming a blue jay pummeling his wife.

Native Americans in the Chinook tribe long warned of the blue jay as trickster. Since the birds were believed to lie and cheat, a blue jay around a home meant deceitful people were preying upon its residents. Mystics associate blue jays with transformative change. Some believe recurrent sightings of the bird indicate it's time to reassess the people you allow into your life.

When you search for information on blue jays, you'll find the internet rife with tales of both avian havoc and, equally, their symbolism—blue jays as totems, as spiritual guides. I'd honestly never given a single thought to the blue jay until my first encounter with one near my house in Los Angeles on the first day after I was fired.

The house I rent and have lived in for nearly a decade is part of a ramshackle duplex with crumbling Spanish-architectural charm. It's on an objectively beautiful, tree-lined street, a private circle really, surrounded by lavish and newly renovated homes, plus a few rental units occupied by upper-middle-class-renter schlubs like us, holdovers from when Los Angeles was a place where those of many income stripes could afford to live. Our rented house is located on, and is slowly slipping down, a steep hill, the floors at such a tilt that if you place a marble at one end you can watch it quickly make its way to the other, a trick I've used to entertain the children and animals who visit my home for years.

There are two ways off the hill. In one direction, a secret staircase leads to the famous Sunset Boulevard, a place where shirtless, over-tan men pace back and forth in front of trendy coffee shops scream-ing "FUCK" as loud as their lung capacity allows while miniskirt-clad coeds scurry around them, nine-dollar matcha lattes in hand. The other direction is more scenic—more trees, more hills, eventually an expansive reservoir, a sparkly-tranquil, fenced-in city lake, to be admired from afar. This way off the hill is the more relaxed option if you're not up for city bustle and its accompanying human chaos. Or if you're going on a nice little walk to try to process one of your life's more bruising shames.

It's midmorning when I set out on my first day of post-job free-dom. I exit the house into the warmth of the late-spring Los Angeles day, squinting at the sun. Save a single gardener and his leaf blower, the block is empty, quiet, and calm. This is not the case for my brain, which, post-firing, remains a glitching pinball machine, fast-moving thoughts pinging about. *Maybe I should've said yes to that story my boss suggested about closet organizing.* PING! *Were those security guards there for me the whole day?* PING! *Oh, THAT'S why Nora was so weird at lunch. She knew.* PING PING PING!

My mind is tuned to and stuck on the YOU GOT FIRED Channel, the show currently playing is a *CSI*-level forensic analysis of every detail leading up to the moment of termination, investigating each scene for clues I should have spotted, over and over, on a loop. After this, I'll contemplate the growing list of post-firing logistics, mentally calculating the sum of all our bank accounts, each of our upcoming bills, and how long we can afford to live without my pay.

It's in this ping-ponging state that I start down the hill, away from the stairs and toward the reservoir, down around someone's cactus garden, up past the spot where the sidewalk is cracked and juts up, where I've tripped enough times to know instinctively how to avoid it. I'm lost in my thoughts. Lost enough that I don't register the blue jay perched innocuously on a wire far above my head.

I amble a few steps further down the road. Then I hear it: a prolonged whirring buzz, an aggressive sound that's unlike any birdcall I've known, more a throaty lizard's jeer. The almost-midday sun is bright and glaring, but I stop and look up anyway, lifting my head to scan around for the sound's origin. Within seconds, the whirring-buzzing jeer is audibly closer. Then, quickly, it's clear: I've looked too late.

In the corner of my eye, I spot a blurred flapping, feel an eerie, unfamiliar flutter of air. Suddenly, the blue jay that was *just* on the wire above me is there, mere inches from my cranium, the alarming sense that something had fallen from the sky immediately present. Even if you've never been attacked by a bird, you've most likely experienced the feeling that you *might* be attacked by a bird, had a bird fly too close, its presence startling you into a specific panic, reminding you of the utter wildness of this world.

The first time the blue jay dives toward and attacks my head, a feeling best described as a skull tap, I instinctively fall to my knees, a reflexive Hail Mary, a *help this lapsed Catholic from this flying monster, God, please*. When it pecks at my scalp a second time, when I can feel the force of the point of its beak, I run, an out-of-body run, awkward and lumbering, limbs flailing, like I'm five again and fleeing a bully, like my mom's going to find out soon.

It's the first time I've ever been attacked by a bird, but it won't be the last. The next blue jay attack happens on the same day as the first, in the same place, on my walk home. Then it happens again, the following day, while I am walking the dog. By this time, I know it's not a fluke.

A Latin root of the word "fail" means "to trip, to cause to fall or stumble." Psychologists believe feelings of failure after the loss of a job often give rise to grief; grief in one area of life can stir up other areas of despair, rekindling in the brain past feelings of sadness, longing, and loneliness. The jolt from a failure may uncover additional heartache the psyche's found a way to protect us from; it can shatter the container, the false self, the deep-down hidden repository where we've been holding it all.

The week after I am fired, I am a broken vessel, a shaken beer can shot up with holes, spilling and spewing, spraying in all directions at once. At the time I felt wholly ashamed for existing in this state; for failing to quickly pull myself together, the voice in my head—*Get over yourself, WHAT'S WRONG WITH YOU?, Suck it the FUCK up*—trying desperately to break through.

I remain a zombie for weeks. I host our kid's eighth birthday party in a daze. During cleanup, I forget to put away what's left of the ice cream cake, wake up the next morning to a river of old milk. I sleepwalk through two meetings at the school. When, later, Alex asks what happened, I can't remember. I forget to feed the cats, run dangerously low on gas. Out for drinks with an old pal, I mindlessly chainsmoke so many cigarettes that when I go to light another, my friend places her hand over mine, stares at me intently, and says, "Jenn. Stop."

I relive the firing continuously in my mind. I am shocked by the fact that I cannot find a pithy processing avenue, an everything-happens-for-a-reason positive spin. What's becoming apparent is, I am no longer up for soldiering, for bending reality to my will. Something had changed in me, a shift I could not articulate, but could no longer avoid. It was like I'd lost the passwords to my brain. None of my old coping strategies worked. Not the boot-strappy methods I'd written about in my too-inspiring book. Not the breezy, don't-over-think-it steps I'd outlined on conference stages for years. Not the secret "tough love" ways I'd always spoken to myself, nitpicking every syllable I uttered, shaming myself for any hair out of place. I was in new and unfamiliar territory now. I had to relearn how to be. I wasn't sure what to do or where to go next, but one thing was clear: I could no longer use emotional beatings to whip myself toward success.

People talk a lot about burnout, especially in recent years, especially after we've lived through years of a plague in a country with few social safety nets, a pandemic that left most everyone outside of the one percent traumatized, abandoned by our country's current brand of billionaires-take-all capitalism. When we talk about burnout, we most often discuss feelings of overwhelm; the physical, emotional, and mental exhaustion that occurs after periods of overwork and excessive stress, how we become numb, unable to achieve or even dream of what future achievements could be.

But we less often talk about burnout in terms of grief, the grief for what you thought your career could be, what you thought *you* could be, the grief for the time you'll never get back, the grief for having given yourself over to something unworthy of you, the grief that springs from cruelty and mishandling, of never being given as good as you gave. The sadness that comes from reaching the top of a summit you'd set your sights on, only to get there and feel *Is that all there is?*

Truth was, I'd been burned out for years. I was post-burnout, existing in a kind of dissociative fugue state, next to zero connection to
the person I was before. In the months leading up to my firing, I'd
sit in my office staring, sometimes for hours, watching the messages,
commands, demands roll in like endless, mindless waves, unable
and unwilling to meet yet another set of unrealistic goals. I was post-
ambition, post-anxiety, post–caring at all.

A profession is not a personality, a columnist at *The Atlantic* will
tell you; work won't love you back, says yet another antihustle book.
But if a career was no longer my personality, what was? I'd spent the
entire first half of my life living and working in dysfunctional systems,
my waking hours dictated by inflated-ego monsters and incompetent
adults who behaved like children; swimming in the whiny-briny muck
of rich-people stew; lured by the promise of titles, promotions, status,
awards, and fiscal comfort. My many learned trauma responses—my
time as a female on a planet that secretly and not so secretly reviles
females; my endless validation seeking; my all-consuming need to be
a good girl who succeeded at work, who never let a ball drop, who
exceeded any and all expectations; the violent shame spirals I'd experience at even a hint that I'd let someone down or done something
wrong—all of it set me up to keep working at an unnatural pace for
longer than one naturally could or should.

The grief I felt the day after I was fired presented as a kind of
nauseous rage, an aching remorse for what I'd allowed and toler-
ated over the course of my career. Decades when I was verbally harassed, sexually harassed, my boundaries crossed, my self-esteem
trampled by bullies young and old. Sold to me as the price of admis-
sion, *part of the job, what you signed up for, you're lucky, so lucky, to be
employed*.

And it wasn't only that. I grieved for my complicity, my inability
to show up better than I had; the moments when I chose dominance
over kindness; the moral culpability inherent in the company lines I
toed; the draconian rules I'd followed; the foul, inequitable systems

I'd protected. No amount of personal success is achieved without at least a bit of cost to someone else. I was better than most of my kind, I knew, but I also knew that by participating in and supporting toxic systems of oppression, I was far from beyond reproach. Getting fired punctured an inflated fantasy of myself, woke me out of an ego dream state. And, if getting fired hadn't fully awakened a new kind of monster in me, repeated attacks from a bitchy Los Angeles blue jay finished the job.

When I arrive back home, I Google my new nemesis.

A blue jay tells you to speak up since closed mouths do not get fed, I discover on WorldBirds.com.

Then, on the "symbolism" page of the same site: *If you are constantly seeing Blue Jays around you, then it is an indication that you need to speak up for the greater good of all. It is time to find your voice. It is time to clearly establish what you will and will not accept.*

Over the next year, the blue jay will attack Alex and a few of our neighbors. Eventually someone reports the attacks and the bird is humanely removed. But that first month, a month when I am wandering the Los Angeles hills feeling vulnerable and afraid, the blue jay seems to intuit my weakness. The bullying fucker chooses only me.

The attacks occur with a good deal of regularity for weeks, a declaration of war, but I don't have it in me to fight. Instead, I surrender, start wearing a bike helmet on dog walks. One afternoon I catch my helmet-clad reflection in a car window. The helmet is hot pink, the circles under my makeup-free eyes are deep purple, I'm wearing a ratty old green sweatshirt. I'm a wild mess of a human color wheel, in no shape to look for new work. I decide then and there to use the money we'd saved for a fixer-upper house to put a pause on my career and address the fixer-upper that is my head.

As anticipated, the bird swoops and taps on my way down the hill that day, and again a week later, helmet or no. I become resigned to it. Even if I run, I reason, I cannot outrun whatever this is.

I'd always had a strange relationship with birds. When I was growing up, we kept a series of them, floating in a cage on an eye-level perch in the dining room, covered with a heavy curtain at night. The first set, four zebra finches, came to us through death, inherited from my great-grandfather. The birds, who were old but seemed healthy enough, began pecking at one another soon after they arrived. Their gray feathers grew rough and mangy, balding in spots; their bright orange beaks, dull. Eventually they began dropping dead, one by one by one. I'd find them stiff at the bottom of the newspaper-lined cage, eyes open, feet rounded over, petrified in midclasp.

Most all of our pets died like this; unlikely, untimely deaths, mainly due to neglect. An entire family of rabbits perished by cannibalism after we failed to feed them; cages full of hermit crabs were posed forever naked, out of their shells, searching for water we failed to provide; there were turtles we lost and forgot about, ones we'd uncover in the back of a closet months later, ashen, now food for the earwigs that appeared when we shook their dead turtle shells. The parakeet named Sunny who died within weeks of arrival, the same fate that would unfortunately befall Sunny 2. The family cat my parents told us died by suicide was really run over in our driveway after sleeping near my dad's car, searching for warmth.

When we see death like this, we become desensitized to it. In the presence of haphazard care, children can't fully grasp its opposite. Responsibility is expected of kids, but when it's not modeled, responsibly, they fail (and are then blamed for failing) to learn. When one of us finds the dead birds, we're insensitive jerks. We yell to my mother, unaware of where she might be in the house or what she might otherwise be doing at that moment. "Mom! Mom! Dead bird! Another bird died! Mom! Mom! Mom!"

A bird will not die of fright but from a surplus of stress hormones which present when frightened.

Keep your new pet's environment calm: a bird's small, fragile heart cannot handle too much stress.

In the late 2000s, Pat Monaghan, a researcher at the University of Glasgow, conducted a study on the effects of stress on nearly two hundred newborn finches. Starting twelve days after they hatched, Monaghan fed seventy of the birds food laced with CORT, a stress hormone; the others she left alone. The artificial stress raised the birds' CORT levels to those they'd typically experience while under duress. She repeated this exercise twice a day for two weeks, after which she left the chicks to grow up undisturbed.

Three years after this, Monaghan studied the birds. More than 30 percent of the CORT-fed finches had died—twice as many as their peers who experienced chickhood relatively stress-free. Monaghan concluded that consistent exposure to stress early in their lives had a significant impact on the birds' survival. At the time of death, none of Monaghan's finches were diseased. They weighed the same as their peers and showed no signs of injury or infection.

Perhaps more surprisingly, high levels of stress had a significant impact on not just the CORT birds themselves but also on their significant others. Research has long shown that animals exposed to stress are less likely to find mates. But Monaghan's study took this one step further: Her CORT birds grew up to become undesirable adult partners who posed a health risk to their companions. When paired up, the traumatized finches shared the impact of early hardship with their partner birds, who, in turn, became stressed to the point of premature death too.

According to a 2011 *National Geographic* article on Monaghan's study by journalist Ed Yong, "Zebra finches form strong social bonds when they pair up, and like many other back-boned animals, these bonds are accompanied by higher levels of a hormone called oxytocin. This buffers them against stress, making them less sensitive to difficult environments and bolstering their health. But if a partner is sensitive to stress themselves, they're less able to provide this 'social buffering.'

So it's not that the CORT birds were actively harming their partners; they just weren't helping them."

———————

Symbolism is rarely understood in the moment; neither is the reality of our lives, if such a thing exists. Our great human flaw is living forward or backward, wanting and wishing for something other than the present, reminiscing about the pleasures of some nonexistent past.

On the morning of his thirtieth birthday, Alex and I wake up to find a sparrow flying inside our Brooklyn apartment. The windows were not open; to this day, we don't know how the bird managed to arrive. But there it was, small, brown, and panicked, race-flying from room to room, searching for escape.

It's just past dawn, mid-May. We're in our underwear in our bright shared apartment, in love's first blush. Years later, when our lives are stretched, events like this will seem an intolerable nuisance, turn us against each other, our anger misplaced and unrestrained. But in this moment we are young and buoyant, sleep-faced but happy, on a shared mission to save our bird visitor, a team in this avian chase. With a little coaxing, the bird flies out as quickly as it flew in. We fall back into bed, satisfied, sleep the midmorning weekend sleep of those responsible to nothing but themselves.

In ancient Greek mythology, sparrows were considered a symbol of love.

In Indonesia, it is believed that if a sparrow flies into a house, a member of the household will soon marry or give birth.

A few seasons later, on our honeymoon, we head to Rome, the place of my ancestors, a place neither of us has been. We stay in a neighborhood called Campo de' Fiori, our "hidden gem" hotel just off a square with a sprawling Italian market of the same name. For twelve days, we follow an agenda I've meticulously cobbled together, composed of recommendations from well-off, well-meaning friends with

bank accounts ten or more times the size of ours, our magazine colleagues, our ostensible peers. We're—or, more accurately I'm—afraid
to look and feel unsophisticated, can't bear to miss out on the "best"
the city has to lend.

Italian trains are notoriously late, a fact we never catch in the
guides. We miss a train in Naples, or it never comes, our Italian too
weak to sort out which. Alex and I spend hours in the then-rough-
and-tumble Napoli Centrale, bear witness to physical altercations
and petty crimes. A man in front of us in the ticket line is agitated,
screams out intermittently. Another bleeds from his face. Across
the station, an American couple's bags are stolen; there's fuss. We
don't want to be dumb like them or assholes either, so we sit dutifully atop our luggage and wait, slowly absorbing the chaos of the
scene.

We're married; but we have few tools for processing stress together,
missed the class on how to responsibly lend space and gentleness, to
communicate with care. Later that night, cold in our too-thin jackets,
lost in Florence, searching for somewhere still open to eat, we'll walk
into the first of the trip's petty quarrels, yell so loudly at each other the
Italians stare.

The trip turns good once we slow down, once I stop acting like a
FOMO bitch with a spreadsheet. We cancel all our side excursions
and spend the last five days where we began, in Rome. We wander
the city streets agenda free; discover quiet shops, churches, cafés we
would not have otherwise found. One night just before dusk, we're
strolling the Tiber River just past the Vatican when the sky suddenly
becomes dark. We look up to see a flock of birds in formation, a
swirling black cloud, packed together so tight they eclipse the early-
evening sun.

The birds are starlings, we'll discover later, an invasive species of
blackbird with an iridescent purple-green sheen. Starlings travel in

flocks of thousands, sometimes millions, a superswarm known as a
murmuration, common in Rome from October to March. A murmuration is a self-protective measure named for the sound the birds make
together, a sound that is not what you think when you imagine a murmur, but more overwhelming: a high-pitched screeching, a synchro-
nized primal scream.

Starlings feed on oil-heavy olive groves in the Italian countryside,
then return to roost in the city because it's warm. At night, the birds
produce enough thick excrement to create an urban-ecological crisis,
with slippery traffic and hazardous walking conditions, the pedestrians
forced to carry umbrellas to avoid a rain of oily, hard-to-remove shit.
The shit is the price for the murmuration, an awe-inspiring nightly
nature show that stops you in your tracks, leaves you humbled, trans-
fixed.

*Starlings are symbolic of communication, of your relationship with your
fellow members, and your standing in society.*

*Starlings are a symbol of unity; these birds have learned that we are
always stronger together than alone.*

*To experience a murmuration is to experience firsthand how little we
understand about the power and mystery of the natural world.*

At home on the hill in Los Angeles, we wash dishes while looking
out over treetops, bear witness to the city's wilder wildlife. One day
there's a pack of coyotes patrolling our streets; the next, a mountain
lion chilling on a neighbor's lawn. A flock of wild parrots flies over our
house most summer afternoons, briefly fills the soundscape with a ser-
enade of squawks. The parrots swoop and swoosh over the stoic red-
tailed hawk who sits perched atop the telephone pole just down the
hill. The hawk remains still even when there are other birds around it,
even the one day when I look out the window and find it repeatedly
attacked by a blue jay.

Some believe blue jays are meant to send a message to form long-lasting and trusting friendships and to invest yourself in your community instead of going outward.

A blue jay sighting may be asking you to stop diverting your energy into areas other than the people you love.

Message received.

Ghosts

A separation from work necessitates a reunion with yourself, with life. Even if the self and the life you return to are not always what you remember or what you want to see.

Facing myself without the cover of my career was not what anyone would call fun. Outside of work, I'd never been the easiest person to know and, in two decades hiding behind "busyness," I'd become more of my worst parts: impatient and demanding, selfish, and if I'm truly honest, at least a bit of a bully. I was intermittently kind and compassionate; I always showed up in a crisis. I never missed an important life event. I sent thank-you cards and Mother's Day flowers, consistently proffered generous, thoughtful gifts. But I'd devoted myself to my career for so long, I failed to truly see or value much else. Including, most shamefully, the people in my life.

Someone once told me that 80 percent of how you conduct yourself in relationships comes from the behavior modeled by your parents (the other 20 percent comes from your own experience and stuff you read). Like my parents, I approached interpersonal conflict like war. When I felt vulnerable, I struck preemptively—better to hurt before I could be hurt myself. I shut down arguments by yelling louder (loudest), created intimacy through "passion." With Alex, I'd taken the power grab one step further: I filled my life with so much work there was little room for him. When he complained about my behavior, I reminded him that I earned most of the money. I made myself simultaneously unimpeachable and unreachable, emotional armor to disguise how fucked up and terrified I was inside, how afraid I was he'd sort out how bad I was and leave.

But getting firing leveled the playing field. I no longer earned the big money, no longer carried big-job demands. There was no place left to hide.

We call the couple's therapist "Jeffrey" because after the first session I can't remember his real name so we settle on "something like Jeffrey," and it sticks. We see him for the first time in his sun-dappled midcentury-designed office, part of an expansive house in an east side neighborhood of Los Angeles, one with a stone fountain and surrounded by elaborately landscaped grounds. Jeffrey begins our hour with an intake. He introduces the "dialogue of intimacy," hands us worksheets, asks if it's something we practice, and, if not, can we start.

He discusses "naked playtime" and wonders whether we still engage and just how often, if we do. After fifty minutes attempting and failing to practice "uninterrupted listening," confirming that our interactions are "highly reactive," we leave feeling defeated, more than a little cliché. We were once free-spirited weirdos, wary of institutions, *we got married, on a whim, in City Hall!* We convinced ourselves that by staying independent and somewhat cool ourselves we'd avoid monogamy's scam, the banal pitfalls of marriage, this most embarrassing game adults play. "It is so tiring to hate someone you love," the smart, difficult, complicated writer Simone de Beauvoir wrote, ostensibly about her smart, complicated, and even more difficult partner, Jean-Paul Sartre. Who were these exhausted people? How did we get here? Would the other people ever return?

Later, we debrief at a bar.

"I thought he was good," I say, sloshing my bartender-recommended orange wine, which smells, and mostly tastes, like old slime.

"Yeah, better than I expected. Should we split the brussels sprouts and get one more drink?"

That afternoon Jeffrey asked what was working in our partnership. After a long pause, I blurted out "Nothing!" in a schmaltzy yada-yada voice, the way you'd deliver a "Take my wife, please!" joke. No one laughed.

"Do either of you carry resentments?" Jeffrey followed. Neither of us knows where to begin. Neither of us knows what's been lost, if we're too far gone to come back. We're here to sift through the ashes of this burned-down relationship. We've come to see what remains.

Here's the worst part, the part I don't like to talk about, the part that's almost too painful to type. While I was out chasing titles and money, building other people's companies, overcompensating for feelings of inadequacy by over-competently supporting other people's lives, my baby, my now second grader, had been struggling for years. I'd tried to solve the problem, threw money and experts at the problem, held my five- and six- and seven-year-old accountable for a problem a child of that age could not possibly be expected to solve. For years, I sensed that what the problem required was my undivided attention and time, time I could not give as I worked all days far past 5:00. Time I resented, felt unable to and failed to find.

The trouble started all the way back when I was working at the start-up, which is when I began to receive the Calls. From teachers, from principals, from earnest camp counselors, from field trip chaperones, once, from someone at the zoo. "Your child is disruptive," one says. "I've never seen a student less eager to please adults," explains another.

Alex and I don't know how seriously to take the situation. We argue over courses of action. He doesn't see a problem at all; I think something is off, but I don't know what. Attempting, as always, to find the sweet parenting spot between neurotic and neglect. Eventually, dutifully, I insist we get the behavior checked out, the way you would a rash. We consult with behaviorists, family therapists, pediatricians. No one can find anything wrong.

When I request time away from work to handle the issue, my executive bosses poo-poo the problem. They advise that a private school will solve it; public school, they suggest, only makes situations like this worse. "They can't deal with your kid *and* the free lunchers," one explains, while also recommending I need additional full-time help at home; "the system is already stretched." Their children struggled too! Now they are thriving, they say, raised by night nurses and nannies, *look at our school, no, look into mine, here's the brochure, it starts in pre-K, it's $40K a year.*

One summer, our kid's kicked out of five camps: Gymnastics, Science, Theater, "Sports," and Swimming. All the dismissals involve a common theme: Our child has an intolerance for forced fun, contrivance, and injustice, and has now discovered the fact that childhood—and especially children's summer camp—is filled with all three. The caregivers seem concerned, but we're tentatively not. Our kid is hyper-articulate, quirky, opinionated, reads college-level books by age five. We decide it'll be fine.

However, by the spring when I am out of work and am home all the time, the spring our kid is eight, I begin to see things in a different light. With more careful observation, the quirks start to seem extra quirky; emotional outbursts a hair too big. I begin volunteering at school, mostly so I can spy. I see a lost kid completely disengaged; I see a frustrated teacher at the end of her rope. I consult more professionals. By the time Alex and I are sitting with the psychiatrist who's conducted a multihour, multivisit, eight-thousand-dollar-out-of-pocket neuropsych assessment, I'm beyond concerned, I'm alarmed.

"So, what you're saying is our child is high-functioning with some neurodiversity?" I ask the doctor.

"No, Ms. Romolini, what I'm saying is your child is barely functioning at all."

Whenever I'd fantasized about getting fired, I always imagined the first few weeks would look like one of those movies where a middle-aged heroine journeys to a musty old country home in search of transformation. I imagined that an early release from high-pressure-job jail would inspire a kind of thrilling optimism, hope for the future. I thought the person I was outside of work would reveal herself quickly, that I'd throw open the drapes and all the windows, uncover the furniture, beat the dusty rugs, bend into a few yoga poses, blow the cobwebs off ye olde typewriter, roll in a fresh sheet of paper, and a reunion with my most authentic self would commence. *Here we are! Let's start over, fresh.*

Instead, I remain in bad shape for weeks, unrecognizable to myself. I manage well enough through our family's morning routine. Make breakfast, pack lunch, "do you have your homework," "brush your teeth," car ride to school. But after drop-off, I drive around aimlessly, sobbing in the California sunshine, past the palm trees, the sunshiny people who jog. Los Angeles is not a terrible place, but it is a terrible place to feel sad. The city doesn't want to see your self-esteem in the shitter: *How dare you wallow,* it's seventy-one degrees with a light breeze outside!

About a month after I'm fired, word's out that I no longer work at my high-profile job, and I start receiving offers for other high-profile jobs, all in "fast-paced environments" where "you'll wear many hats." I'm approached about positions for projects that make little sense, executive arrogance and ignorance and not much else on display in the slickly designed big-idea pitch decks I blindly swipe through, ideas not worthy of the elaborate NDAs I'm forced to sign for the privilege of these views. Ideas that fail before or just after they're launched.

Everything feels intolerably false, stabbingly performative, like sugar penetrating a rotting tooth. I'm cynical and angry, both overwhelmed and checked out, the professional walking dead. I've got a messy home life to rebuild, a child who requires my focus and care. The only job I'm up for is ghost.

I'm privileged enough to find spotty freelance work by calling up former colleagues, people I've done right by who are kind enough to hand over whatever behind-the-scenes tasks they have. I write a four-hundred-caption gift guide for a site for young, career-minded women, flexing my *Lucky* caption-writing skills for the first time in years, selling bullet journals, elaborate daily planners, affirmation cards, feminist-power tees, various and sundry successories to the site's aspiring girlboss clientele.

I take on a short-term project for a "cultural expert" looking to grow her digital footprint, increase her follower count, become more influential, and expand her personal brand ("It's really all about showing my authenticity, I want it to be *real,* you know?").

I work back-of-house at a women's empowerment conference to support a friend in a jam, moving furniture and handing out lanyards, and while doing so witness the conference boss—a well-known and well-respected female executive—scream at and threaten her staff. I overhear the employees say they're afraid to eat in front of their boss. "You know how weird she is with food," one says as they huddle in a corner scarfing noodles out of take-out containers after putting in a twelve-hour day. I have flashbacks to my own career at their age; I want to tell them it's not worth it, to run now, jump off the train, but I know they won't hear me. Instead, I sweep up the room we're in and get on my way.

"You're playing small," a lawyer I've hired says after reviewing what is, apparently, a bad freelance deal. "Is this even what you want?" I don't know, I tell her, but I know I don't want to play big.

The first ghostwriting project I land is for a business book that seems, from the proposal I'm sent, right in my wheelhouse. After several phone meetings, I meet the author at a downtown L.A. coffee shop with a counter full of seven kinds of milks. She's in her thirties, married to a man who works in finance, a go-getting SHE-E-O. She's white, thin, and fit with an ultrabright smile and a forehead as smooth and shiny as freshly cleaned glass. It's my first time taking on a project like this. I've researched her career, read and reread her proposal, and made a list of questions, notes on how we should start.

After we settle in, I start asking my questions, but before I can get the first one out fully, the SHE-E-O stops mid-almond-latte sip, shakes her head, and puts a finger to her lips. She interrupts me to say she doesn't actually want the book to be like the proposal—she had another ghostwriter write it, and she doesn't trust this ghostwriter anymore, the proposal never reflected what she wanted to do. She leans in close, looks at me knowingly, says, "You know, people will write *anything* in a book proposal, you just want to sell the book."

We've already signed the paperwork, the deal is done. In this initial meeting, the SHE-E-O tells me she wants to bring in anecdotes from other successful women, women she calls "she-roes." We should be strategic about the she-roes we choose, she explains; they should have big social media followings. She also wants quizzes in the book and lists of tips, and she wants to tell her story—of working her way up, working white-collar jobs, not liking those jobs, starting a company (with her husband's help, but don't say that part). She wants other women to be able to do what she did. That's what the book should be—practical, a how-to guide.

I take notes on all of it. A month later, when I am thirty pages into writing the book of the SHE-E-O, I hit a wall. I can't find an actual story or point of view. I consult my notes. I look at the now-loathed book proposal, at her college thesis, her LinkedIn page, her website, more. I Google and Google and Google and dig and look for something to turn into a book that's more than a fortune-cookie-fortune remix of advice.

The next day, I call her, panicking, that old bad-kid feeling arising, sprinkled with shame. "I'd love to record some of your stories about building the business, hard times you had to overcome and the lessons you learned." She's just returned from a multiweek trip to Africa and wants to talk about that instead, tells me, "Everyone needs to go to Africa." Before hanging up, she says, "You're my fairy bookmother!" in a lilting voice that sounds like a coo. At one point, in one of our conversations, the SHE-E-O reminds me that while I'm writing I should make sure to "carve out her TED Talk." She says this twice. I know because the first time I think maybe it's a well-executed deadpan joke, a funny Bookzilla versus the words butler prank. The second time, I know it's true.

After months struggling to turn a book about nothing into a book about something, nights when I stay up overnight, chain-smoking, squinting at the screen, fiddling with structure and form, with chapter titles and active verbs, I finally hand over a book I'm proud of, a book that makes sense as a book. The SHE-E-O approves what I've written, and we turn it in. When we get on the call with the publisher, the editor calls it a "killer manuscript" and gives us just two notes. I'm conflicted about the ethics of this accomplishment and also thrilled, the part of me that still lights up when praised, aglow. But the SHE-E-O does not take the news the same way.

Her reaction reminds me of the young starlets I used to interview at *Lucky* cover shoots, often their first, how I'd watch them complain to the point of meltdown about gorgeous clothes they objectively looked good in, clothes they didn't choose, hair and makeup they didn't want, watch their faces fall as they felt increasingly out of control. The SHE-E-O appears irritated that the book she failed to communicate ideas for does not include more of her ideas. But what I sense even more is this milestone doesn't feel as she'd expected it would. It's a hollow victory—not fully, enjoyably hers. When we pay someone else to hit the pellet button, the pellet rarely tastes as good.

"I have to be honest, it's a good book, but it's not a *great* book," the SHE-E-O tells the editor. After this meeting, she frantically writes extraneous chapters herself, adds more quizzes, more lists. After this, she doesn't pay my fee when she's supposed to pay. After that, she posts a multiimage post:

- *First pic: A selfie, no makeup, tears in her eyes, holding up a freshly printed copy of the manuscript: "Publisher finally accepted the manuscript for my book! So happy I cried! Writing a book was a DOOZY. I had to overcome so much fear!"*

- *Second pic: A beautiful, well-appointed desk: "My home base for writing. Spent so much on printer paper lol."*

- *Third pic: A picture of the manuscript neatly organized into multiple piles on a gleaming hardwood floor, light pouring in: "The hardest thing I've ever done. I've cried, I've gotten lost, I considered quitting so many times, but I stuck with it, I stuck with my dream."*

If she didn't quit, neither should you.

What do you want?

A friend asks, the therapist asks, my agent asks, my husband asks, my siblings ask, the reporter who is interviewing me about my old book asks, a mom at my kid's school asks.

What do you want?

I want to buy a house (lie).

What do you want?

I want to fall back in love with my husband, I want my kid to be okay, I want to be a better friend, I want to show up appropriately, I want to feel useful, I want to find work that doesn't make me feel dead inside, I want to let go of the past.

What do you want?

I want to stop feeling afraid of myself.

The Irish Job

The fall after I'm fired, my friend Quinn and I spend Saturdays in a Los Angeles community woodshop, at first learning to make spoons, then bowls, then chairs. Woodworking is careful, considered, straightforward, precise. The machinery is loud and intimidating. One false move and you'll lose the whole project, if not an arm. I begin to approach my life at home with the same delicacy. There's peace in my marriage, but it's tentative, fragile; we're still sorting it all out.

I begin to prioritize internal contentment over external success, train my brain to spot the difference, to stop saying yes when I mean no. In therapy, for the first time, I commit to staring down the ghosts of my past, talk about my life openly without fear or shame, begin to understand the puzzle of who I am and what it means. I'm diagnosed in quick succession with PTSD and ADHD, the diagnoses validating, a relief. I'm not dumb, like I'd always thought, an emotionally reckless monster, the girl my young mother painted me to be. Only when we identify the sickness can we start to heal it, the therapist says, everything else is just a shot in the dark.

My lack of high-powered, high-paying work's left our bank accounts shaky, but, as much as I've lost financially, I've gained in other ways. To cut costs, I live the life I'd once outsourced: I scrub the tub, walk the dog, stroll the grocery aisles, cut my own hair, leave my nails polish free; do more with less. I wrap up work each day by 2:00 P.M. to make it in time for after-school pickup, stop for two-dollar ice creams on the way home, eat mine slowly while we talk about the day, about playground gossip, how to deal with popular girls, multiplication tables and nouns. I no longer answer emails on my phone, turn down clients who want me to labor after hours, turn down anyone and anything that doesn't align with my values, even if at first I'm terrified no one will ever ask me to work again. Each step away from my old way of working is hard earned; like learning to walk again, it's awkward, humbling, unhurried by design.

In the late afternoons, I help with homework, build elaborate props for the school talent show, relish preparing dinner without distraction or rush. I show up with everything I was unable to give before— consistency, patience, presence—our kid's mental health improves by the day. So, incidentally, does mine.

Our crumbling house on the hill needs constant work in order to crumble less. Workers arrive to try to secure the foundation outside; inside Alex and I are securing a foundation too. We are learning to pass the work baton, to talk to and support each other, collaborate and share. We're changing our relationship with time and who we give it over to, start treating it as fleeting, a commodity of highest value to be guarded fiercely, the best we can.

About a year after I am fired, my consulting work leads to a steady job I want, a job no one thinks I should take. I'm compressing the time line a bit; it's not that easy, or fast. One afternoon, I have coffee with an old friend who is now a top executive at a top place, a man who seamlessly swings from one top-paying job to another, the way kings of the jungle swing from vines. In the time that I'm a working ghost, former peers like him have all become wildly successful. One buys a $3 million house, another begins collecting art, specifically busts.

My top executive friend and I meet at a just-opened café with oat-milk lattes whirling out of a tap. It's located along a newly cleaned-up stretch of the Los Angeles River, a former garbage dump. Now you can rent gleaming cruiser bikes here for twenty-five dollars an hour, or visit a boutique that sells trendy three-hundred-dollar tops. We are having coffee next to the remaining Beastie Boys, now gray-haired Beastie Men, one of whom is arguing into his phone about the details of a business transaction while the other stares out at the concrete river's trickle and smokes.

My executive friend tells me about his latest job in publishing, makes conversation and shares insider information about topics I once cared and thought about a lot. He tells me how the future of media is all intellectual property, how no one assigns stories in the same way anymore, that was the old days. Now it's about getting Hollywood buy-in first, editors anticipating what the studios want so they'll option your ideas, pay you extra to own the rights to what you push out. *Forget traffic! Forget ads! Forget playing social media's game! No more pivots to video!* There's a new revenue driver. It's reverse-engineering assignments as star vehicles: Pay a writer to write that deep dive into Patsy Cline once you know Gaga wants to star in the biopic first. "It's a seller's market, they *need* original content. They're gobbling our stories up fast," my friend says. "Sure, sure, most of the projects will never get made, but the best part is we still get paid."

We have known each other since New York, since we were young and idealistic, since he was floppy haired and tender, an aspiring Brooklyn novelist in dad jeans. He's a slick photograph of himself now, lit up by dealmaking, refers to famous people by their first names.

"You know I get offered so much work now, I have to turn half of it down?" he says. I recognize the swagger in his voice as something we once shared. He looks at me differently now, greets me with a pitiful "You good?" pat on the back. I'm no longer the same animal in the ambition zoo, chest-beating out my accomplishments the way I always had, meeting his achievement howls with my own.

My executive friend swigs at his foamy oat-milk drink and proceeds to list out all the work he's recently declined, a list that mainly involves man gear, man books, man sports. Except for . . . this one website about weed.

"I mean CBD is snake oil, but weed is still hot," he says authoritatively. "I told them maybe, *maybe* I'd consider coming on as an adviser, but they're going to have to offer a *shit ton* of equity to make it work."

The job clearly sounds silly and stupid to him, but it sounds like easy money to me. I'm intrigued.

"Huh, I don't know, that actually could be cool," I say. "If you don't want it, would you mind passing it to me?"

Turns out, the weed site is run by an international conglomerate, a board of enterprising prospectors hoping to strike gold in the late 2010s cannabis rush. The company is literally all over the place: owned by a Canadian billionaire, overseen by a New York executive, operated by a team of young, enthusiastic Irish tech engineers.

The Irish guys are the ones I'd be working with. They happen to be in town. We agree to meet. They're two twentysomething lads wearing matching polo shirts. They barrel into the over-air-conditioned Hollywood WeWork conference room their boss has rented for the occasion and begin chattering guilelessly about the L.A. heat, the legal weed here, their families back home, all of it a bit too fast and loud, unpolished in a way I immediately cherish. When we get down to business, they lay out their plan for the site. It's refreshingly honest. I don't know if it can work, but it makes sense. We spend two hours discussing the project and their vision. I genuinely like them; our conversation feels natural, lighthearted, even fun. Later that day, I send a scope of work and my fee for consulting. That's cool, they reply, but what we *really* need is an editor, am I available? I can't take a full-time job, I explain.

What if this wasn't full-time? What time could you give?

There are rules to careers, rules we're meant to follow, rules to which we all agree. You're supposed to somehow manage your way out of college and land an entry-level job, to get another job, and—if you're lucky—another after that. After this, you should climb a straight-up career ladder or a circuitous jungle gym; whatever it is, you climb. Each job/role/position/project is meant to be higher than the next, each salary/fee/contract increasing at scale. If you fall, you're supposed to climb up again, this time with more knowledge (fail faster!), your ascent swifter than before.

Nearly every person I tell about the weed job urges me not to do it, emphasizing their concern with a series of "alwayses" and "nevers", catastrophizing on my behalf: I would *always* be associated with weed, I would *never* again be considered for C-suite positions, I could *never* expect to command a "real" salary if I allowed myself to take scraps now. "This is a joke job," one friend-adviser explains sharply. "It will look terrible on your résumé. It's the kind of job you take when you have no other options or when you want to ruin your career." Instead of listening to the experts, I decide: *Fuck it*. This job seems like fun.

The title of the weed job is junior to my level, at first, simply "editor." The job pays enough to cover my share of the household bills— including à la carte health insurance, which it does not include. I will report directly to the executive in New York, a man I like and respect, and collaborate with the team of Irish twenty-five-year-olds several time zones and a full continent and ocean away, assign and edit internet-search-bait stories, such as "Can Marijuana Cure Herpes?" (Answer: No.) The job requires few things: that I travel to Ireland for one week every two months; that, while at home, I host a staff meeting over Zoom each workday at 6:00 A.M. Los Angeles time, 1:00 P.M. GMT. I'll need to attend one other mandatory meeting on Fridays at 5:00 A.M. The rest of the week's schedule is mine to decide.

The staff of the weed site is based in Newry, a sleepy Northern Irish border town equidistant from Dublin and Belfast, population 26,000. Most days I work from home in L.A., spend afternoons chauffeuring my kid to kid's appointments after ending my workday by 2:00. But every two months, I fly out of Los Angeles on a Friday night after kid bedtime, land in Dublin the following day. From the airport, I check into a hotel, a cheap favorite, where, during certain times of the year, you can upgrade to a high-floor suite with a bathtub, a balcony, and a view, the kind of place where, if you ask nicely, the upgrade is free.

The hotel is close to the city's main train station and close to Trinity College, though the city is small and everything's close. After checking in, I call home before cleaning up and heading out into the night. Arriving a day early allows me to stave off jet lag, be more productive once the week starts. But I'm mainly paying out of pocket for the luxury of a stolen night of freedom—the thrill of walking alone in a foreign city getting me higher than the weed I'm here to talk about ever could.

Here are the perfect first hours upon arrival in Dublin, if you're lucky enough to have such a thing. Leave your hotel and find your way to the river Liffey, a waterway in the center of the city where Vikings once sailed. Cross the river at the Ha'penny Bridge, a two hundred-year-old pedestrian overpass lit up with hand-carved metal lanterns and, on Saturday nights at least, enthusiastic young Irish people bouncing and chattering, out for a good time. From there, make your way to the best restaurant in Dublin, hidden over a charming bookstore, up a winding set of wooden stairs. The restaurant's named after a Yeats poem and serves Scotch eggs, red-wine-braised venison, chocolate and stout pudding, five different kinds of sherry. If you're not that kind of eater, you get the fish and chips, wash it down with a Prosecco the waiter calls "austere."

After dining solo, wind through and past the Temple Bar area—cute drunk Irish boys, abundant hen parties, a sight!—until you stumble upon a tiny old pub all the tourists ignore. You sit by a fire with a book and your drink, a Guinness if that's your thing, whiskey if it's not, until the space fills, until the harder partiers show up and you tap out. Buoyed by a slight buzz, you jump on a city bike, ride a mile or so along the cobblestone streets, wind blowing through your hair. The next morning go for a brisk walk to stretch off the travel, take your tea and stroll the grounds of Trinity College before anyone's up and around.

My time in Ireland is the first extended period I'm on my own in decades. After years of corporate travel, when I had little control over my schedule, at the weed site, I demand to set my own pace, to build in rest to balance my labor. As a result, I experience what it is to wander a foreign city alone for hours, to eat whatever I want and stop wherever I like. Halfway across the world and free of obligation to meet the needs of others, I witness myself as an independent person not defined by work or marriage or motherhood. I become reacquainted with my most earnest preferences and desires, what I'm curious about and drawn to. For the first time in my life, I find solace in my own company, get to know my adult self in a new way. The freedom of these trips is intoxicating to the point of erotic. I savor every small pleasure of life on my own terms.

After a blissful mom's-night-off in Dublin, I ride the two-hour train up north, a train called the Enterprise, a train that runs along the eastern coast of Ireland, where I frequently spot rainbows, a train so civilized it has train waiters who serve your order on a ceramic plate and with a cloth napkin, your beverage in a glass.

Upon arrival in Newry, I check into another hotel, the Canal Court, a crumbling, sprawling palace in the center of things, an old-world-meets-modern-tacky structure that appears to have been built in the 1800s and updated in the 1980s, with a grand central staircase, scratchy sheets over lumpy beds, and four bizarrely configured cafés and bars. On the top floor is a run-down fitness center and spa that serves as the local gym, an Irish community Y. In my weeks there, I treadmill next to swole Irish weight-lifting bros who earnestly teach me their tricks, steam in the steam room with a grandmother who doesn't care that I'm American but is concerned that I've had just one child and also believes I'm twenty-five.

Come Monday morning, I walk the ten blocks to work, past two churches, a narrow canal filled with ducks, and a bakery manned by two old Irish ladies wearing bonnets, where I stop to buy office treats. I arrive at the crowded office, head to the kitchen to make a black tea before settling in, and find the team's bought me my own mug with a "J" as a "glad you're here" gift.

The office is a family affair, run by two brothers, two six-four former rugby players named Josh and Jonny. When I arrive they deliver bear hugs and chat me up, seem genuinely interested in what I have to say. Over the course of these trips, I come to love these brothers in a way I hadn't anticipated. They come to feel like my own.

The work I'm here for is a site that promotes the medical benefits of cannabis, an authoritative resource for the "canna-curious," essentially breaking down any lingering "Just Say No" antidrug bias and outlining how the plant is not only beneficial but safe. I manage young writers and editors who've never written or edited before. I remember what it's like to teach people how to write clear sentences, how to outline their ideas, work I love and have missed.

Everyone works in the same room. HR consists of one female employee with a gold service bell on her desk, which she rings whenever anyone gets out of line. The brothers curse and the bell rings—ding!—the actual teenagers who run social media gossip too loudly and the bell rings again—ding! ding! One twenty-four-year-old's upset because she's not getting enough bylines, another's fired for plagiarizing, which she didn't know was a thing. A junior editor gives terrible edits to a twenty-nine-year-old single mom who's having none of his bullshit; she kicks the situation to me. When I gently correct him, he argues his case loudly, but I stay calm, and he eventually comes around. It's raucous, it's chaos, it's raw and alive, it's work in its purest form. Instead of feeling bogged down, I delight in all of it. This is how I'd always wished it would be.

I'm older by decades than everyone in the office, more experienced, wiser too. But I resist the urge to flex, to take over, to jockey into a position and prove what I know. I'm relearning how to work without overworking, to stop anticipating every possible problem and making it mine to own. I'm training myself to stop chasing every success avenue, to let go, to stop always having something to prove. Instead of white-knuckling the wheel of this ship, I'm a passenger this time and smart enough to know it. I'm here to enjoy the ride.

The crew stops at a decent hour, and in the spring when I visit, the lot of us head to an outdoor bar adjacent to the sea. We drink pints of hard cider, share baskets of fries, make fun of each other's accents, talk about travel, our families, our futures, who and what we'd like to be. I like them all, but Jon and I are instantly connected and most aligned. He's married; he and his husband and their two dogs live in a tiny stone house in a town nearby. On weekends, they bake bread and make soap. One night after work, Jon drives me to his house in Dundalk to meet his husband and dogs. Later, we stroll down to and sit in a pub, and another co-worker joins. These people are strangers. I'm in a strange place. But I can't help but notice how happy I feel, more comfortable in my skin than I've felt in years.

Once, right before Christmas, the whole weed site team rides in a bus to a ramshackle whiskey distillery in the middle of nowhere. There's a bonfire outside. Someone knows Irish folk music, someone plays the guitar, someone else sings. We smoke cigarettes by the fire, under the stars. It's as magical as it seems.

The people I work with don't earn a ton, but they have social safety, guaranteed healthcare and thirty state-sanctioned days off a year. Their jobs are far from perfect, but they prioritize camaraderie and loyalty, are in-your-face assertive and give each other—and me—the business when anyone's full of themselves, full of shit. Working with them reminds me of Philly and home, the best parts of my working-class roots, a side of myself I'd compartmentalized and hidden for years. There are no she-roes here. These are not game players. There's not the same American career ladder to climb. The goal is to do the best job you can, but not at the expense of your life.

When I'm not with the staff, I spend some evenings running through the mostly empty hotel in a pair of old running shoes, use its long halls and hidden stairwells as a kind of track, clearing my head. On other nights, I wander the town's misty streets alone; an American in a pink raincoat hiding in plain sight. Turns out, hiding from the world can give you space to stop hiding from yourself. Turns out, racing down the career ladder is a fuck ton more fun than climbing up.

One June night after work, Jon takes me and another co-worker to see a centuries-old castle located in the center of a sheep farm. We park on the road and climb right up to and through it, marvel at the structure and the grazing sheep. Near the top, we pass around a joint in silence while sitting on the ledge of a stone wall, staring out over endless green. My companions are both younger than I am, with their whole lives in front of them; their sense of the future is sprawling and wide. Spending this kind of unstructured, carefree time with them helps me remember all the life I have yet to imagine for myself, that there's quite a bit of mine left to live too.

After the castle, we drive back to the hotel just as the sun is setting, watch the moon rise over the fields. I'm forty-six years old. This is what I'm getting paid to do. The job will last just over a year before it all goes to hell, multicontinent, multination white men and their egos ruining the vibes for everyone else. I won't try to save it, even though I sense that I could, see the fight I could take on, the control I'd need to wrangle, the choke-holding overhaul, the stress. I know enough to know that in saving the job I'd ruin everything I love about it, everything that's good.

Alone in my hotel room on my last visit to Ireland, I reflect in my journal, what I've done here, where I've been, what I might want next. Before I close the book, I scrawl:

I want to make things for myself, not a boss or a company.

I want to write something that means something to ME.

In the time I've worked the weed job, I've developed new dreams, smaller in some ways, bigger in others, all involving, for the first time, not a climbing, clawing, one-size-fits-all idea of a successful life, but something more spacious, private, and quiet, something made for the moment I'm in. Something made for me.

Epilogue

O n the August afternoon when my dad calls, the news doesn't come as a surprise. I'd been expecting his call for weeks. After two years in which she'd survived Covid, three bouts of pneumonia, and a battle with sepsis; at the age of ninety-one, my grandmother Dolores, our family's fighter, was finally gone. My father was by her side when it happened. I'd soon be by his.

"It looks like it will just be our main family," says my mom when we're sorting out travel for the funeral. "Your siblings' spouses aren't coming, they don't want to bring all the kids. I'll set up the air mattress for your brother in the living room, you can sleep in my office, Michele can take the bed in the front. The three of you should stay here."

My parents have retired along the Jersey Shore, settled in a beachy cottage a half block from a bay and a few miles from the sea. The area is residential and underdeveloped—a place of tall dunes and buggy trees, a nature trail where they ride bikes in the morning, a backyard big enough to maintain a robust vegetable garden—a twenty-minute drive from where my dad goes to fish.

We coordinate logistics over text. There's an extra day built in before the funeral, a bright, hot summer afternoon we decide to spend at the beach. When we arrive, the ocean is calm and temperate. My brother, dad, and I jump in, float around, ride the familiar Atlantic waves. Tan boogie boarders fly past us in neon board shorts, an aerial-banner plane trails an ad for local grinders and hoagies overhead. We narrowly avoid a raucous game of Marco Polo played by a group of heavily accented Philly tweens. Past the break, there's a strong undertow; when we accidentally drift too far toward the rocks, the lifeguard whistles and gestures us to move closer to shore. My brother wonders aloud when was the last time the three of us were together like this. None of us can remember—years? decades?—but we don't press. In the joy of the moment, it's best not to recall the past.

In the years since I left my parents' house, there have been dozens of visits, family dinners, birthday parties and celebrations. Still, I've never felt sturdy enough to come home to my family, not really, not like this. Into my adulthood, I accomplished so much outward success, but it did little to resolve my internal shakiness. No matter what titles I held or how much professional power I gained, I'd still feel undone in my parents' presence, find even the suggestion of their disapproval outsize and intolerable; their most minor tonal shifts would leave me destabilized for days.

Once-a-decade confrontations by my mother lead to subsequent months-long estrangements, her rage too much to carry, to sift through even, the weight of our collective disappointment too great to bear. I was forty-five the last time my mother and I argued like this, the last time we spiraled into insults, accusations, and teeth-gritting screams. I'd been fired a few months before. There was no endless-scroll inbox to retreat into, no big career to hide behind. I begin therapy right after, wrap myself up in a self-healing cocoon. I learn it's not selfish or "bad" to show up for myself before I show up for my job, family, friends—anything else. I learn that forgiveness is not nearly as essential as acceptance. I begin to see that in order to accept and appreciate my parents for the good they gave me and not solely fixate on the bad, I have to reckon with my childhood on my own terms first. That in order to love and know my parents as their adult child, I need to put in the work to emotionally grow up myself.

After the beach, we all take showers, rinse off the sand. My mother pours wine, begins preparing our meal. We ask if we can help and she refuses. She *likes* doing it, she says. *When am I going to have my family together like this again?* Within an hour, a feast is set before us: thinly sliced roasted red peppers to layer on crusty bread; broccoli rabe sautéed with garlic alongside wedges of sharp provolone; crabs she's bought fresh and carefully released from the shells, seasoned with chopped parsley and olive oil; a pin-neat caprese salad with creamy mozzarella, just-ripe tomatoes, and bright basil snatched from my father's garden earlier that afternoon.

We eat quickly and in silence, reach greedily for more, serve ourselves second and third helpings until all the plates are empty, the food rapidly gone. Afterward, my sister, brother, and I load the dishwasher. My mother wipes the table, pulls out the after-dinner glasses and a large stack of photos, pours us each a Fernet. She's more mellow now than she's ever been, less controlling with us, more accepting, content. In the years since we all left home, she's built a rewarding career for herself, an independent life of travel, community, clients, and (many) friends.

"The funeral home will have easel-like stands," she explains, giving us our marching orders, raising her hand to chest height: *about this high.* We're to organize two poster-board-size photo collages to place upon the easels; these, we've been told, are customary and important features of a funeral service, things the people who attend like and need.

Before us are dozens of snapshots of my grandmother's life, ninety years of time jumps, in next to no chronological order, from infancy to a few months before her death. There she is in her teens, sitting in my great-grandfather's barbershop chair, sexy in a tight sweater and gold hoops. Here she is at forty-three, wearing red pants at Christmas, holding my infant sister in her arms, a hand on my five-year-old head. Some of her baby pictures were once black and white, but someone's colored them in with marker. A more formal portrait is a bit tattered;

she's in a beehive, my father (age three?) dressed up in a tiny hat and a gangster's suit.

"Don't forget to include your cousins!" my mother yells over at our work area. She's redoing our cleanup effort, extra scrubbing the sink. "They're her grandchildren too!" In the corner of the room, my dad sits on the sofa wearing reading glasses, working on his eulogy, writing it out by hand. When he gets stuck, he calls me over and I help him make a transition, tell him he needs a joke. Then I return to sorting out the photos, and my brother and I start arguing over glue. The reason we're together is heavy, but there's lightness between us, easy connection. We're a busy, industrious unit, working as a team.

Sorrow is not generationally agnostic. It morphs and hides and slithers sneakily through family time lines, quietly devastating until someone holds it up to the light. In the years I'm in therapy I grieve the childhood I didn't get, the support I needed and deserved. Session after session, week after week, I wallow in the sorrow of all my parents couldn't give. Eventually, I rise to the surface of my own grief and see the picture more clearly, understand how much my parents were hurt themselves; and my grandmothers before them. I'll stop striving as I sit more firmly in myself, knowing we're all swimming against the pain in our lives, doing our best to survive one big sorrowful sea. It's an imperfect resolution, an ongoing process. It's the way it needs to be.

On the morning of the funeral, my mother makes us coffee. We eat a quick breakfast together, take turns with my parents' iron smoothing wrinkled sleeves and crumpled hems. Afterward, we solicit each other's opinions about tie and belt options, this shoe or that.

"I don't *really* have to wear black, do I?" asks my mother. "I feel like white is more of a celebration of life."

The funeral home is ninety minutes away from my parents' house. When it's time to leave, we all take off in separate cars. About fifteen minutes into the journey, the dashboard of my rental car lights up, flashes a menacing symbol that looks like an exclamation point over a wavy stream. I panic. I have no clue what this means. I call my dad from the road. He does.

"Oh yeah, babe, the air in your tire's low, you might be close to a flat," he says, immediately shifting into dad mode. "Pull into the next gas station, there's one right at the fork on Route 47. Go to the air machine. You want all the tires set to thirty-five. The leak's most likely small. You should make it fine to the funeral home and the rental place after that."

He's got a lot on his mind. He'll soon greet relatives he hasn't seen in years, deliver a heartfelt eulogy, watch as his mother's ashes are lowered into the ground.

Still, no matter what his day entails, I'm forever my father's child. He calls to check on me and the tire three more times before I arrive.

––––––––––

"Happy endings are only a pause," Jeanette Winterson tells us in *Why Be Happy When You Could Be Normal?* "There are no happy endings in history, only crisis points that pass," Isaac Asimov explains in *The Gods Themselves*.

In leaving behind the crisis of my all-systems-go career, I imagined so much loss, but I never understood what I'd gain. The opportunity to know and accept myself, to give myself grace; to know and accept my family, my partner, and, most of all, my child for who they truly are, not an idea of someone else, who I wish them to be. In letting go, I allowed myself the space to cultivate new, sustaining friendships; seek out new creative collaborators; walk a professional path less taken, more precarious, a path true to me.

A few days after the funeral, I'm back in Los Angeles. I walk out of therapy and right up to an exact replica of my first car, an '88 Nissan Sentra I bought, with every last cent of my summer waitressing tips, for fourteen hundred dollars, negotiated down by my dad from two grand. I wanted this car so bad, but he'd prepared me: for any negotiation to go well, you have to be ready to walk away. I kept my poker face that day and got to drive my new car off the lot. For the next almost ten years, I kept driving it away from everything I knew—home, college, a bad first marriage, friends who were somehow no longer friends—trying to land somewhere that felt right, always negotiating, always ready to walk away.

It took me years to discover there's no dream job to chase, no have-it-all fairy tale, no happy ending in which to escape. The story is never so pretty or so neat. The best is often what's right in front of you; the hardest, most ambitious goal is to stop running from yourself.

Acknowledgments

This book would not exist without the talent, vision, integrity, and unfailing commitment of my editor, Kate Napolitano. Writers wait their entire lives for a collaboration like ours. I am so lucky. And to everyone at Atria Books, especially Sean deLone, for helping us shepherd it all through.

Thank you to Nicole Tourtelot, the agent of my dreams, for believing in me, for picking me up from the professional dead, dusting me off, and pushing me back into the world.

To Quinn Heraty, for gently suggesting I stop playing creatively small and, when I failed to listen, suggesting it again.

To Stephanie Hitchcock, who told me to stop hiding myself in other books and write this one instead.

My sincerest thanks to the friends and colleagues who read early drafts of *Ambition Monster*, who sent smart critiques or just words of encouragement: Kim France, Samantha Irby, Megan Stielstra, Minna Proctor, Ashley C. Ford, Claire Dederer, Angela Garbes, Kimberly Harrington, Molly Savard, Glynnis MacNicol, Rei Hance, Julie Mervine, Kristen Lisanti, Liz Flahive, Cristina Mueller, Felicia Sabartinelli, Katharina Bitzker—I am deeply indebted to all of you.

I wrote a podcast while writing this book—there's no question that producer Mary Knauf's generous feedback made me and, by extension, this work, better and stronger.

And to my therapist Patrick Jensen, who did the same.

This book was written over two years in California, New York, and Iceland; on planes and trains, in a cabin in Laugarvatn, at a rented desk in Silver Lake, on a hotel bed in New York City, and in a tiny house on an Altadena farm.

My thanks to Victor Quinaz, Alda Sigurðardóttir of the Gullkistan Center for Creative Arts, along with the kind people at The Marlton Hotel and Zorthian Ranch for sheltering me and my work.

Crafting a memoir is an emotional excavation that impacts not only the writer, but those who are closest in their lives. Alex Pappademas steadfastly nurtured my messy, ambitious heart through the process and never flinched. It can't be easy living with two writer parents. Thank you to CJP for putting up with us.

Finally, my life and this story would not be possible without the unwavering love and support of my parents and my siblings. Thank you for teaching me bravery and grace. I am never not proud to be a Romolini.

References

Page 203:   The Workaholics Anonymous Book of Recovery: Second Edition Paperback—August 6, 2019 by Workaholics Anonymous World Service Organization

Page 237:   Measuring workaholism: content validity of the Work Addiction Risk Test. Bryan E. Robinson.

Page 257, 263: Worldbirds.com "Blue Jay Symbolism & Meaning (+Totem, Spirit & Omens)," September 24, 2021 By Garth C. Clifford

Page 258:   Lafebar.com "Ask Lafebar: Fright death," June 9, 2021

Page 259:   *National Geographic*, "Finches die earlier if they're paired with highly strung partners," Ed Yong, August 17, 2011

Page 260:   Sparrow Kirkland, "About Us" page

Page 260:   "When Sparrow Falls," Mark L Briggs marklbriggs.com

Page 262:   Sonomabirding.com, "Starling Symbolism and Meaning (Totem, Spirits, and Omens)"